COGS IN THE WHEEL

COGS IN
THE WHEEL

THE FORMATION OF SOVIET MAN

MIKHAIL HELLER

ALFRED A. KNOPF, INC. NEW YORK 1988

THIS IS A BORZOI BOOK
PUBLISHED BY ALFRED A. KNOPF, INC.

Library of Congress Cataloging-in-Publication Data

Heller, Mikhail.
   Cogs in the wheel: the formation of Soviet man.

   Translation of: Mashina i vintiki.
   Includes index.
   1. Soviet Union—Social conditions—1917–
2. Soviet Union—Politics and government—1917–
3. Soviet Union—Economic conditions—1918–
4. Communism—Soviet Union—History. I. Title.
HN523.G447 1988   306′.0947   87-46075
ISBN 0-394-56926-1

Manufactured in the United States of America

FIRST AMERICAN EDITION

CONTENTS

INTRODUCTION

Three years have passed since the Russian edition of this book first appeared. The developments that have taken and are continuing to take place in the country of the "cogs" have served to confirm the topicality of my subject. The scraps of information I had to gather from Soviet and non-Soviet publications are now flooding onto the pages of magazines and newspapers, even television screens. It has been announced officially that the Soviet Union is going through a crisis. In the last years of Leonid Brezhnev's life there was no longer any doubt about the reality of this crisis. Yury Andropov, who succeeded him as general secretary, spoke of it openly, but the brevity of his tenure in the top post (November 12, 1982, to February 9, 1984) allowed him to do no more than draw up a program of action. His successor, Konstantin Chernenko, ceased altogether to talk of a crisis. He held on to the post of general secretary for just over a year (February 13, 1984–March 10, 1985).

The depth of the abyss to the brink of which the Soviet Union had been brought was made clear by the next general secretary—Mikhail Gorbachev—who was elected to the post the day after Chernenko died. The "possibilities of socialism," Gorbachev said, were not being properly exploited in industry, agriculture, the social sphere, culture, rail transport, the health service, and so on.[1] On January 27, 1934, Stalin had proclaimed: "There was no point in overthrowing capitalism in October 1917 and building socialism for all these years if we do not succeed in enabling people to live in a state of prosperity."[2] Fifty-three years later, on January 27, 1987, Gorbachev declared that prosperity was still a long way off.

The Soviet Union is certainly going through a very serious crisis, and Gorbachev now has been talking about it for more than two years. But this is not the first crisis in Soviet history. In 1921 the Soviet regime experienced—in Lenin's words—the gravest crisis in its brief history. The reason then was the unwillingness of the peasants, who constituted the overwhelming majority of the country's population, to accept the policy of "instant Communism" that was being put into practice by the Party, under Lenin's leadership. Persuaded that it was impossible to break the resistance of the peasantry by force, Lenin took a "step backwards," and initiated the New Economic Policy (NEP) which D. Ryazanov has described justly as a "peasant Brest." In March 1918 Lenin had concluded the "Indecent Peace" with Germany in the Treaty of Brest-Litovsk, sacrificing territory to buy time in which to consolidate his power. He repeated this kind of maneuver in 1921 with the NEP. Stalin concluded in the late 1920s that all the advantages that NEP could offer for consolidating the regime were exhausted, and he then set about producing a crisis artificially. In an effort to compensate for Lenin's "step backwards" he organized a "great leap forward." In the process of collectivizing Soviet agriculture, the peasantry was eliminated as a class relatively independent of the state. The state became completely homogeneous: everybody was declared to be equal, everybody became a slave of the state.

There are no hostile forces in the Soviet Union today. The roots of the present crisis can therefore be seen to reach back to the remarkable success achieved in the formation of Soviet man, *Homo sovieticus.* That charlatan Trofim Lysenko, without realizing what he was doing, described the principal peculiarity of the regime: "In our Soviet Union people are not born. What are born are organisms. We turn them into people—tractor drivers, engine drivers, academicians, scholars and so forth."[3] In the course of seventy years of building socialism the regime has succeeded in "making" people who have lost all interest in work because they are convinced that those who "made" them are also obliged to guarantee their needs once they have adapted themselves to life in special Soviet conditions.

It is no accident that the proclamation of a "state of emergency" and the public recognition of the Soviet Union's catastrophic situation coincided with the appointment of a new general secretary. The possibility of crisis at such a juncture is an essential element in a single-party system. Since the Party has in its hands all the levers of power, there is no reason why a general secretary should not remain in power for life. The situation in China and Albania, in Czechoslovakia, Romania, Hungary, Vietnam, East Germany and Cuba is clear confirmation of the universality of this rule. The Party machine, the *apparat,* which he creates and by means of which he rules, goes on ruling along with the general secretary, and every time a general secretary dies or is replaced the same thing happens: Each new one (beginning with the first, Stalin, elected at Lenin's suggestion to the previously nonexistent post on April 2, 1922) immediately sets about dismantling his predecessor's Party machine and creating his own. It took Stalin almost a decade to get rid of Lenin's Party machine. Despite some initial success, Khrushchev suffered defeat in this process after a ten-year battle. For the first time in the history of the Communist Party of the Soviet Union (CPSU) he wanted to carry out, without actually realizing it, a genuine reform of the Lenin-style Party. Khrushchev succeeded in getting the Central Committee to pass a resolution dividing the CPSU into two sections, one for industry and one for agriculture. That this would inevitably lead to the emergence of two parties, even if both Communist, was so obvious that the conspiracy to remove Khrushchev was successful. The reform was a threat, not just to a few leaders, but to the "party of a new type" that Lenin had invented. Brezhnev quickly set about purging the *apparat* of those who had supported Khrushchev's reforms.

Every new general secretary begins by revealing the "true" situation and by shocking the population by candid talk about things well known to everyone. Suddenly words coincide with deeds and reflect the real state of affairs. The most powerful trump in each new general secretary's hands is the fact that, in exposing the errors in his predecessor's behavior, he is speaking the manifest truth—not all the truth, but at least the truth about how the country arrived at the brink of catastrophe. That is what happened after the death of Stalin, after the removal of Khrushchev, and after the death of Brezhnev. In the first case the cause of all the trouble was said to be the "cult of personality," in the second case "voluntarism," and in the third "apathy and corruption."

Each time there is a danger of losing control over the process. Khrushchev's struggle against the "cult of personality" threatened on several occasions to get out of hand, although he had indicated very precisely the point at which Stalin ceased to be "good" and became "bad" (December 1934, when the "leader of genius" organized the murder of Kirov and directed the instruments of terror against members of the party). Brezhnev had to maneuver between "voluntarism" and a return to the "cult of personality." The most important means to keep control is to set a strict limit to the period covered by the crisis: there must be no suggestion that the disease is endemic. So a critical question for Gorbachev is, When did the crisis begin? His reply is, In the late 1970s and early 1980s.[4] He attaches no importance to the fact that it was in those very years that he was made a secretary of the Central Committee (November 1978) and became also a candidate (and later a full member) of the Politburo (November 1979). What is important for him is to lay the blame on Brezhnev.

Predictably, the new general secretary identified the crisis as being the work of his predecessor, and he has proposed a miracle cure—the replacement of the old Party machine by a new one. The process of acquiring power is carried on, of course, under the slogan of correcting the mistakes of his predecessor, who had not known how to "exploit all the possibilities of socialism."

The general secretary of the Central Committee of the CPSU has the possibility of acquiring absolute power, but that power does not come into his hands automatically. He must know how to exploit all the potentialities that his job offers. No reforms are possible, even if he wishes to bring them about, unless he has the requisite power. So all the reforms he carries out as he gathers strength are aimed at increasing his own power. The political scientist and publicist F. Burlatsky, discussing the possibilities and impossibilities of reforming the Soviet system, composed a dialogue between two fairly high-ranking Party officials. One, representing the old *apparat,* had already been pushed out; the other was the new man installed in his place. The older man says that he has heard it all before:

This is the third time in our memory that we have come up against these questions. The first time was after Stalin died. . . . That was all they talked about—reforms, democracy, social self-management. And what came of it all? . . . The second time was in 1965, when the Central Committee announced the beginning of the economic reform. Again nothing came of it. Everything slipped back into the old track and got lost in the sand. . . . It's not our way of doing things. It goes against the system.

The new secretary sees everything differently: "The fact that we have already begun to talk about reforms several times just shows how inevitable they are. In those days we did not have the courage and political will. Now we do."[5] Burlatsky does not find it necessary to say in whom the "courage and political will" are now embodied. It is obvious.

Gorbachev declares that the present crisis is so serious as to require a "change of direction of a revolutionary character."[6] Another revolution is needed! By using a word that has not been employed for more than fifty years to describe Soviet domestic policy, Gorbachev hopes to shock the minds of his Soviet people. He speaks vaguely and imprecisely about the need for "revolutionary changes." The writer Valentin Kataev, who used to sing the praises of Stalin's great wisdom and of Brezhnev's outstanding literary talent, now has claimed to hear the "music of revolution" in Gorbachev's appeal for people to "rid themselves of falsehood and corruption, and to promote honesty."[7]

A theoretical article appeared in *Pravda* in 1987 that was mainly concerned to establish what kind of revolution is *not* wanted today in the Soviet Union.

> We are not talking about a social-political revolution, in which the foundations of economic relations in the old system are destroyed and a fundamentally new political regime is established. . . . It is not a question of ending the public ownership of the means of production but of confirming it and of making better use of it. It is not a question of rejecting the basic principle of socialism—"from each according to his ability; to each according to his needs"—but of a more consistent application of it in the interests of social justice. We are not talking about destroying the power of the state but of a further strengthening of the national state, the extension of socialist democracy and socialist self-management.

But what sort of a revolution is it if it leaves everything in its place and aims only at consolidating the existing system? The *Pravda* article indicates the model for the Gorbachev revolution: "It invites comparison with collectivization and the revolution in cultural affairs."[8]

The model and the source of inspiration for the change "of a revolutionary character" that Gorbachev is directing are to be found in Stalin's "revolutions from above": collectivization (1929–34), in the course of which the peasants were turned into collective farm workers by terribly cruel means; and the cultural revolution (1928–31), during which the Party asserted its authority over the spiritual life of Soviet citizens. These were the two most important stages on the way to the creation of the Stalinist model of the totalitarian state or, as *Pravda* now says, "they signified the country's further advance along the path of socialist revolution and the completion of the task begun by the October Revolution."[9]

Like all general secretaries, Gorbachev declares himself to be the direct—and only—heir of Lenin. "Why do I spend so much time with volumes of Lenin?" was the rhetorical question he put to a group of writers with whom he had a private conversation just before the 8th Congress of the Union of Soviet Writers in July 1986. The answer was obvious: he was seeking inspiration from the father of the revolution and the Soviet state. But the main source of the ideas, slogans and tactics of the Gorbachev era is actually Stalin, the very first general secretary, who possessed an abundance of "courage and political will."

In the early 1930s Stalin completed his "inexorable ascent" to absolute power, resolutely overcoming resistance on the part of the "human material" in the process of building a totalitarian state. In different circumstances Gorbachev has come up against a similar problem: he is trying to attain absolute power, and meeting, as the expression goes today, resistance from the "human factor." But while Stalin had to deal with the "human material" in the course of forming Soviet man, Gorbachev has to deal with the finished product. In this connection he has no need—for the time being at least—to resort to mass terror. He makes use of other instruments from Stalin's rich arsenal.

The Miracle, the Mystery, and Authority—the three forces of Dostoevsky's Grand Inquisitor—remain the three basic forms in which the various instruments for influencing Soviet man are used. A peculiar feature of Gorbachev's policy is his use of the Mystery as the Miracle—the extension of the amount of permitted information is offered as a miraculous remedy capable of curing all the ills left by Brezhnev.

Gorbachev gives the miracle a name: *glasnost*. This is exactly how Lenin understood it, having employed the word forty-six times in his writings and asserting in particular, *"Glasnost* is a sword which itself heals the wounds it inflicts."[10] *Glasnost* has been taken into the political vocabulary today with exceptional speed to become the symbol of the new, Gorbachevian era, and has entered the vocabulary of foreign countries in official Soviet translations that distort its meaning. In French, for example, *glasnost* is now translated, following the lead given by the Novosti feature agency, as *transparence*. But the pre-revolutionary Russian-French dictionary, which remains an irreplaceable work of scholarship, translates *glasnost* as *publicité* or *notoriété*.[11] In Russian, *glasnost* means giving publicity to something that is already well known.

In Gorbachev's terms *glasnost* represents permission to speak publicly about the ills of the system that have long been apparent to everybody. It is permissible to talk about the disastrous effects of alcoholism, about drug addiction, about corruption, false statistics, and the lack of social justice. Gorbachev has spoken of the presence of "social corrosion."[12] There is talk of a "decline in the quality of education" due to the inability of the schools to defend themselves from the "arbitrary behavior of the local authorities and education bodies." "Claims for hundred percent success on the part of whole classes, schools, regions and republics," along with a decline in the quality of education, are to be explained, according to Gorbachev, by "a decline in the quality of the people working in education—the teachers, head teachers and inspectors." There is criticism also of excessive centralization and the formation of a too-rigid hierarchy which finds expression in particular in the establishment of a monopoly over information ("because the person who disposes of more information also has more power") and in a hostile attitude to trade, which is treated as profiteering and ill-gotten gains, and so on.[13]

Glasnost, strictly controlled from above, pursues two aims: to shock the Soviet citizen by showing him the brink of the precipice at which the country has arrived, and to accuse the preceding leaders of having been the ones who brought the country so close to disaster. *Glasnost* on a large scale is the most important instrument for destroying the old Party machine. At the same time it is credited with miraculous healing qualities that become apparent when a new Party machine, headed by the new general secretary, emerges in place of the one being destroyed.

A number of criteria can be applied to determine the character of the changes connected with the Gorbachev era. First of all, there is his attitude to the past. By making the late 1970s–early 1980s the dividing line between the period of success and the period of decline, Gorbachev categorically rejects the need for any serious study of history. In an unpublished conversation with Soviet writers Gorbachev explained: "If we started probing into the past we would use up all our energies. We would come into direct conflict with the people. We must go forward. We will deal with the past later." In a public speech the general secretary made it clear how he would "deal with" the past: "You have to see history as it really is. There were all sorts of things; there were mistakes, and serious ones, but the country continued to advance. Just take the periods of industrialization and collectivization."[14] The mistakes of the past (the distant, pre-Brezhnev past) are of no importance because, as he announced proudly, "It fell to our lot to be pioneers." What was most important was to be going in the right direction. So long as the Party was going in the right direction all the rest was secondary. As Lenin wrote: "Our mistakes and shortcomings are just the growing pains of the new socialist society."[15] Lenin was not put out, the Party's theoretical journal explained, "if something conceived and decided by the Party did not work out in practice quite as planned or not at all as expected."[16] And if Lenin was not put out by such setbacks, those who continue his work today will naturally not be put out either.

The most important guide to the real intentions of the Soviet leaders is the vocabulary they use. In a logocracy—as I explain in this book in great detail—the word is the most important instrument of power. The provenance and source of the words used by the regime is significant, determining the new sense of the word and creating new associations to supplement the meaning.

All of Gorbachev's catchwords have been taken from the vocabulary of Stalin's day—*glasnost, perestroika* ("restructuring"), and *uskorenie* ("acceleration") were the most commonly used appeals of the 1930s. In those days *glasnost* was called *kritika i samokritika* ("criticism and self-criticism"), *perestroika* was *rekonstruktsiya,* and *uskorenie* was *tempy* ("tempo" or "speed"). Gorbachev proclaims: *"Glasnost,* criticism and self-criticism are simply essential for us as a matter of principle."[17] Fifty-seven years ago, Stalin said exactly the same thing: "We cannot manage without self-criticism. . . . without it it will be impossible to avoid stagnation, the decay of the *apparat,* the growth of bureaucracy and the undermining of the creative initiative of the working class."[18] Gorbachev in his turn declared that *uskorenie* is the basis of his strategy of "revolutionary change." More than half a century before that Stalin taught that "in the period of reconstruction, speed decides everything." Gorbachev insists on the importance of the "human factor," repeating Stalin's famous dictum: "Of all the valuable forms of capital in the world the most valuable and the most decisive are people, cadres."[19]

The use of material incentives for the working people is one of the fundamental elements of the "strategy of acceleration." Good work must be better paid than bad work, and a skilled worker should receive more than an unskilled one. But, according to Gorbachev, the idea of "egalitarianism" has taken root in people's minds. To violate "the organic link between the measurement of labor and the measurement of demand not only deforms the attitude to work, restricting the growth of productivity, but also results in a distortion of the principle of social justice, and that is a matter of great political importance."[20] In 1934 Stalin spoke out against the incorrect understanding of the word "equality" and described "egalitarianism" as a tendency to "level out" people's needs, saying that "Marxism is strongly opposed to the level-ling-out process."[21] Commenting on Gorbachev's appeal for people to fight against distortions of the principles of Marxism and socialism, the philosopher T. I. Oizerman states: "The concept of socialism is incompatible with egalitarianism in reward for labor. The fight against egalitarianism makes possible the full revelation and the optimal realization of the advantages of the socialist system over capitalism."[22] This conclusion was drawn just fifty-two years after Stalin made his appeal.

Gorbachev's proposal "to extend further internal Party democracy" as part of the "general policy of the further democratization of Soviet society" was treated—mainly outside the Soviet Union—as a major sensation and indisputable evidence of a sincere desire to carry out revolutionary changes in the USSR. Gorbachev proposed that "we may introduce a procedure whereby Party secretaries, including first secretaries, will be elected by secret ballot at meetings of the appropriate Party committees."[23] This proposal might well be regarded as sensational if the secret ballot for the election of Party bodies had not already been written into the Party's statutes, and if, in February 1937, a meeting of the Central Committee had not approved a special resolution based on a report by Andrei Zhdanov which required "the reorganization of Party work on the basis of the unconditional and complete application of the principles of inner-party democratism laid down in the Party statutes," including "the introduction of the secret ballot for candidates in elections to Party bodies."[24]

It is worth noting that Gorbachev's speeches often contain close (though concealed) quotations from Stalin. For example, his speech on the Party's personnel policy ends: "Bolsheviks can achieve everything," paraphrasing Stalin's well-known statement that "there are no fortresses that Bolsheviks cannot take."

It is a peculiarity of the Gorbachev epoch that an only slightly touched-up Stalinist vocabulary is used with exceptional effectiveness. Slightly extending the range of permitted information, it has become possible to present Soviet society as though it were open. All that was needed was to publish newspaper reports of earthquakes in Tadzhikistan, a collision between two ships in the Black Sea, an ecological catastrophe in Uzbekistan, and so forth. Each dispatch of this kind was intended to demonstrate the results of the bad work put in by Gorbachev's predecessor, who had let the people get out of hand, and at the same time to underline the breadth of view and the openness of the new general secretary. The Soviet leaders do not now rely only on their own means of mass communication, however: they have turned to Western public-relations specialists for assistance. Robert Dillenschneider, president of the world's biggest public-relations firm, Hill and Knowlton, said in an interview published in an Italian magazine that, following the explosion of the nuclear reactor at Chernobyl, in the Ukraine, he was invited to the Kremlin, where he obtained a contract to "sell" to the world the Kremlin's version of the disaster.[25] The preoccupation of the Soviet information and disinformation services with foreign policy and Western public opinion was evidenced, similarly, in February and March 1987 when some 130 prisoners were released whose names were known in the West but whose release was not mentioned at all in the Soviet mass media, though their names were announced at press conferences given at the ministry of foreign affairs. Gorbachev the Liberator thought it important that his benevolence should be properly appreciated by public opinion in the West.

Gorbachev's prestige and his reputation as a reformer and revolutionary, which he acquired with such remarkable speed, are to be explained mainly (since the concrete results of his moves are still not apparent) by skillful exploitation of the mass media to project his image. Perhaps even more important has been the intensive use of Soviet "cultural" activists—writers, artists, and film people. Not since

Stalin's time has a general secretary enjoyed such affection on the part of the Soviet "masters of culture." In the course of his well-known meeting with writers, Gorbachev put to them a straight question, On whose side are you, masters of culture? Today their reply is practically unanimous, On *your* side, Mikhail Sergevich!

It must be admitted that the Soviet "masters of culture" have every reason to be nice to Mikhail Gorbachev. In the years 1985–87 films previously banned by the censor were screened, some writers and poets whose names had previously been excluded from the history of Russian literature (Gumilev, Nabokov, Ivanov) were rehabilitated, and some manuscripts that had been lying for years in writers' desks were allowed to be published. These were changes that one could only rejoice at. But one cannot help recalling the Trojan high priest Laocoön who warned his fellow citizens: I fear the Greeks even when they come bearing gifts. Gorbachev's gifts evoke apprehension primarily because they are indeed gifts and even, one might say, bribes. They are offered out of the kindness of his heart, because it is the monarch's will. But no law has been passed abolishing censorship, nor one to protect the writer, artist, or film-maker from the arbitrary actions of the regime. It is a striking fact that the only writers to be "rehabilitated" are ones long since dead, and that publication has been permitted of manuscripts that have been lying around for decades and may be completely out of date. Artistic affairs continue to be regulated (as the literary critic Viktor Shklovsky once said) like a railway timetable. But here one must not forget that Laocoön was cruelly punished for his suspicious attitude by the angry gods, and his fellow citizens joyfully welcomed within the walls of their city the Greeks' gift—the Trojan horse.

A notable feature of the Gorbachev "revolution" is the total absence from it of young people. There are no young people among the officials surrounding the general secretary, nor are there any among the journalists, writers, and artists whom Gorbachev has seduced. The places that have become vacant following the purge of the old *apparat* are being filled by party officials advanced in years. Unlike the situation in the post-Stalin period, Gorbachev's appeals have not awakened any enthusiasm among either young students or young workers. The artificial character of the "revolutionary change" proclaimed by Gorbachev is underlined by this apathy on the part of the young. History knows of no revolutions that have been carried out by old men alone. The apathy of Soviet youth can be explained by reference to their upbringing, but also, perhaps, by the fact that they sense the insincerity in Gorbachev's catchwords.

The Miracle and the Mystery—two elements in the triad of the Grand Inquisitor—produce results only if they are exploited by Authority. The only obvious and indisputable result offered in more than two years of "change" is that there is in the Soviet Union today only one Leader, only one Authority—Mikhail Gorbachev. Never before in Soviet history has a new general secretary created a cult of his own personality with such speed.

The technique of creating a "cult" has, once again, been borrowed from Stalin, who showed the way. Gorbachev's most striking gesture—his telephone call to Sakharov—was a straight imitation of Stalin. A quarter of a century ago, in his novel *Life and Fate*, Vasily Grossman described a telephone conversation between Stalin and a nuclear physicist called Shtrum. Grossman depicted in one conversation the miraculous effect of Stalin's phone calls. "Stalin and his telephone calls! Rumors would go round Moscow once or twice every year: 'Stalin's phoned Dovzhenko, the film director! Stalin's phoned Ilya Ehrenburg!' There was no need for Stalin to give direct orders—to ask that a prize be awarded to X, a flat be allocated to Y, or an institute be set up for Z. Stalin was above such matters; they were dealt with by subordinates. . . . If Stalin gave a man a quick smile, his life would be transformed overnight. . . . Dozens of notables would bow down before him—Stalin had smiled at him, Stalin had joked with him on the phone."[26] In the same way members of the Academy of Science gave Andrei Sakharov a joyful welcome when he returned to Moscow after Gorbachev's phone call, although a short time before that, before the phone call, they had known only the words used to condemn their colleague.

Today it is only Gorbachev who speaks—on every question—with writers, engineers, collective farmers, film producers, Young Communists, artists and journalists, peace fighters and foreign statesmen and politicians. He alone puts forward new ideas, issues instructions, advice, and directives, and teaches people to work well and live "honestly." In his talk with writers Gorbachev described the situation in the country in these words: "There is the population which wants changes and even dreams of seeing changes take place, and there is the administrative *apparat,* the Government *apparat* and the Party *apparat* that do not want to see any changes taking place or to lose some rights arising out of their privileges." That means that it is the people and the general secretary who want changes. They are obstructed by Brezhnev's *apparat*. Once the barrier between the people and the general secretary has been destroyed, changes will take place about which the Soviet people are dreaming. The dream will become reality. So we have drawn up for us the ideal (traditional) Soviet pyramid of power: Lenin (the source of legitimacy), the general secretary (today Gorbachev), and the People. In a conversation with the general secretary of the Argentinian Communist Party, Athos Fava, Gorbachev complained: "They want to turn me into a god, but I am not a god. If there is a god in the Soviet Union, it is our people."[27] People began to regard Stalin as a god only toward the end of his life.

The general secretary's authority derives from the party's indivisible authority in the country. "No one should forget," Gorbachev reminded people, "that our party is the ruling party."[28] Time and time again he stresses that "our party is the ruling party."[29] The leading role of the party in the life of the country and its right to govern the country remains an axiom, to doubt which is a crime. Neither *glasnost* nor criticism and self-criticism extends to this subject; they are strictly forbidden. In 1926, when the first general secretary was busy destroying Lenin's party machine, it was still possible to talk of such matters. Nikolai Bukharin said then: "A certain section of our Communist cadres, both young and old, may degenerate through having exclusive power. Since our Party is the ruling party in the country, and since our regime is a form of dictatorial power, there is, of course, a great temptation to make use of one's position." Nine years after the Revolution, Bukharin was already noting the party's tendency to degenerate and turn into a "hierarchical system."[30]

What is the nature of the changes that have taken place in the Soviet Union since March 1985? The question may be formulated in a more concrete way: Is it possible to imagine a ruling party carrying out reforms aimed at reducing its authority? Doubts whether Gorbachev's "changes" are genuinely revolutionary, i.e., are changing something essential in the system, derive from the fact that appeals similar to Gorbachev's and actions, projects, and promises of a similar nature have been repeated before so many times. Doubts also rise because of certain frank statements of opinion by both theorists and practitioners in today's Soviet society. E. Ligachev, said to be the party's chief ideological guardian, declared: "The sum of the party's activities since the April [1985] Central Committee meeting amounts essentially to a confirmation of the close links between ideology and real life." A corresponding member of the Academy of Science, G. Smirnov, summed up the situation: "The current changes are being carried out on our own socialist foundations and are aimed at consolidating those foundations and their development worldwide, at the completion and perfection of socialism and the transformation of Soviet society into a fully developed socialism."[31]

In a speech dealing with a proposal for a new program for the CPSU and with the main directions to be taken by economic and social advance in the USSR up to the year 2000, Gorbachev set out with admirable clarity the aims of the ruling Party: "Our Party must have a strong social policy embracing every aspect of a man's life, from the conditions in which he works and lives, cares for his health and occupies his leisure time to his attitude to social classes and other nationalities." To embrace every aspect of a man's life is to continue and develop on the threshold of the third millennium Stalin's dream of people as cogs who "keep our great state machine in working order."

The satisfaction, joy and sometimes enthusiasm which Gorbachev's activities evoke are easy to explain. The oppressive immobility of the Brezhnev era, which lasted for eighteen years, was so hard to bear that even the appearance of movement is a relief and seems like a step in the right direction. But the joy is somewhat clouded by the fact that it has been experienced so many times before and has led only to bitter disappointment. Half a century ago the German writer Lion Feuchtwanger visited the Soviet Union at the height of the Terror. He felt himself to be fortunate in having escaped from "the oppressive atmosphere of false democracy and hypocritical humanism into the lively, health-giving atmosphere of the Soviet Union," and he concluded his account of his trip—*Moscow 1937*—in a striking manner: "It is a real tower of Babel which is being built, not to bring people closer to heaven, but to bring the heavens down to the people. And they have succeeded."[32]

Have they really succeeded?

April 1987   *Mikhail Heller*

I drink to the simple people, *ordinary* and modest, to the "cogs," who keep our great state machine in motion.   STALIN

Someone must keep an eye on the cogs. . . .   KHRUSHCHEV

Our Party must have a strong social policy embracing every aspect of a man's life. . . .   GORBACHEV

I

THE GOAL

1

The Beginning of the
Experiment

The October Revolution, as Soviet ideologists rightly assert,
was an unprecedented phenomenon which gave birth to a new era. Its
nature and significance remain to this day the subject of heated controversy: was it a step forward, a step backward, or did it merely mark
time? But on one point there is agreement: October 25, 1917, must be
marked as a red-letter day. On that day, for the first time in history,
a revolution was carried out whose goal was not simply to seize power
over what Lenin called the "state machine," but to create an ideal
society, a political, economic and social system new to mankind. The
October *coup d'état* was carried out with the purpose of implementing
a project and attaining a great goal. The authors of the project, who
were not in power, knew that the goal could be achieved only if they
created a New Man, and they also knew how to proceed: "Proletarian
coercion in all its forms, beginning with the firing squad is . . . the way
of fashioning the communist man out of the human material of the
capitalist era."[1]

The task was clearly and unambiguously defined. Influenced by his
study of the French Revolution, Alexander Herzen had formulated in
1862 the "great, fundamental idea of revolution": "Wishing to consider

the people as having come of age, and to give them back their freedom, the revolutionaries treated them like an object of welfare, a *chair au bonheur public,* a sort of liberation-fodder not unlike Napoleon's cannon-fodder."[2]

The leaders of the October Revolution were full of contempt for the "people's freedom" and determined to look upon them as immature children. From their very first days in power they set about remolding this "human material of the capitalist era," this "liberation-fodder."

Maxim Gorky, a contemporary witness, commented on the revolutionary events of 1917 in his newspaper *Novaya zhizn' (New Life)* from the day of the Bolshevik *coup* until July 1918, when the newspaper was closed down by Lenin. He tirelessly reiterated that "the working class cannot fail to understand that Lenin is only performing a certain experiment on their skin and on their blood"; that Lenin "works like a chemist in a laboratory, with the difference that the chemist uses dead matter. . . . Lenin, however, works with living material"; that "the People's Commissars treat Russia as material for an experiment; to them the Russian people is that horse which bacteriologists inoculate with typhus so that the horse produces antityphoid serum in its blood"; that the proletarians are being used as material for "an inhuman experiment"; that the Bolsheviks "are performing an extremely cruel scientific experiment on the living body of Russia"; and that revolutionaries were treating the people "as an untalented scientist treats dogs and frogs intended for cruel scientific experiments."[3]

Day after day, in his *Untimely Thoughts,* Gorky repeated his accusation that the Bolsheviks, led by Lenin, were conducting a "brutal and scientific experiment on the living body of Russia," the Russian people, and the Russian proletariat. He stressed the cruelty of the "scientific" experiment; to this witness of the Revolution, it was only too clear that the goal was the very refashioning of living human matter. Decades later the experiment still continues.

In 1917 Gorky was convinced that the commissars' experiment on the Russian people was "doomed in advance to failure." Horrified by the Revolution for which he had done so much, the famous writer thought that the "worn-out, half-starved horse may die."[4] Today, opinions differ about the results of the experiment.

At one time it seemed that it had proved a resounding success. In 1949, *Pravda* was in no doubt that "the traits of the communist future, once as far away as the light of the distant stars, today are close at hand: visible, palpable and alive."[5] These words were soon echoed in a 1950s novel: "It was Vladimir Ilyich who said that 'the struggle for the consolidation and completion of communism is the foundation of communist morality.' This was in 1920. Nearly three decades have elapsed since then, and we have created a new society and a new type of man."[6] *The Soviet People,* published in 1974 by Politizdat, asserted that the Soviet Union—"the first realm of freedom on earth for the working man"—had become the "motherland of a new and higher type of *Homo sapiens: Homo sovieticus.* "[7] With the utmost clarity the authors proceeded to draw up the balance sheet of the experiment they considered to have been so brilliantly executed: it had taken millions of years for the cell to advance to the stage of *Homo sapiens* and to reach the level of man endowed with reason, but only sixty for him to be cleansed of all impurities, and for the highest type of *Homo sapiens,* a new biological specimen by the name of *Homo sovieticus,* to be born in the Soviet Union. Leonid Brezhnev declared in his report to the Twenty-Fifth Party Congress in 1976 that Soviet man represented the "most significant achievement of the last sixty years."[8]

More recently, however, doubts have begun to undermine this unshakeable certainty. In 1981, Mikhail Suslov, then the Party's chief ideologist, was forced to concede that Soviet man had not yet been perfected, and so did not yet satisfy all the Party's requirements.[9] Two years later, the new ideological chief, Konstantin Chernenko, insisted on the need to continue with the experiment, emphasizing that "the formation of the new man constitutes not only an important goal but an indispensable prerequisite for the construction of communism."[10]

Outside ideological circles, opinions also differ on the extent to which the task has been completed. In his prison diaries Edward Kuznetsov noted that "the spiritual realm has become the object of the crudest manipulation, whose ultimate goal is to produce a new man." According to him, this is both a project and a goal yet to be attained.[11] Alexander Zinoviev, on the other hand, believes that the task has been accomplished: ". . . we were the first to produce this new type of man."[12]

But all agree on the central fact—the creation of Soviet man is a process which began in the first days of the revolution—and disagree only on how soon the goal will be attained. During the decades since

1917 the model for Soviet man has changed: in the 1920s the accepted model was the revolutionary, the destroyer of the old world (the iron commissars, the Chekists), a model that was succeeded by the creator of the new world (Industrial Man, Scientifically Organized Man, Perfect Communist Man, the builder of utopia), from whom the Party demanded energy and initiative as well as ideological commitment. Then Stalin proclaimed the "cog" to be the ultimate ideal: Soviet man should consider himself a mere "cog" in the gigantic wheel of the Soviet state. Khrushchev announced in 1961 that this "cog" would certainly be created by 1981, would combine "high ideological commitment, broad education, moral purity and physical perfection."[13]

But these external changes in the model have served only to obscure the fact that its content has remained unchanged. The goal is still to create an instrument to build the new world. As early as the 1920s, the great writer Andrei Platonov warned that this process could only lead to the emergence of a new type of citizen: the "state's man." Indeed, the fundamental characteristic of each of the models of the new Soviet man has been his feeling of belonging to the state, of being but a particle (a "cog") in the state machine, a member of the collective. Three years after the Revolution, Evgeny Zamyatin described the state of the future, a state in which the relationship between the individual and the system is defined with mathematical precision:

> ... take a pair of scales: on one side there is a gram, on the other—a ton; on one side "I," on the other "We," the One State. Is it not clear that to suppose that the "I" can have some sort of "rights" in relation to the State is exactly like assuming that the gram can counterbalance the ton? Hence the rights go to the ton and the duties to the gram: and the natural path from nothingness to greatness is to forget that you are a gram and to feel instead that you are a millionth part of a ton.[14]

Zamyatin here formulates a fundamental law governing the formation of the New Man: in order to attain the goal, it is essential not only that the leaders should want to melt the "grams" into the "ton," but also that the led—the grams themselves—should *wish* to be merged into the "ton," welded together into a collective. The success of the operation to produce a new type of person depends on the extent to which the individual is ready to surrender his "I" and on the intensity of his resistance to a process which in the 1930s came to be described in metallurgical terms as "reforging."

Today, after seven decades of Soviet power, doubts as to the success of the operation still persist, because *Homo sovieticus* in his pure form remains a relatively rare phenomenon. In Gorky's play *The Lower Depths,* Satin, who utters the celebrated words, "Man . . . that has a proud sound," explains that Man is not just you, or I, or he; Man is you; I; he; Mahomet; Napoleon—all in one. *Homo sovieticus* is an amalgam of the qualities and characteristics which can be discerned in varying proportions in all those who inhabit the Soviet Union and breathe its air. In 1982 the French critic Louis Marcorelles expressed his amazement after seeing a Soviet film at the Venice Film Festival: "the protagonists and the director are like visitors from another planet and another era." His astonishment was understandable. But if he had looked more carefully around his own country, or Italy, or any other country of the non-Soviet world, he would have discovered in its people many of the qualities of Soviet man; or a readiness to acquire them. It is remarked that wherever a Soviet-style regime is set up, it immediately undertakes to create the New Man. When the North Vietnamese army entered Saigon in 1975, the "formation of the new man, a new type of people and a new mentality," began immediately, as the 1983 Statutes of the Institute for Cultural Relations with France in Ho Chi Minh City (formerly Saigon) made clear: "The only cultural and propaganda materials which can be imported, kept and circulated are those which . . . promote the creation of the new man in Vietnam."[15] And in Mozambique the new president announced, "We are waging a class war for the creation of the new man."[16]

The determination "to transform human nature by force" that Bertrand Russell discovered in Moscow in 1920[17] is apparent sixty years later in a growing number of countries, which now include nearly a third of mankind. From Moscow to Saigon, Maputo to Tirana, Prague to Phnom Penh, Warsaw to Beijing, the experiment is in full gear. The new man is being created, and with him a new language and a new civilization. A "new world" is being built, in which the state becomes a "school of social conditioning," as the leader of the Socialist Revolutionaries put it four years after "October."[18]

The experiment continues, but with erratic success; different countries march towards the great goal in different ways. One of its results, however, is indisputable: the characteristics of Soviet man can all be found to a greater or lesser degree (some are more apparent than others) in *Homo sapiens* himself. In Soviet-style regimes, as a result of the process of social conditioning, these qualities begin to develop, grow, and become dominant. Every human organism contains tuberculosis bacteria, and under favorable conditions they will trigger the disease and take over the entire organism.

I offer . . . paradise, an earthly paradise,
and on this earth there can be no other
kind of paradise.   DOSTOEVSKY

2

Sketch for a Portrait

In his study of socialism as a phenomenon in world history, Igor Shafarevich points to a striking similarity between the structure of present-day communism, the utopian communism of the Middle Ages, and primitive communism at the dawn of mankind. He concludes that there is a yearning for death and self-destruction in both "the personal experience of individuals" and "the psyche of mankind as a whole." And according to Shafarevich, socialism is "one of the aspects of the impulse of mankind's yearning for self-destruction and nothingness."[1] The author's arguments are convincing, but in order to accept them one must also accept the proposition that humanity's death-wish has been so powerful and seductive as to have been a prime mover in thousands of years of history. The utopias of Plato, Thomas More, Campanella, Müntzer, Babeuf, Winstanley, Fourier, Saint-Simon and Marx have all attracted fanatic adherents. People all over the globe have never stopped trying to create an earthly paradise, which invariably turns out to be a hell. But this does not discourage others, for the people summoning us to the "golden age" have always been those who considered themselves New Men cleansed of impurities, who can promise their followers purification and rebirth.

For centuries the dream of the New Man was closely bound to the idea of God. Only through acceptance of God and by God's grace could man experience rebirth and achieve perfection. Later, in the nineteenth century, the dream was transformed: the wish to become new and perfect remained, but the new man was now seen as the incarnation not of God's design, but of a scientific plan. Only by conforming to the laws of science and history could man hope to achieve regeneration.

In the 1920s, the young Soviet state began to search for its ancestors in the revolutionary movements of the past, discovering such precursors as the Anabaptists who in 1534 captured the city of Münster and established there a "communist state"—the New Jerusalem. Soviet ideologues detected a direct parallel between Lenin's actions after the October coup and those taken by the Anabaptist leader Jan Bokelson who, after the seizure of Münster, had introduced "certain communist principles" (the obligation to work, the partial expropriation of working instruments and consumer goods) and "in defending the city from internal and external enemies had resorted to terror."[2]

Hundreds of books have been written about the Russian idea of Bolshevism and the Russian precursors of the October Revolution and Soviet power. There is no doubt that if an October-type revolution were to take place in England, France, or any other country, it would be very easy to find antecedents for it in that country's history as has been the case since 1945 wherever a Soviet-style system has been set up: in China and Poland, Albania and Cuba, Cambodia and Czechoslovakia, historical precursors who had over the centuries been preparing the ground for the advent of socialism have been sought and found.

Bolshevism's Russian ancestry has been much better researched— the pedigree of millionaires is always more fascinating than that of petty functionaries, and is of interest to the historian and the contemporary layman alike. The basic outline of the concept of the New Man (or Soviet man, as he became after the Bolshevik victory) appeared for the first time in the 1860s as a preliminary sketch of the Man destined to be both Instrument and Goal.

The new idea found its first, striking expression in the 1862 underground proclamation *Molodaya Rossiya (Young Russia);* signed by a mysterious "Central Revolutionary Committee," this was the work of a twenty-year-old revolutionary, Peter Zaichnevsky. The proclamation made no attempt to conceal its ancestry:

We have studied the history of the West, and this study has not been wasted on us: we shall be more consistent not only than the wretched French revolutionaries of 1848, but also than the great terrorists of 1792. We shall not take fright if we find that in order to overthrow the established order we have to spill three times as much blood as was spilt by the French Jacobins. . . .

Young Russia then demanded the "transformation of the existing despotic regime into a republican union of federated regions" with power transferred to a National Assembly and regional assemblies. Believing that the "imperial party" (by which Zaichnevsky meant the supporters of the "despotic regime") might rise in defense of the Tsar, *Molodaya Rossiya* proclaimed:

> With complete faith in ourselves, in our own strength, in the people's support for us, and in the glorious future of Russia, to whose lot it has fallen to be the first country to realize the great cause of socialism, we shall cry: "pick up your axes" and then . . . then, strike down the imperial party without mercy, just as they do not show us any mercy today, strike them down in the squares, strike them down in the houses, strike them down in the narrow alleys of the towns, strike them down in the villages and in the hamlets. Remember that he who is not with us is against us, and he who is against us is our enemy, and enemies must be destroyed by every possible means.[3]

Five years after the Revolution, with Lenin still alive, M. N. Pokrovsky, the first Russian Marxist historian, detected in Zaichnevsky's proclamation the first outline of the Bolshevik program. "What was envisaged by the authors of *Young Russia* has become ordinary, everyday reality."[4]

The *Young Russia* proclamation contained the first important elements of the nascent ideology. The goal was clearly stated: socialism and a social democratic republic. The enemy was clearly identified: all those opposed to the goal. The method of struggle against the enemy was defined just as clearly: destruction "by every possible means." (Maxim Gorky's celebrated phrase, "If the enemy does not surrender, he is destroyed," was lifted virtually word for word from the *Young Russia* proclamation.[5]) Finally, the proclamation identified the "motive forces" of the Revolution: "Our main hope rests with the young people of Russia. . . . Remember, young people, that from your midst must emerge the leaders of the people, that you must head the movement." In other words, on one side are the "leaders" whose task is to lead; on the other the "people" who must be led, and who, according to Zaichnevsky's confident prediction, will follow—*must* follow—the leaders.

The theory of the New Man and his role in the revolution was elaborated by Pyotr Tkachev, who was only seventeen when he formulated his first thoughts on the subject: freed in 1861 after a brief stay in prison for his part in some student disorders, Tkachev declared that the revolution's success would be assured if all inhabitants of the Russian Empire over the age of twenty-five had their heads chopped off.[6] (More than a century later the leaders of the Communist revolution in Cambodia succeeded in implementing Tkachev's project.)

Tkachev, however, very soon abandoned this simple and radical idea, and went on to elaborate a theory of revolution which was to form the basis of Lenin's plan for the creation of a "party of a new type." The people were incapable of saving themselves; left to their own devices, they could not build their future in accordance with their real needs; nor could they, by themselves, carry out the social revolution which Tkachev maintained they so badly needed. It was essential, therefore, to create a "revolutionary minority" (Zaichnevsky's "young leaders"), for only such a minority could lay the "rational foundations of a new and rational social order." Revolution was the seizure of power, and "to seize power a conspiracy is needed, and a conspiracy requires discipline and organization." The influence of Blanqui is clearly discernible here, but it is at the same time both a development and an extension of Zaichnevsky's thought. It is obvious to Tkachev that under the leadership of a revolutionary minority the people would act as a destructive force. The people, the mass, the crowd, must therefore await the spark, the revolutionary leader.[7] In his 1868 article entitled "People of the Future and the Heroes of the Petty Bourgeoisie," Tkachev described the people of the future, the person of the future: the New Man, the highest type of human being, the revolutionary; and contrasted him with that inferior creature, the petty bourgeois *(meshchanin)*. The distinguishing characteristic of the "man of the future" is that "his entire activity, his whole way of life, is governed by one ambition, one passionate idea: to bring happiness to the majority of people, to summon as many of them as possible to the banquet of life. The realization of this idea becomes the sole imperative of the actions of the men of the future, because it coincides exactly with their notion of their own happiness."[8]

The purpose, the meaning of the life of a revolutionary "man of the future," is to produce happiness—or, in Tkachev's flowery language, to summon the majority of mankind to the "banquet of life." But not all mankind: the enemy must of course be excluded; and the enemy (in the words of a Soviet writer of the 1920s) can be anyone who "shows physical, mental, social, moral, or any other signs of disagreeing with the ideal of human happiness."[9]

There is nothing philanthropic about the ideal of bringing happiness to mankind that motivates the "men of the future," the "revolutionary minority"; they want to make other people happy because in doing so they make themselves happy. Tkachev points out that one should not talk about the sacrifices made by the "men of the future"—they are actually doing it for themselves.

Tkachev also formulates a fundamental principle governing the behavior of the "men of the future": moral relativism. If revolution is the "historical law" Tkachev proclaims it to be, the revolutionary is justified in using every possible means to attain his principal goal, the destruction of the "established authorities' den." Tkachev explains:

> There is a principle according to which we should not practice deceit. But deceit comes in many forms. In one case nobody's interests may be affected; in another one person's only; in a third, those of an entire party or social estate; in a fourth, the whole people may suffer, and so on. . . . We must give every individual the right to adopt, in every individual case, a critical and undogmatic attitude towards moral laws.[10]

In 1869, a year after Tkachev's *People of the Future,* a new political text appeared that soon achieved worldwide renown. *The Catechism of a Revolutionary,* a chilling blueprint for the ideal "New Man," was the manifesto of a secret society called The People's Revenge *(Narodnaya rasprava),* and was published in *Pravitelstvenny vestnik (The Government Herald)* just as its members went on trial. The official government newspaper can scarcely have had many readers, but the document, the trial, and the personalities of the members of this clandestine organization attracted Dostoevsky's attention, and provided him with material for his novel *The Devils (The Possessed).*

Although the *Catechism* is closely identified with Sergei Nechaev, its authorship has been a matter of debate and controversy. Some historians have attributed it to Nechaev, others to Bakunin; still others have opted for Nechaev *and* Bakunin as coauthors. The 1966 publication of a previously unpublished letter from Bakunin to Nechaev found in the Paris archive of Herzen's daughter settled the matter: it proved that Bakunin could not have been the author of the *Catechism.* [11] This was followed by the publication of excerpts from the diary of Georgy Enisherlov, a Petersburg student who had taken part in the student movement of 1868–69, and who had formulated what might be called the new principles of revolutionary activity, in particular the theory of "party honesty": "there is no such thing as absolute honesty—there is only party honesty." The members of the circle in which these new ideas were debated included a then totally unknown schoolteacher by the name of Sergei Nechaev. Enisherlov recalled that "a lean, beardless youth, with an embittered expression and a convulsively compressed mouth, came up to me, shook me warmly by the hand and said: 'I am with you forever. You can never achieve anything by the straight path: they will tie our hands. . . . Jesuitism is precisely what we have been lacking all this time. Thank you. You have argued it through and said it.' "[12]

At that time Nechaev was a friend of Tkachev and a member of his group. It can therefore be said that in Russia in the late 1860s in primarily student circles a program was drawn up for a social revolution to be carried out by means of a conspiracy organized by a group of revolutionaries and a party. (From then on, the word "party" began to acquire its modern meaning in Russia.)

The twenty-six paragraphs of the *Catechism* enumerated with extreme frankness the indispensable qualities of the "revolutionary," the New Man whom Lenin later called the "professional revolutionary":

Paragraph 1: The revolutionary is a doomed man. He has no interests of his own, no affairs of his own, no feelings, no attachments, no possessions, not even a name. Everything in him is absorbed by a single thought and a single passion—the revolution.

Paragraph 4: The revolutionary despises public opinion. He despises and hates the existing public morality in all its expressions and manifestations. For him everything that contributes to the triumph of the revolution is moral, and everything that hinders it is immoral and criminal.

Paragraph 6: Severe towards himself, he must be severe towards others.

All the tender and disarming feelings of family relations, friendship, love, and gratitude, and even honor, must be stifled within him by a cold and single-minded passion for the revolutionary cause.

By their very nature, Tkachev's journalistic and theoretical writings, the secret *Catechism of a Revolutionary,* and the *Young Russia* proclamation could not reach a wide audience, as to possess or distribute them constituted a criminal offense. But many of the ideas they promulgated, including the theory of the New Man, became known throughout Russia thanks to what was unquestionably the most influential novel in the history of Russian, even world, literature, N. G. Chernyshevsky's astonishing *What Is to Be Done?* The novel was written in 1862 in the Peter and Paul Fortress, where the author was awaiting trial, and was cleared by the censor and published in 1863. The censor's action was quite logical: the book seemed so bad to him that he decided no one would read it. It really *is* very bad; but it is literature of a special kind: ideological literature. Reflecting on the subject of the "good bad books"—a phrase coined by G. K. Chesterton—George Orwell asked himself who had better withstood the test of time, Arthur Conan Doyle or George Meredith. Orwell said that the best example of the "good bad book" was Harriet Beecher Stowe's *Uncle Tom's Cabin,* [13] and he was right: the influence of this novel, held by some contemporaries to have been one of the causes of the American Civil War, can be said to have been in inverse proportion to its literary merit. But the impact of Chernyshevsky's novel on Russian society and Russian history, and, consequently, on world history, was much more profound.

Its very title, *What Is to Be Done?,* was the question that was to determine the individual's place in Russian society until 1917. Tkachev's answer to the question was: "Make revolution." In his own *What Is to Be Done?,* written in 1902, Lenin echoed Tkachev's answer and added that they must begin by creating an organization of professional revolutionaries. The remarkable writer Vasily Rozanov, unwilling to succumb to the current fashion, announced that he had two answers to the question of "what to do": in summer, gather berries and make jam; in winter, drink tea sweetened with the home-made jam; he was immediately ostracized.

The most striking feature of Chernyshevsky's novel, and the reason for its success and influence, is its main character. *What Is to Be Done?* is subtitled "Some Tales About the New People," and it is a family chronicle of these "new people." The hero, Rakhmetov, has no connection with the main theme; the author introduces him into the novel in order to describe the new, revolutionary and consequently human, hierarchy. The novel's principal characters are the "new people," who are "new" because they possess qualities which distinguish them from their compatriots: they have dedicated their lives to the revolution and have rejected "bourgeois morality." But however they may tower over the rest of society, they themselves in turn are dwarfed by Rakhmetov, the Super New Man, the Hero, the Leader. Even before Rakhmetov makes his first appearance, Chernyshevsky warns the reader, "people like Rakhmetov are scarce. I have met but eight (of whom two were women)."[14] Rakhmetov represents a superior breed of men, the breed of which Tkachev and Nechaev dreamed when a few years later they drew up their blueprint for the ideal revolutionary. He is the first *Homo sovieticus.*

Rakhmetov lives only for the revolution. For it he has disowned his parents, rejected love of woman, and renounced friendship. What distinguishes him from the others is his unusual self-esteem: he knows the revolution needs him, so he builds his physical strength by training hard (he goes in for sports), his intellectual strength by reading books (but only "useful" ones) and his strength of character by sleeping on nails—something that had a special influence on generations of radical Russian youth.

Perhaps his most striking feature was the "dialectical nature of his behavior." The principles that governed his life included: no luxury in food, no money wasted on things he could do without. For example, he never bought white bread, sugar, or fruit, but when invited out "he ate with relish many dishes which he denied himself at his own table." It is not difficult to see why: what he ate as a guest cost him nothing. Nevertheless, there were some dishes he would not eat even as a guest. For "whatever the people eat, though only at intervals, I may eat also, when occasion offers. I must not eat that which is entirely out of the reach of common people." Therefore, "when fruits were served, he always ate apples but never apricots; . . . at Petersburg he ate oranges, but refused them in the provinces."[15] Rakhmetov—the ideal revolutionary hero, the prototype of the New Man, the "salt of the salt of the earth," as Chernyshevsky calls him—lived by uncommonly subtle and highly dialectical rules and principles.

Fifteen years after the publication of *What Is to Be Done?* (by which time the novel had been banned), Turgenev wrote a prose-poem called *The Threshold* that demonstrated the extent to which the character of Rakhmetov had permeated the spirit of the Russian intelligentsia. A young girl stands on the threshold: she has decided to dedicate herself to revolutionary action. A mysterious voice lists the trials ahead of her and asks if she is prepared to face them: "Do you know what awaits you there: cold, hunger, hatred, ridicule, scorn, insults, prison, illness and death itself?" "I know," answers the future revolutionary. She is ready to endure "estrangement and total loneliness," a complete break with her family and friends. "Are you prepared to commit a crime?" asks the voice. "Yes," answers the young revolutionary, "even a crime."

The poem ends with the words: " 'Fool!' say some. 'Saint!' say others."[16] Those who said "Saint!" constituted a majority of the Russian intelligentsia; only a minority considered her a fool. Dostoevsky was moved to ask: "How do you know that it is not only possible but necessary to transform human nature?"[17]

His question fell on deaf ears. The Russian intelligentsia had come to believe that it was imperative to bring happiness to the people. "The basic moral judgment of the intelligentsia," wrote the philosopher Nikolai Berdyaev, "can be expressed in the formula: 'Let truth [*istina*] perish, if its disappearance will make the life of the people easier and happier. . . .' "[18] And many members of the intelligentsia became convinced that only social revolution could bring the people happiness, and that the people could achieve this revolution only under the leadership of the New Men who already possessed the qualities everyone else would acquire later. The new men were needed to make the revolution whose aim was to turn everyone (except those incapable of regeneration) into New Men. The intelligentsia's self-confidence was based on science; the gods it revered were materialists and atheists like Vogt, Moleschott, Büchner. In the words of one memoirist: "Büchner's *Force and Matter* exploded among us one fine day like a bomb. . . . The ideas of Büchner and Feuerbach immediately took hold of the Russian mind, and the reactionary elements proved powerless in their later efforts to turn society back to the naive beliefs of the past."[19]

When Marxism came to Russia at the end of the nineteenth century, the ground was already well prepared. Lenin, who most fully embodied the radical spirit of the Russian intelligentsia, believed in science and revolution before he became a Marxist. The official biographers of Lenin and Leninism worked carefully over the ancestry of the leader of the Party and the Revolution, retaining only his "noble" ancestors—first and foremost, Chernyshevsky. There can be no doubt that Chernyshevsky's *What Is to Be Done?* played a tremendous role in the formation of Lenin's character as a revolutionary. "It ploughed me over" was Lenin's own comment.[20] But no less powerful was the influence of other revolutionaries—above all, Tkachev and Nechaev—whose names were, from the mid-1930s, expunged from the pantheon of the forerunners of "October."

Although Lenin's writings make no direct reference to the leaders of Russian youth in the late 1860s, the first historians of Bolshevism did not hesitate to mention these important precursors. "In Tkachev's prophetic foresight," wrote Pokrovsky, "we detect, fixed upon us, the gaze of Bolshevism."[21] Lenin's close friend and associate Vladimir Bonch-Bruevich remembered how close Chernyshevsky was to Lenin, and added that "after Chernyshevsky, Vladimir Ilyich attached great importance to Tkachev, whose works he advised one and all to read and study."[22] There is no doubt that the leader of the October Revolution made good use of Tkachev's strategic plan:

> . . . the revolutionary minority, having liberated the people from the oppressive yoke of fear and terror of the powers that be, opens up [to the people] the opportunity to display their destructive powers, skilfully directing it towards the annihilation of the enemies of the revolution, it [the revolutionary minority] demolishes their strongholds and deprives them of all the means of resistance and counteraction. Then, by using its power and authority, it introduces new, progressive, communist elements into the people's life.[23]

No one has formulated better the program implemented by Lenin after the Revolution.

Sergei Nechaev contributed some "tactical innovations" to the stock of Lenin's ideas. Writing in 1926, a Soviet expert on Nechaev's life and work insisted, "for the triumph of the social revolution, Nechaev chose the correct means, and what he failed to achieve in his time the Bolsheviks accomplished many years later, implementing more than one of his tactical tenets."[24] Bonch-Bruevich relates that Lenin "often pondered over Nechaev's leaflets," and that Lenin was outraged by the sly trick that "the reactionaries played on Nechaev following the example of Dostoevsky and his loathsome but brilliant novel *The*

Devils." Lenin thought very highly of Nechaev's "special organizing ability" and his "special techniques of conspiratorial work," but—as Bonch-Bruevich emphasizes—what Lenin admired most of all was Nechaev's ability to "put his thoughts into such striking words that they remained imprinted in one's memory for the rest of one's life." Students of Lenin's use of language have ignored this very important stylistic model. The leader of the revolution was delighted with Nechaev's answer, in one of his leaflets, to the question, "which members of the imperial family should be liquidated?" Nechaev's answer, Lenin stressed, could not have been more precise: "The whole great litany." (The great litany was the public prayer for the health and salvation of the members of the imperial family.) Lenin enthusiastically asserted that Nechaev's answer was intelligible to even the "simplest reader": The whole Romanov clan must be wiped out![25] Lenin's own slogan— "Rob the robbers!"—was coined on the eve of the October Revolution, and became the most popular revolutionary slogan precisely because it was so simple and accessible—formulated in accordance with the "Nechaev model."

For Lenin, the encounter with Marxism meant the discovery of the Science of Sciences, a philosophy that called for the transformation of the world and formulated the laws governing such a change in man and society. The formula, "Being determines consciousness," was the first step on the road to the creation of the New Man. Simply to change this "being" would be to build socialism, and to liquidate in the process not only the "imperial party" (Zaichnevsky's somewhat vague and unscientific notion), but all classes hostile to the Revolution: an enemy sufficiently concrete, yet at the same time sufficiently abstract; and an adversary, moreover, who had been condemned by the laws of history.

The Communist Party of the Soviet Union proceeds, and has always proceeded, from the premise that the formation of the New Man is the most important component of the entire task of Communist construction.   SUSLOV

3

Homo Sovieticus Sum

Medical students in the Soviet Union begin their Latin course with the sentence, *"Homo sovieticus sum"* ("I am Soviet man"). In their first year, at the very outset of their medical studies, the future doctors learn that there are two types of human being: *Homo sapiens* and *Homo sovieticus.*

The persistent assertion that these two types of men are fundamentally different is an important characteristic of the Soviet system. Although all nations are convinced of their own superiority, only the Soviet Union claims to be producing a new type of man. The Nazis based their division of mankind into Aryans and non-persons on the concept of "race" as an absolute, immutable category: either you were an Aryan or you were not. The Bolsheviks proceeded from a similar premise, the only difference being that their division of mankind was based on a different but equally immutable criterion: social origin. To be born into a proletarian family, of proletarian parents, guaranteed one a privileged position in the post-revolutionary social hierarchy. But just as in Nazi Germany the non-Aryan could not rid himself of the stigma he carried from birth until death and passed on to his children, so, in the Soviet Republic, the non-proletarian individual could never get away from his origins; his only solution was to conceal it and move to another part of the country. With the typical candor of the self-righteous fanatic, one of the leaders of the omnipotent political police, the Cheka, explained to his subordinates in 1918: "We are not waging war against individual persons. We are exterminating the bourgeoisie as a class."[1] As early as the mid-1920s, in a poem dedicated to Pushkin, Mayakovsky explains to the great poet, who was killed in a duel, that in the Soviet era the authorities would have had no difficulty at all in dealing with his murderer, D'Anthès; they simply would have asked him, "What was your occupation before 1917?" and "Who were your parents?"

As the Soviet system was consolidated and "impure" elements were liquidated, the proletarian ruling class began to lose its hegemony and privileges. Instead, two groups began to take shape: on one side, the leaders who possessed the qualities of Soviet man; on the other, the mass of the led, equal in their imperfection and their desire to cleanse themselves of the "impurities" that prevented them from attaining perfection.

Cliché-ridden remarks on the inscrutability of the Soviet Union continue to fill the pages of historical monographs and spy novels, political memoranda and economic analyses. As a rule, these studies ignore the crucial question of the formation of *Homo sovieticus,* a new type of man who has turned the Soviet system (created for him and by him) into a phenomenon unprecedented in world history. The nature of Soviet man explains why the analogical method cannot be applied satisfactorily to the Soviet Union. Analysis based upon more traditional categories—Russian Empire/Soviet Empire; Westernizers/Slavophiles; Right-wing/Left-wing; Progressive/Reactionary; economic crisis/modernization—is equally unsatisfactory. No one studies contemporary Britain by taking as his starting point the outcome of the Wars of the Roses; yet you seldom come across a Sovietologist who does not refer to the Mongol yoke or Ivan the Terrible.

Russian writers, thinkers and poets who accepted the October Revolution as a natural, if stormy, continuation of Russian history were the first to resort to the analogical method. It was perfectly natural that Russian thinkers who had faced this unprecedented cataclysm would start to look for its causes in the past of their country and people. They searched for the Russian ancestors of the Revolution and found them without difficulty. The poet Maximilian Voloshin voiced most elo-

quently the feeling—especially widespread among the intelligentsia—
that even in the Revolution's terrible reality it was still possible to
recognize certain familiar features:

> What has changed? The insignia and titles are new?
> But on all sides the same hurricane is in view.
> The spirit of autocracy is in the commissars,
> And the gusts of revolution are in the tsars.[2]

The image of the Revolution as a purely Russian phenomenon took no
account of the fundamental point, the determined attempt to transform
human nature. Bertrand Russell was one of the first to draw attention
to this basic characteristic. Visiting Soviet Russia in 1920, he discovered
to his horror that he had arrived in a true Platonic utopia. "The
ultimate source of the whole train of evils," he commented, "lies in the
Bolshevik outlook on life: its dogmatism of hatred and its belief that
human nature can be completely transformed by force," and he pre-
dicted that for the world this could only mean "centuries of darkness
and futile violence."[3] In the 1930s and 1940s, Berdyaev did much to
spread the idea that there was a *"Russian* Communism." In an earlier
book, written soon after his expulsion from the Soviet Republic, when
his impressions of life in the "new world" were still fresh, he spoke of
the emergence of a "new anthropological type," a "new young man—
who is an international, rather than a Russian, type." Berdyaev pre-
dicted: "The sons and grandsons of these young people will quickly
come to resemble substantial bourgeois types, the masters of life. These
gentlemen will fight their way to the best positions in life by means of
the Cheka and an unprecedented number of executions. . . . The most
ominous figure in Russia is not that of the old Communist, who is
doomed to die, but that of this new young man."[4]

Work on the creation of "this new young man" has continued
without interruption. In 1975, half a century after Berdyaev's prediction, the editor in chief of *Pravda* stressed the immutability of the task:
"The educator influences the intellect and feelings of man, transmits to
him and instills into his consciousness information, the content of
which is socialist ideology: he aspires to make this ideology the guiding
principle in all his deeds and practical activities."[5] The editor of the
newspaper of the Central Committees, a corresponding member of the
Academy of Sciences, one of the "generals" on the ideological battle-

field, was saying in all seriousness in 1975 what had been proclaimed as long ago as 1926 by an ideological bureaucrat and fanatical worshipper of the Soviet system in Andrei Platonov's satire, "Gradov City": "Man no longer has any time left for a so-called private life, for it has been replaced by governmental and socially useful activity. The state has become his soul."[6]

The sketch of the New Man was made long before the Revolution. A description of Soviet man (a being in gestation or, as some would have it, already born) can be found in the works of Soviet ideologues and in the travelogues of distinguished foreigners visiting the first socialist state in the world, led by experienced Soviet guides. Following his 1923 visit to the Republic of the Soviets, the American journalist Albert Rhys Williams concluded that the October Revolution has "supplanted the Second Coming of Christ," and observed that the morality of the Soviet people was now based upon the "principle of collectivism." "They acted collectively and submitted to the collective wisdom of the Party, but this did not diminish their individual freedom by one iota."[7] The American journalist had mastered to perfection the sharpest weapon in the Marxist arsenal, the dialectic: submission to the Party's collective wisdom does not reduce individual freedom—a dialectic whose true meaning Orwell later revealed in the formula: Slavery is Freedom.

The introduction to *The Soviet People*, headed "Homo sovieticus," gives a list of the basic attributes of Soviet man:

> The first and most important quality of a Soviet man is his total commitment to Communist ideas and his devotion to the Party. . . . Whether or not he is a member of the CPSU, his Party-mindedness manifests itself in his entire world outlook, his clear vision of the Ideal, to which he is selflessly devoted.

The authors are at pains to give as detailed a picture as possible of this fruit of so many years' labor in refashioning human matter:

> We are pondering over a difficult task—how to characterize the New Man. . . . Words are not enough, for this human being cannot be made to fit into mere formulae. But we do have something to say about what sort of man *Homo sovieticus* is . . . he is, first of all, a Man of Labor . . . he regards work as the most important thing in his life . . . he is also a man of the

Collective . . . a man infinitely loyal to his socialist multinational fatherland . . . he is a man who feels responsible for everything . . . there is nothing that does not concern him, be it an event of global significance or simply the life of his neighbors on the same landing . . . he is a man of lofty ideals . . . he actively champions the ideas of the Great October . . . he is a harmoniously developed human being . . . he is a man about whom the state cares a great deal. He is aware of this concern and feels its results everywhere. His children go to kindergarten or school, his parents are treated by the best doctors; he himself has just received a new apartment. . . . Cities grow, green parks abound, new goods are put on the market, scientists are concerned about clean air—and all this is for him, for Soviet Man, and free of charge or at very little cost to himself. The state's concern for him is tangible and visible. His comrades, whom he has elected to governmental bodies, decide matters of state, and he knows that this is done in his name, for his benefit.[8]

Stripped of the embellishments required by propaganda (e.g., the state gives the Soviet citizen everything at little or no cost to himself), the main elements of this portrait coincide with the attributes of Soviet man as enumerated by Alexander Zinoviev in his satirical novel, *Homo Sovieticus.* In the official version, Soviet man lives only for his work, is deeply devoted to his homeland, is a member of his collective, always interested in the lives of his neighbors and the inhabitants of this planet; he knows the state has assumed responsibility for looking after him. In Zinoviev's definition,

Homo sovieticus has been trained to live in comparatively foul conditions; he is ready to face adversity and constantly expects even worse; he obediently complies with commands emanating from the authorities; he seeks to frustrate the actions of those who violate the customary norms of behavior; he fully supports his leadership; he possesses a standardized and ideologized consciousness; he feels responsible for his country as a whole; he is ready to sacrifice himself and to sacrifice others.[9]

It is not by chance that the Soviet propagandists and the Soviet satirist paint an identical picture, for both portray an ideal *Homo sovieticus,* as they enumerate qualities found to a greater or lesser degree in every inhabitant of the world of "mature socialism" (and those who were raised in that world). In 1927, the physiologist Savich defined revolution as a process of "unloading" in which man discards everything he has acquired in the course of his cultural development. Criticizing the work of this "bourgeois" scholar, whose book *The Foundations of Human Behavior* had gone through two editions, Leopold Averbakh, the leader of the Proletarian Writers, admitted that Savich had "gone to the essence of the problems of the cultural revolution" that "serves one cause: the re-fashioning of human material, the creation of a new type of man." Averbakh agreed that it was during the cultural revolution that the "unloading" mentioned by Savich—the liquidation of old feelings and the "primitive accumulation of socialist emotions"—would take place.[10] The foremost Marxist philosopher of the 1920s, Abram Deborin, provided a theoretical foundation for the plan to produce a new type of man: "Since socialist ideas can conquer our thinking, they are also capable of being transformed into emotions." Having become socialist emotions, socialist ideas can transform "the whole human being and his psyche, in all their complexity."[11]

From whatever point of view one chooses, Soviet history is in the final analysis the history of the formation of Soviet man, the creation of a special set of conditions in which man no longer behaves as the obsolescent *Homo sapiens* did (and in some backward parts of the world still does), but begins to "accumulate socialist emotions" and to think and feel in a new and different way. Each new generation learns to take the newly created conditions for granted, and future generations will come to regard them as the only normal ones. In one of his stories, the Polish writer Stanislaw Lem describes a distant planet whose inhabitants are indistinguishable from humans. The regime ruling the planet demands that the inhabitants live in, or even better, *under* water. "Gurgling" is their only means of communicating with one another. The official propagandists spare neither efforts nor resources to persuade the citizenry that to be wet is the best thing in the world, while to inhale air—physiologically absolutely essential—is virtually a political crime. The inhabitants of the planet suffer without exception from rheumatism and fervently dream of living for at least a few minutes on dry land. But the propagandists insist that living like a fish, and in particular breathing underwater, is the Ideal, the Goal toward which all citizens must strive.

In the decades since the Revolution the social environment has changed, and under the new conditions the inhabitants of the land of "mature socialism" have developed special attributes. The 1970s emigration from the Soviet Union brought the West its first real contact with products of the new world, for although the émigrés who left Russia immediately after the Revolution left it for good, after crossing the frontier they remained within the bounds of that same civilization. The wave of Soviet émigrés who left Russia during the war years consisted of people who had been breathing Soviet air for almost twenty-five years—a considerable time, but apparently not long enough for a definitive reforging of human nature. The "third wave" of émigrés had known no other environment than the Soviet one.

This does not mean that the émigrés of the 1970s were ideal Soviet men and women: their very desire to leave their native land was proof of serious weaknesses in their Soviet education. Nevertheless, when these former Soviet citizens came up against the non-Soviet world, the differences between the Soviet and non-Soviet mentalities and attitudes toward the world were immediately highlighted.

In 1890, less than a century ago, the Russian humorist Nikolai Leikin wrote a book entitled *Our Folk Abroad.* It describes the journey of a young couple from the provinces, the young merchant Nikolai Ivanovich and his wife, Glafira Semyonovna Ivanov, to the Paris World Exhibition, and their return home. The book was an extraordinary success with Russian readers, who laughed at the young travellers just as they laughed at Mark Twain's *Innocents Abroad,* Leikin's model.

Leikin and Twain described the natural predicament of people who travel to an unfamiliar country, of whose language and customs they have little or no knowledge. Having crossed the frontier, their heroes remain within the bounds of their respective civilizations. Glafira Ivanov is astonished to find that Parisian hotels do not put out the samovar in the late evening, and Nikolai Ivanovich is unhappy with the (by his standards) small portions served in Parisian restaurants. But the possibility of foreign travel, the freedom to exchange rubles for francs, and the general availability of a wide variety of goods seem perfectly natural to them.

To the Soviet travellers of the 1970s, on the other hand, the non-Soviet world's abundance of consumer goods, its wide range of choice, the freedom of movement, the relationship between state and citizens, the particular forms of freedom and unfreedom, are frighteningly alien. Theirs was an encounter between two civilizations—one terrestrial, the other extraterrestrial—with the latter proclaiming itself the Ideal, the crowning achievement, of the entire course of human history.

The fate of Soviet prisoners of war between 1944 and 1947 is a tragic instance of the incompatibility of the two civilizations. The Western Allies could not understand why many of the Soviet officers and soldiers they had liberated from Nazi camps, were unwilling to return home. The former prisoners of war knew very well that, at best, they would be sent to another prison camp, but the British and Americans were quite incapable of grasping this, and they forcibly handed over more than two million of these former prisoners to the Soviet authorities. On the other hand, the Soviet authorities, who themselves had liberated tens of thousands of Allied officers and soldiers, could not understand why former prisoners were welcomed home as heroes in Britain, France, and the United States.[12]

An American film showing the arrival of a spaceship from another planet was called *Close Encounters of the Third Kind.* The 1970s' arrival in the West of a large number of Soviet émigrés could also be called an "encounter of the third kind," one that raised a series of highly topical questions: How is the human race transformed? How is the New Man— *Homo sovieticus*—created? To what extent is the reforging of human material that has been going on in the Soviet Union for seven decades a universal process? Can it be extended to other countries and continents?

Fly, our locomotive, fly full steam ahead.
The commune is the terminus.

FROM A SONG

II

THE VECTORS

In the entire course of human history there has never been such an experiment in the accelerated mass production on a strictly scientific basis of New Men. Lenin's party had seized power with only a very general idea of what it had to do; there was no carefully worked out plan, only the Great Goal—and the means by which it was to be attained. The study of Soviet history reveals a system in what seemed to contemporaries to be a series of fortuitous, uncoordinated, and chaotic acts.

The system for the creation of Soviet man consists of vectors—the main ways in which the human raw material is to be treated—and the instruments with which the work is to be carried out. The vectors may appear to change as the model for Soviet man changed in the post-revolutionary period, the 1940s, and the 1980s. (Nadezhda Mandelstam, one of the most perceptive observers of the Soviet scene, remarked upon the change that had occurred in the outward appearance of the model, in the "physical appearance of Soviet functionaries,"[1] over the decades), but just as a compass needle invariably returns to magnetic north, so all the changes in the vectors were ultimately variations in the same general line, which continued the same basic direction. The goal remained unchanged: the creation of a citizen belonging to the state and the formation of a man who considered himself a small cell in the state organism.

The two main vectors are reality and consciousness. According to Marx, any change in objective reality automatically produces (with a little push, if necessary) a change in human consciousness. As one Marxist has written: "Marxist scholars have observed that human beings are much more adaptable than was earlier assumed."[2] Transformation of the real world means, first and foremost, the destruction of the old state, economic, and social systems, with one of the most powerful blows inflicted on society.

The human relations that make up the society's fabric—the family, religion, historical memory, language—become targets, as society is systematically and methodically atomized, and the individual's chosen relationships are supplanted by others chosen for him, and approved by the state. Man remains alone, face to face with the state Leviathan. Only by melting into the collective, by becoming a mere drop of the "mass," can a man save himself from his terrifying loneliness.

One of the principal means of remolding human consciousness is the infantilization of Soviet man.

We shall prove to them that they are not weak, that they are nothing more than pitiable children, but that the happiness of childhood is the sweetest of all.
DOSTOEVSKY

4

Infantilization

Differences of opinion as to the extent to which the process of creating Soviet man has been completed are an integral part of the animated debate over the effectiveness of ideology as an instrument for remolding human consciousness in the countries professing "real socialism." There are two reasons for the academic nature of these discussions as to whether or not the inhabitants of the zone of "real socialism" in which a third of mankind now lives believe in the official ideology. One is that many Western experts and ex-Communist memoirists exhibit an insatiable nostalgia for the era of revolutionary enthusiasm, the "flight of youth," the time when nothing (apart from millions of victims) could cloud hopes for better times. The second reason is the total absence of research into the effect upon the human brain of decade after decade of uninterrupted ideological intoxication compounded by total control over the means of communication.

It may be considered a mere accident that the effect of detention in Hitler's concentration camps has been studied by psychologists, physiologists, and specialists from all branches of medical science, while no one has studied the prisoners of Soviet camps. After examining several hundred officers and men who had returned from Korean camps, Robert J. Lifton concluded:

> The brainwashing of the prisoners in Korean camps was essentially an attempt to destroy the individual's previous personality and remould it in terms of Communist ideology. It is a process of death and rebirth; and though few left the prison camps as convinced Communists none emerged from the ordeal unscathed.[1]

Lifton draws attention to a fact of exceptional importance: the effect of "brainwashing" and its methods is felt even by those whom he calls "apparent resisters," those who seem not to succumb to the intoxication. His study showed that they do assimilate what has been hammered into their brains, but the effect comes only some time after their liberation, like the explosion of a delayed-action bomb.[2]

It is not hard to imagine the effect of "education" and "reeducation" upon the Soviet citizen who is exposed from the day he is born to brainwashing, and is bombarded all day, every day, with all sorts of propaganda and persuasion.[3] This intensive treatment of human mentality is especially effective because it is carried out in the closed territory of a country cut off from the rest of the world by a strictly guarded frontier. From the first days of the Revolution, the inhabitants of the Soviet zone (it is no accident that the prisoners call the prison camp the "small zone" and the Soviet world beyond the camp gate, the "big zone") have been subjected to extremely severe forms of stress. No studies have yet attempted to measure the destructive effect on the human organism of such permanent forms of stress as fear, chronic shortages of goods, inevitable queues, cramped accommodation, abominable public transport, innumerable prohibitions and the constant need to defy them, and a feeling of total isolation.

In the 1970s the word "stress" became fashionable among Soviet journalists who stressed the harm caused by "stresses" in "capitalist societies rent by socio-economic contradictions."[4] At the same time, Soviet geneticists, newly allowed to engage in a science which in the Stalin era for many years had been denounced as "bourgeois," pointed to the beneficial effect of certain forms of stress as factors promoting the consolidation of hereditary changes.[5]

The Soviet Union is like a gigantic ghetto whose inhabitants develop special qualities that allow them to adapt themselves to life in the ghetto. Semyon Gluzman, a psychiatrist from Kiev who was sentenced to seven years in labor camp followed by many years of internal exile for his exposé of the criminal methods employed by Soviet psychiatry to suppress opposition, took advantage of his confinement to study his fellow prisoners' mental state. He discovered, in particular, that political prisoners who had spent twenty or twenty-five years in the camps developed a special attitude he called "fear of freedom." According to Gluzman, this "fear of freedom" is experienced by political prisoners who even in the camp remain true to their ideas and stick to nonconformist opinions, while ordinary criminals, even if they spend many years in detention, continue to long to leave. Gluzman says this is because criminals who adopt a conformist attitude in the camps do not expect to find different moral and psychological norms from those that governed their lives in camp on the "outside," while political prisoners know that "by comparison with life in the camps, they will experience in freedom a considerable curtailment *a*) of their inner freedom and *b*) of the possibility of defending their dignity against encroachments by social institutions."[6]

Gluzman concludes that political prisoners in the camp live in a psychologically healthy climate, in a group in which moral and spiritual values are given pride of place. Their "fear of freedom" is the fear of healthy individuals apprehensive about reentering an unhealthy society. Yet Soviet psychiatrists have officially declared "dissent" a mental illness; they regard society as healthy, and anyone accused of casting doubt upon the ideal nature of Soviet society as mentally ill. From the point of view of the brainwashing experts this assessment is perfectly logical: dissidents are nothing but the junk of society, rejects who have not capitulated, who have preserved their individuality, and have proved incapable of "loving slavery."

The criteria of "health" and "sickness" in the "new world" under construction were eloquently formulated by the author of the first Marxist history of Soviet literature: "For the sake of the means, the Revolution has to forget about the goal for a long time to come, and it has to banish its dreams of freedom in order not to weaken discipline." The Marxist critic asserted that "it is essential to create a new enthusiasm for the new slavery," and "to learn to love our chains so that they will come to feel like the tender embrace of a mother."[7]

Orwell's novel *1984* ends with the words, "He had won the victory over himself. He loved Big Brother." In Zamyatin's novel *We,* which served Orwell as an important source for *1984,* the character whom the hero (tempted by freedom and realizing its futility) falls in love with is called the Benefactor. In a moment of despair, before loving the Benefactor and betraying the woman he loves, this inhabitant of the One State sorrowfully confesses his dream: "If I had a mother, like the ancients: mine, yes, precisely—*my* mother." But the citizen of the One State, who is known by a number instead of a name, had neither father nor mother. Like the other inhabitants of utopia, he had the Benefactor; just as Orwell's Oceania had Big Brother. The state supplants the family, and the Benefactor–Big Brother replaces the parents. The state must be loved like a parent, and the chains of serfdom become like "the tender embrace of a mother." Evgeny Zamyatin develops the metaphor to its logical conclusion: the Benefactor is the High Priest who personally executes those who break the laws of the One State, as a father punishes his wayward children. The Benefactor's portrait ("Before me sat a man as bald as Socrates"[8]) leaves no doubt that it is a portrait of Lenin.

In April 1918, Lenin outlined his program for transforming man and society: "We, the Bolshevik party, have *convinced* Russia. We have won Russia from the rich for the poor, from the exploiters for the working people. Now we must *rule* Russia."[9] The program was simple: the Party must rule Russia, the people, and every individual citizen. The Party, the people's rulers, assumes the role of omniscient leader, the father who must guide his people (Russia) to Paradise. Lenin drew a clear distinction between "We" and "They." "We"—the Party—must rule "Them"—the mass. We are the fathers; they are the children. The program for transforming human material required infantilization of the individual. In a country marching towards the Supreme Goal, leaping from the "kingdom of necessity" into the "kingdom of freedom," a complex hierarchical system emerged, a new pyramid of privilege. But the principal dividing line ran between the rulers who knew the way things were going—the fathers—and the ruled, ignorant ones who had to have their eyes opened—the children.

The individual thus becomes a child for whom the state replaces parents and friends. The ideal standard for the behavior of Soviet man is furnished by literary characters or such mythologized zealots of the new faith as Lyubov Yarovay and Pavlik Morozov, who sacrifice their own blood relationships for the sake of their spiritual father.*

Drawing on his experience as a prisoner in Dachau and Büchenwald, the psychiatrist and psychologist Bruno Bettelheim described the behavior of the individuals and masses of people in extreme conditions and concluded that the purpose behind the creation of extreme situations (arrests, beatings, torture, confinement in camps) was to "make the prisoners behave like children" and to accelerate the transformation of adults into docile infants.[10] Bettelheim does not seem to suspect that his analysis of the behavior of executioners and victims in the German concentration camp is at the same time a description of the principal stages in the transformation of man in the Soviet Union. The purpose of the German concentration camps, he wrote, was "to change people's personality and adapt it to the needs of the state." With this goal in mind the authorities set out "to break the prisoners as individuals, turning them into a docile mass which would put up no resistance as individuals or as a group." Bettelheim emphasized that the prisoners' individuality was broken down by a series of traumatic shocks: "They were made to curse their God, to accuse each other of the foulest deeds." As a result, grown men were transformed into submissive children who feared their guards and readily carried out their every instruction—and thus adapted to life in the camp.[11] Iosif Mendelevich, sentenced in 1971 to twelve years in a labor camp for attempting to escape from the Soviet Union, recalls being in a similar situation:

> . . . Just imagine that you have been put into a kindergarten for adults, where you are denied the right to behave as you please, to have your own point of view or even your own facial expression. "Why don't you take part in general cultural activities? Why do you look so sullen? Why are you wearing dirty clothes? . . . For this you will be deprived of something or other—parcels, letters, visits."[12]

---

*Yarovay is the heroine of Trenev's play, of the same name, who betrays her husband, a White Guard officer, who is executed. The play, written in 1926, is still performed on the Soviet stage and has been adapted for a film.

Morozov was a twelve-year-old boy who accused his father of helping the kulaks in 1932. His father was shot, and Pavlik was killed by his grandfather.

Soviet man has also been shaped by a series of traumatic shocks. The history of the USSR has been a succession of agonizingly painful blows, both physical and mental. The first shock was the Revolution itself: it destroyed the existing social hierarchy and affected both those who had been at the top of the social pyramid and now found themselves at the bottom, and those who had been at the bottom and now rose to the top. People in the first group suffered from the suddenness of their fall, from their loss of privilege and their accustomed way of life, and from their often impotent anger. People in the second group suffered from the novelty of their new position and the unlimited possibilities opened up for them by unbounded power, which demanded in exchange complete submission to the Idea.

The next shock was terror. Among Lenin's writings extolling terror, demanding its intensification and demonstrating its indispensability and efficacy, one document in particular is remarkable for the candor and precision with which it sets out his thoughts. In this letter, dated March 10, 1922, addressed to the members of the Politburo and marked "strictly secret," Lenin gives detailed instructions for a new assault on the clergy and the bourgeoisie. The letter was written after the end of the Civil War and the adoption of the New Economic Policy, a period (1921–28) of extreme liberalism by Soviet standards. Lenin demands the arrest and execution of a "very large number" of residents of the small town of Shuya, where the faithful had opposed the confiscation of consecrated articles from local churches, and writes: "Now is the time to teach these people such a lesson that for decades to come they will not dare even to think of such opposition."[13] It was not by chance that the leader of the Soviet state chose the verb "to teach": mass executions were intended primarily to perform a pedagogic function, to teach; and for the lesson to be effective, it was important for the shock to be as profound as possible.

From the outset the makers of the New Man realized that the infantilization of Soviet citizens must be universal, that it must embrace the entire population. The concentration camp, a new instrument of terror created in the summer of 1918, had not only a punitive function but an educational one as well.[14] Felix Dzerzhinsky, the chairman of the Cheka, declared it to be a "school of labor."[15] The Cheka acquired the right to confine in concentration camps "those persons who are unable to work without a certain degree of coercion," who "are not conscientious in their work," who work badly and "without enthusiasm," who are late for work. In November and December 1982, at the behest of Yury Andropov, the newly elected general secretary of the Central Committee, police patrols in every Soviet city carried out spot checks on Soviet citizens, treating them like children playing truant from school: "Why are you not at work? What are you doing on the streets, at the cinema, in the baths, during working hours?"

Terror, although absolutely indispensable, was not the only instrument used to infantilize the Soviet population. Immediately after the Revolution, the authorities simultaneously opened the front of the struggle against counter-revolution, the economic front, and—along with others—the front of the "struggle against illiteracy." Drastic measures were adopted to bring about the "liquidation of illiteracy," which had been a chief scourge of pre-revolutionary Russia. (In 1897, only 22.9 percent of the population could read and write.[16]) The principal reason for this widespread illiteracy had been the low rate of urban growth; as late as 1926, more than 80 percent of the population still lived in rural areas.

No one doubted the need for literacy. It could be achieved in one of two ways: normally, by enabling those who felt the need to acquire the necessary knowledge themselves; or by force, by applying Lenin's method of liquidating illiteracy by decree. The word used to describe the chosen method—"liquidation"—was borrowed from military and police lexicon; it was a cruel word that left no room for hope. Lenin himself set out in clear, unambiguous terms the meaning of the widely publicized campaign. "An illiterate person stands outside politics and must, therefore, learn the alphabet. Without that there can be no politics."[17] Lenin regarded the liquidation of illiteracy primarily as a means of "educating the people," or involving them in his policies. "It was only in Russia," Nadezhda Mandelstam was later to comment, "that the idea of popular education was replaced by the political notion of indoctrination."[18]

The decree of the Council of People's Commissars "on the liquidation of illiteracy among the population of the RSFSR," signed by Lenin on December 26, 1918, began by stating the goal: to make it possible for "the entire population actively to participate in the political life of the country." Consequently, "The whole population of the republic between the ages of eight and fifty who cannot read or write are obliged to learn to do so." Paragraph eight of the decree warned that: "those attempting to evade the obligations laid down in the present . . . will have criminal proceedings instituted against them."[19] No other document illustrates so clearly the peculiar features of the new world being created. Learning to read and write has become a duty, an obligation, a kind of tax. The regime has sent the entire population back to school and, like a stern father, is making sure the "children" acquire the knowledge the regime requires.

The first Soviet census (1926) revealed that five million adults had "liquidated their illiteracy." This made it obvious that the post-revolutionary tempo of adult education was more or less the same as that of the last decade before 1917. But the campaign for the "liquidation of illiteracy" was of great significance in the future shaping of Soviet man, because it instilled the conviction that even in the field of education (not to mention other spheres of human existence) coercion was the best means. It inculcated the belief that the citizens of the Soviet Union could never achieve anything on their own, not even in their own interests, unless the State compelled them; and so the regime had to be thanked for all achievements.

The State reserved to itself the most important of parental prerogatives: the education of children. And along with the system of primary, secondary, and higher education, a new system of adult education was gradually built up. Despite the fact that according to statistics the Soviet population has become literate (99.7 percent in 1979[20]), propagandists and activists continue to read newspaper articles out loud in factories and offices during the lunch hour, and political lectures continue to be organized on a gigantic scale as "an important method of Marxist-Leninist propaganda." In 1980, Znanie (the All-Union Society for the Dissemination of Political and Scientific Knowledge) had 3.2 million lectures. In 1979 alone, more than 26 million lectures were given to audiences totaling 1.2 billion people.[21] The lecturers-agitators are trained in special courses and at universities of Marxism-Leninism, and give their talks in workplaces and even in people's homes.

The most important stage in the shaping of the New Man was the shock of collectivization, which for decades traumatized the minds of contemporaries and their descendants. Collectivization constituted a great political and psychological victory for Stalin; it was the realization of the plan to bring about the infantilization of the Soviet peasantry, as the overwhelming majority of the population was uprooted from its traditional way of life and deprived of its independence. Alone among the Soviet writers, Andrey Platonov understood and described the building of socialism as a process aimed at transforming the country's inhabitants into children living in fear, obediently carrying out their elders' absurdest instructions, deprived of their traditional ideas and beliefs and subjected to constant bombardment by radio, newspapers, and propagandists. "Stop that noise! Let me answer it!" the hero of Platonov's *The Foundation Pit* appeals in vain, "in the midst of the noise which kept pouring from the loudspeaker."[22] But the noise continues to pour uninterruptedly from the loudspeakers, and the parents teach their children and make them into "new Soviet men."

Collectivization was the greatest shock in Soviet history because it was associated with the genocide of the peasantry. Robert Conquest has estimated that "collectivization and the famine associated with it were directly responsible for the death of approximately fifteen million peasants."[23] This genocide was an essential element in the construction of the Socialist utopia, because it proved that man had become an abstraction, a number, a mere statistic. Half a century after the event, Soviet histories of collectivization provide precise figures for the livestock losses, but do not contain even estimates on the number of human lives lost. The massacre of the peasantry allowed the state to turn the survivors into a submissive, inert mass of state citizens, as the peasants, now transformed into "collective farmers" deprived of all rights and tied to the state's land, became the "bottom" of the Soviet hierarchical system, the base of the social pyramid. The internal passport, introduced in 1932 as a means of controlling domestic travel and resettlement, was not issued to rural dwellers; it was only in 1976 that the *kolkhozniki* began to be given passports.[24] This process was supposed to have been completed in 1981, but by the mid-1980s there were still many collective farmers who had not yet received passports.*

Soon after the end of collectivization, the Soviet population was subjected to another terrible shock, the four years during which the country lived in a state of terror in which everyone was equal in lack of rights. The campaign of total terror was conducted under the slogan "No one is innocent": from the bottom to the top of the social ladder, all citizens were presumed guilty of what they had—or had not— thought. The finishing touches were being put on a system in which the

---

*Collective farmers are not actually handed their passports (identity cards). They are kept in the office of the village soviet, and it requires special permission for a passport to be handed over to a *kolkhoznik*, who cannot leave the village without it.

country's entire population was turned into children obedient to the will of a terrible and merciless father. ("Our Own Father" was now added to the list of Stalin's official titles.) In 1938, Soviet citizens of all ages were issued a new catechism to study, *The History of the CPSU (b): Short Course.* The entire country was sent back to school to master the new text, which provided the answers to all questions.

The monstrous losses sustained by the Soviet Union during the Second World War (yet another shock, another trauma) resulted not only from Hitler's surprise attack on his ally Stalin, but also from the ruthless attitude of the leaders (the "fathers") toward the "children," whom they regarded as easily replaceable human raw material. After the war, these losses (no precise figure has ever been provided, and talk of 20 million victims is "unofficial") were used to justify all the mistakes and crimes committed by the authorities before 1941. The wartime losses also served to excuse chronic economic difficulties and an expansionist foreign policy; the 20 million victims became a check that the Soviet leaders kept on presenting to both their own people and the rest of the world: they demand reimbursement for the "price of victory" and use the war casualties to persuade people that *anything* is better than war.

Infantilization is meant to turn the socialist country's population into children who are obedient, intimidated, devoid of initiative, and at all times awaiting instruction "from above," from their "parents." In the 1960s and 1970s, Soviet literature, which regularly supplies new models of the ideal hero, began to describe lovingly the rural dweller, now a collective farmer, who preserved the best traits of the Russian *muzhik*: love of the land, the feeling of an indissoluble bond with nature, love of hard work. The rapid blossoming of writing about rural life was connected with the emergence of a whole galaxy of talented writers who knew about village life and who sought Russia's national and cultural roots in the old, now virtually destroyed, peasant way of life. The ideologists permitted writing about village life with one small qualification: Soviet writers did not have the right to portray religious believers in a favorable light. Consciously or unconsciously, the Russian *muzhik* has always been religious, but in the 1960s and 1970s the hero of Soviet literature was Platon Karataev, who worshipped the regional Party secretary, not God. The ideal hero, the ultimate object of the process of recasting human matter, had become the Party's child.

The process of infantilization has for the most part been completed. The Soviet man of the 1980s has begun to feel nostalgia for the Stalin era as a symbol of his childhood and youth, a feeling that Alexander Zinoviev expressed with characteristic directness when he entitled his book on Stalinism *The Flight of Our Young People.* Soviet man has begun to dream of his youth—not realizing that even as an adult, he remains a child.

> One cannot entrust to the essentially sim-
> ple mechanism of a clock such a precious
> thing as time.　　　　KATAEV

5

The Nationalization of Time

It was no accident that in 1934 the Soviet writer Valentin
Kataev cast doubt upon the suitability of the clock as an instrument for
measuring time. The conviction that time belonged to them (because
the future belonged to them) was an important, integral part of Leninist
Marxism. The October Revolution was for Lenin the most convincing
confirmation of his prophetic talents: Not doubting for a moment that
he had grasped the laws of history and discerned the Goal, the Leader
of the Revolution set out in the very first months after the Revolution
to nationalize time—now included among the means of production to
be socialized.

In Lenin's mind, the Revolution became a time machine. He expected that within a few weeks the spark thrown out by the Russian
Revolution would kindle a world conflagration. On July 12, 1919, he
stated categorically: "We say with confidence . . . that we shall overcome the difficulties and that this July will be the last difficult July, and
that next July we shall welcome the victory of the world Soviet republic—and that victory will be total and irreversible."[1] Having mounted
the time machine, Lenin drove it hard, so as to reach the goal more
quickly. A few days after the Revolution, in a conversation with Ray-

mond Robins, head of the American Red Cross Mission to Russia, Lenin expounded his program: "I will force enough people to work fast enough to produce what Russia needs."[2] The key words in Lenin's program were "I will force" and "fast enough."

At the end of 1921, no longer in private conversation but in public, Lenin explained what he meant by building communism in the shortest possible time: "We decided that under the system of compulsory deliveries the peasants will provide us with the quantity of grain we need, and we will distribute it among the factories and workshops and thus achieve communist production and distribution."[3] *We* have decided, *they* will give *us, we* will distribute and as a result, *we* (that is, we and they) will achieve communism, and the time machine will arrive at the terminus, Paradise. The fathers will lead their children—under armed escort, if necessary—to the "better future." It was at this stage that Lenin's celebrated formula of the time machine made its first appearance: socialism means careful accounting and supervision.

Lenin had long before discovered the way to resolve political, social and cultural problems: the Party would rule, direct, and supervise everything. In the spring of 1918, he also found the key to the economic problems confronting the Soviet Republic: the Soviet regime, the most progressive of all social systems, must utilize the "most progressive" (in Lenin's words) economic system, that of the Kaiser's Germany. The Soviet state, the "embryo of socialism" in politics; and the German economy, fully centralized and totally at the service of the state, the "embryo of socialism" in economics, would make it possible to surmount all the difficulties involved in the building of the new world. Six months later, Lenin invented his first magic formula: Communism is Soviet power plus the strictly regimented economy of Imperial Germany.

PLANNING

For the first time in history, a planned economy was born in the USSR.
SMALL SOVIET ENCYCLOPEDIA, 1930

The real command of time began after the magical properties of planning had been discovered. In 1919, Lenin took out a patent for his invention: if we could distribute 100,000 first-class tractors and supply them with fuel and the people to drive and service them, the peasant would say, "I am for the commune, i.e., for communism."[4] The most striking feature of this statement was not the unshakeable conviction that "we" know what "they" think, nor was it the familiar post-revolutionary formula, "we" give, "we" take; the stroke of genius was the establishment of a direct connection between figures and the advance towards communism, between figures and the philosophy: 100,000 tractors and the *muzhik* becomes a Communist; 100,000 tractors and the Goal is attained. In 1919 Russia had only a few thousand tractors, and Lenin knew that the United States had more than 200,000; but this argument carried no weight with the Leader of the Revolution.

Lenin discovered how to speed up the march of time: a plan was drawn up, time was divided into short segments, and the conquest of each segment created the illusion of a rapid advance. The figure showing the fulfillment of the plan became an indication that the Goal was drawing near. The first state plan (known as GOELRO), drawn up in 1920, provided for the construction of thirty district electric power plants. Lenin declared it to be the "second party program" and communism's magic formula now became: "Soviet power plus electrification." It might have been "plus tractorization." In due course it would become Soviet power "plus industrialization"; "plus collectivization"; plus "cornification" or "chemicalization."

The link between figures and progress towards the goal came to be regarded as axiomatic, a fundamental element of Soviet ideology, confirmation of the connection between the base and the superstructure.

During the period of the New Economic Policy (1921–28), a breathing spell that saw a temporary slowing of the race to communism, Lenin's heirs became involved in heated political arguments about defining the next stage in the advance towards the goal. The triumph of Stalin's formula "Socialism in one country" marked the beginning of total planification.

The first Five-Year Plan, approved in April and May 1929, became the model. Stalin's attitude toward the Plan revealed his attitude to figures and his understanding of the function and importance of the "planned economy." It took economists nearly three years to prepare the "control figures" for the first Five-Year Plan, which they offered in two versions: a basic or initial version; and an optimal, more ambitious one. As products of the old, pre-revolutionary school, the planners thought the targets should have some connection with concrete reality. They did not understand the character of the new system being created. The optimal plan was adopted first, but it was soon discarded as an obstacle impeding forward advance, and "super-optimal" control figures were approved instead. But this was not enough, and a new idea was launched: "overfulfillment" of the plan. Any target that was set had now to be exceeded, and those who objected were proclaimed "limit-setters," enemies seeking to prevent the victory of socialism. The first Five-Year Plan was "fulfilled" in four years, with some branches of industry reporting that they had met their targets in two or two and a half years.

Stalin then formulated the law of the planned economy: "Tempos decide everything"—another way of saying that "Figures decide everything." The Five-Year Plan, a specific segment on the road leading to Paradise, became the unit of Soviet time. But Soviet time, unlike other units of time, length and weight, had no standard measure. Soviet time, instead, was fixed by resolution of the Central Committee of the Party. The Polish novelist Tadeusz Konwicki depicted 1970s Poland as a country where all calendars had been removed; the only remaining calendar was kept in a safe in the Central Committee! In the Soviet Union it is not only calendars that have been suppressed; clocks have also been removed; and the only time the country knows is that decreed by the Party. The rule that upon arrival at a prison camp, relatives of prisoners must, before visiting, hand over their watches, is highly symbolic.

The controversy over the merits and demerits of economic planning still goes on. The example of the Soviet five-year plan turned out to be infectious. Hitler was the first to realize the advantages of planning and introduced a "six-year plan." Since the Second World War, in spite of some sharp criticism voiced by a few penetrating minds,[5] the idea of the "planned economy" has been spreading its influence both in the countries of the socialist camp and in countries with free-market economies. In the socialist countries, planning aims (on the Soviet model) to establish total control over every aspect of everyday life. In non-socialist countries, "elements of planification" have been adopted. These quantitative variations determine the qualitative differences between countries. The vast possibilities that planification offers the regime suggest that elements of planning are like germs: once injected into the organism they cause disease and degeneration of the organism.

The standard objection to the planned economy is made by economists; and from an economic point of view, it is logical: the national economy is such a complex system that it is impossible to envisage all its mechanisms, to take into account all the factors involved and to foresee all the results. Economists rightly point to the obvious fact that with the scientific and technological revolution of the second half of the twentieth century, economic relations have become steadily more complex. Even Lenin noticed this: a few months after the Revolution he admitted that, contrary to what he had forecast in August 1917, a cook could not prepare meals and govern the state at the same time. In a book written after his emigration, the Soviet economist Igor Birman pointed out how insolubly complex is the task of "determining a country's economic objectives" and how incredibly difficult it is "to choose the best variant at the different levels of the national economy."[6]

It is pleasant to criticize the Soviet planning system because it is so easy. The low standard of living that prevails in socialist countries now is generally recognized. But such criticism based on analogies with the non-Soviet world overlooks what is most important: Soviet-type planning is not intended as an instrument for forecasting economic development, but as a powerful tool for remolding human consciousness. Its creators and custodians have never concealed its true function: "Our plans," the *Small Soviet Encyclopedia* pointed out in 1930, "are the plans for the advance towards socialism." Half a century later, the task remains unchanged: "The state plans have always been and remain an immense organizing and mobilizing force."[7] In the period characterized by revolutionary enthusiasm and great hopes for the achievement of the goal, economic planning and the conquest of time led the authorities to give precise, scientifically founded dates for the attainment of the final stage: Communism. The adoption of the first Five-Year Plan allowed a Marxist theoretician to declare that in precisely fifteen years, in 1944, "our generation will be able to see socialism."[8] In his 1961 report to the Twenty-second Party Congress, Nikita Khrushchev solemnly announced that Communism would be built in exactly twenty years. Yury Andropov, elected general secretary as it became clear that Khrushchev's prophecy had not come true, felt obliged to warn people about the delay, saying that "the country is at the beginning . . . of a long historical period."[9] But he retained the absolute right to fix the moment when the goal would be reached and to regulate the progress towards it—to have control over time.

Power over time transforms the "forward movement," the planning of progress towards the goal, into an ethical category. When he heard that the Kremlin cathedrals had been destroyed during the seizure of power in Moscow in October 1917 (a false rumor), Anatoly Lunacharsky, the first Commissar of Education, tendered his resignation. Lenin, however, persuaded him to withdraw it: "How can you attach such importance to this or that old building, however beautiful, when what is at stake is the creation of a social system capable of creating beauty immeasurably superior to anything that man may have dreamed of in the past."[10]

The plan, the unit for calculating the advance into the future, thus became an ethical category that explained and justified the behavior of the builders of the new world. The positive hero of the period of the Five-Year Plan is categorical: "Morality? I haven't any time to ponder over the word. I'm busy. I'm building socialism. But if I had to choose between morality and a pair of trousers, I'd choose the trousers. Our morality of the creation of the world."[11] And one of the leaders of the era of "mature Stalinism" explains to his wife: "We are engaged in a race with the capitalist world. First one must build the house and then one can hang up the pictures." And when his wife reproaches him for his cruel treatment of people and workers he declares: "You said that I was always going to extremes. There can be no extremes for those who work to strengthen the material basis. Because it is matter that comes first."[12] Then the march forward in accordance with the plan also became a philosophical category.

Planning was, of course, also a political category. The logic behind the idea of planning and the persuasiveness of the arguments advanced in its support were borne out at the beginning of the 1930s by the catastrophe of the world economic crisis. Soviet ideologues had no difficulty proving that it was the result of the unplanned nature of capitalism. In the Leninist vocabulary, *stikhiya* (uncontrolled and undirected movement) always had a pejorative meaning that the Party insisted on using. Planning became a splendid illustration of the infinite opportunities for struggle against evil. "Socialism," a propagandist for the plan asserted in 1934, "is potentially more productive than capitalism, for it relies on a plan, and not on the anarchy of the market. In three or four years, or rather, in fifteen to twenty years, we shall be in a position to ensure for the whole population a living standard higher than that enjoyed today by the average bourgeois in America."[13]

Among the manifold functions fulfilled by planning, it is important to note that in making efforts to bring about the economic integration of the country, the distinctive features and resources of the various regions and peoples were rejected and even scorned. Gosplan (the State Planning Commission), created in 1921, instructed I. G. Alexandrov to elaborate a plan for the rational development of the country's productive forces. "Our idea of creating autonomous regions," wrote the author in support of his plan, "is founded on the utterly new principle of the expedient division of the state on a rational economic basis, and not on the relics of forfeited sovereign rights."[14] The same idea underlay the creation in early 1949 of the Council for Mutual Economic Assistance (CMEA): the integration of the economic plans of East European countries in which the Communists had seized power was intended—in Stalin's mind—to lead to the formation of a mighty bloc capable of annexing the whole of Western Europe by peaceful or military means. As Stalin put it at the time, "The activity of CMEA will be of greater significance than that of the Comintern."[15] This policy of integrating the economies of Eastern Europe was carried further after 1949 and has continued into the 1980s. The formation of a single monolithic bloc operating in accordance with a single plan remains the ultimate aim.

Planning—this is one of its principal functions—enables authorities to control every facet of human activity and to remold human behavior. A few years after the Revolution, Viktor Shklovsky remarked that art must be allowed to function naturally, like the heart within a man's breast; instead, it was organized like a train timetable. Total planning opened the possibility of regulating not only art but every aspect of the life of Soviet citizens.

The plan becomes the law. Everything is planned and the plan is everywhere. There is—it seems perfectly natural—a Five-Year Plan, an annual plan and a monthly plan; this includes educational establishments (achievement plans for the class, the school, the district, the region, the republic), hospitals, restaurants, snack bars, canteens, fire brigades, research institutes, and the police.

The collectivization of the Soviet peasantry in the years 1929–32 was accompanied by the "liquidation of the *kulaks* as a class."[16] What seemed at first a simple enough task was complicated by the absence of a legal definition of the "kulaks." By planning the genocide, the authorities were able to exercise a strict control over the "liquidation" and to regulate the speed with which it was carried out. For example, in a resolution of February 20, 1930, the Politburo decreed that in Central Asia the number of "kulak and landowning families" liable to deportation "must not exceed 2–3 percent of the peasant population." In March 1930, the Central Committee noted that "in certain districts the percentage of expropriated peasants had reached 15 percent."[17] The police fulfill their plan for arresting law-breakers and the interrogators plan for extracting confessions. In schools, teachers cannot give their students low marks because that would "lower the school's success rate." Reports appeared in the Soviet press that a fire brigade in a small town had set fire to buildings so as to be able to put the fires out and thus fulfill the plan.

The Soviet experiment has been successfully applied in other socialist countries. According to the sinologist Simon Leys, when Mao Tsetung was preparing the "great purge" of the 1950s, he fixed in advance the number of executions to be carried out: 0.6 percent of people arrested in the villages, and 0.8 percent in the cities. But Leys is wrong to assume that while Mao alone acted in so deliberate and calculating a manner, Stalin's actions were "primitive, barbaric and chaotic."[18] Stalin always planned everything well in advance; on the eve of the Great Terror he fixed the quota of "unreliables" in the Soviet population at 5 percent. Whatever his contribution to the cause of "mature socialism," Mao Tse-tung, like the other leaders of the "bloc" nations, was simply following in the footsteps of Lenin and Stalin.

The planning system and the associated practice of "socialist competition" demanding compulsory overfulfillment of the plan establish a close link between the "mystical" sense of forward movement and material advantages; overfulfillment of the plan brings wage increases and special bonuses. The omnipresence of the plan thus conditions the behavior of the Soviet citizen. In 1982, after requesting political asylum in Sweden, the Soviet trawler captain V. Lysenko described the irrational forms Soviet planning can take: trawlers have to fulfill a plan not only for delivery of fish but also for the recovery of scrap metal, both ferrous and non-ferrous. To fulfill the first plan, Soviet fishermen resort to catching cod well below the legal limit of 70–80 cm in length (often as low as 35 cm); to fulfill the second plan, they steal metal from shipyards. Lysenko cites cases of Soviet captains refusing to send SOS signals—an accident at sea can result in a loss of bonus.[19] The *Izvestia* correspondent Leonid Levitsky discovered that all the cafés and snack bars in the large Siberian city of Tomsk served the same abominable food. His investigations revealed that the public catering firm to which the city's cafés and snack bars belonged demanded fulfillment of a daily plan for the production of food waste; and so, Levitsky reported, "The soup was burned, the macaroni and sauce stuck together on the plate in an unappetizing lump, and the baked cheese pudding tasted like sawdust."[20] The customers refused to eat this food which had intentionally been badly prepared; but the waste food plan was fulfilled, even overfulfilled. The leftovers were sent to be used as pig feed; the plan was fulfilled. And so the forward movement to socialism turns into a *perpetuum mobile*.

Socialist planning in the late twentieth century has come face to face with the most dangerous adversary it has yet to encounter: the invention and amazingly rapid development of computer technology. The computer constitutes a terrible threat to the system of total planning; the Soviet control over time is endangered. The appearance of the computer has alarmed the inhabitants of Utopia for many reasons. *Pravda* reported on the Turkmenistan Ministry of Construction, which decided to keep pace with the scientific-technological revolution and invested in a Minsk-22 computer. When it rapidly became clear that the computer had to have "a separate transformer unit, linoleum on the floor, walls covered in plastic, and daylight lighting"—in short, the type of comfort provided only for the minister—the machine was relegated to the basement. The *Pravda* article ended with the words: "Computer technology must be brought out into the light of day."[21] But the computer needed more than material comforts; it needed accurate primary data. "Why don't you install a computer?" an engineering student asks of the chief engineer in a Soviet short story. "In the twinkling of an eye it will process thousands of facts and figures and will give you the optimal solution." "Oh, pack it in," the chief engineer replies crossly. "No machine can take into account or predict whether Ivanov or Petrov will decide tomorrow to climb over the wall during working hours and run to the shops for a bottle of port."[22] He considers the computer useless because it cannot forecast the behavior of the Soviet worker. This is true, but it is only part of the truth: the most important truth is that the computer would expose the plans' economic fictions. Igor Birman, who is well informed about the "secrets" of the Soviet economy, says firmly, "The most important secret, the reason why the annual plans for gross output are always fulfilled in all branches of industry and in all the republics, is that at the end of the year all targets are revised in the light of what is really expected."[23]

It is obvious that the Soviet economy has no need for computers. Programmed with false data, computers will produce false results—which can be obtained without them. But computers not only are useless, but do harm. According to the American economist Marshall Goldman, "Soviet planners fear that the use of a computer would in effect transfer their power to decide what should be produced, and how, to the programmers."[24] The introduction of computer technology would turn ideological decisions into economic ones, and would render the Party useless—and that would amount to a revolution.

A 1983 incident at the Volga automobile factory in Togliatti shows why the computer is perceived as a threat. One day, the main computer-operated assembly line stopped suddenly, and the computers and the entire factory, with its more than 100,000 employees, ground to a halt. Six hours passed before work could be resumed. The stoppage turned out to have been caused by a strike of a kind hitherto unknown in the Soviet Union: a programmer dissatisfied with his low salary and slow promotion had made a deliberate mistake and had brought the computer, and the whole factory, to a halt. Having drawn attention to his demands, the programmer corrected his mistake and confessed. A journalist who described this unprecedented strike in detail emphasized the lack of supervision over programmers' work: "a complete verification of the program by another programmer is either impossible or requires the same amount of intensive labor as the composition of the program itself." The Soviet system had witnessed the emergence of a new profession—and a very dangerous one, entirely individual and impossible to control. "Throughout the entire [programming] process," wrote the horrified journalist, "we could only rely on the specialist himself."[25] Most frightening of all was the fact that the programmer's error had been discovered only because he had himself confessed.

Computer technology is penetrating the Soviet system, but only a few restricted areas where it can contribute to the strengthening of "mature socialism": in the arms industry and the organs of repression. Its application remains strictly limited because the Soviet economy can manage perfectly well without it. The absence of any idea of a product's economic cost offers unlimited possibilities that cannot be comprehended by comparing the Soviet system with the non-Soviet world.

Total power over time and material resources allows the Soviet leaders to spend vast sums (quite senseless from a rational economic point of view) to obtain the required results and to produce what is deemed absolutely necessary.

The nationalization of time has increased considerably the scope of Soviet diplomacy. Unconstrained by the calendar, undisturbed by periodic elections (presidential, parliamentary, and so on), Soviet foreign policy operates within a teleological framework entirely in the power of those who keep the calendar locked up in the Central Committee's safe.

> There are three forces, the only three
> forces capable of conquering and enslav-
> ing forever the conscience of these weak
> rebels in the interests of their own happi-
> ness. They are: the miracle, the mystery,
> and authority.   DOSTOEVSKY

6

Ideologization: The Triad of the Grand Inquisitor

In Dostoevsky's *The Brothers Karamazov* the Grand Inquisitor explains to Christ how to make people happy, and in so doing he
formulates with amazing precision and conciseness the principles un-
derlying Soviet ideology. Soviet ideologists from Lenin on have been so
insistent and stubborn in their claims for the "scientific" nature of the
Soviet ideology known officially as Marxism-Leninism that even their
opponents have come to believe them. There are disputes over the
degree to which it is "scientific" and about the mistakes in forecasting
made by "the only ideology providing a truly scientific analysis of
reality."[1] The greatest success of Soviet "disinformation" has been the
presentation of the system created in the USSR and other countries
organized on the Soviet model as the "only scientific" system, strictly
rational and founded on a precise knowledge of the laws governing
world development.

Friedrich Hayek has written that people will in the end understand
that the twentieth century's most widespread ideas (including the
planned economy and fair distribution, replacement of the market as
a form of compulsion) were based on prejudices, in the literal sense of

the word. In Hayek's definition the "century of prejudices" was a period in which people imagined they knew more than they actually did.[2]

THE MIRACLE

Is that not a miracle?
STALIN

The mysterious and irrational character of what had happened did not escape the leaders of the Russian Revolution—certainly not Lenin. The Revolution had been a miracle, and Lenin did not try to conceal the fact. Speaking in 1922 at the last Party congress to be held in his lifetime, Lenin could find only a mystical explanation for the unexpected behavior of the state he had been building for four years: "The machine is snatched out of your hands: it's as though there's a man sitting there driving it, but the vehicle doesn't go where it is steered but where somebody else is steering it."[3] A mysterious hand guided the Soviet state machine to a different place from that where Lenin should have driven it according to the scientific laws he thought he had discovered.

The miracle of the Revolution, and the miracle of what happened after the Revolution . . . Orwell, in the course of underlining the superiority of Zamyatin's *We* over Huxley's *Brave New World,* points first to the Russian author's "intuitive understanding of the irrational aspect of totalitarianism."[4] Orwell speaks elsewhere of the extraordinarily powerful effect the "mystique of the revolution" had on people's minds.[5] Nadezhda Mandelstam confirms Orwell's observation, saying, "The force of the word 'revolution' was such that one wonders why our rulers still needed prisons and capital punishment."[6]

The mystical goal—the achievement of paradise, the repetition on a gigantic scale of Dr. Frankenstein's experiment, and the creation "in accordance with scientific laws" of the New Man, superior in every way to the *Homo sapiens* created so amateurishly by God—turned Marxism-Leninism into an irrational, mystic teaching. The goal—placed well into the future—and the unshakeable conviction that it would be achieved (the most popular slogan was "Communism is inevitable!") transformed the miracle into a recognized necessity, to paraphrase Engels. The promise and expectation of a miracle, the need for a miracle, were the reverse side of Marxism-Leninism's "scientific" nature. Power over material things and power over time allowed one to claim that one could not only foretell the future but also determine the speed of arrival at the goal.

The history of the Soviet system became the history of the promise and expectation of a miracle. Lenin's theory of the weak link that allows the chain to be broken developed into a doctrine of a universal magic key that opened the door to the future. The October Revolution had been the first instance when the "key" was used. Although the Russian Revolution was supposed to set the world on fire, the door had opened only slightly, but that did not worry the magicians.

Lenin's discovery of the direct relationship between the movement towards communism and a number (100,000 tractors and the peasant for communism) gave the miracle a "scientific" basis. The reality of the miracle was confirmed by the number. From the early 1930s the number would be expressed in percentages and would acquire a magical power. Trying to persuade West German tourists of the superiority of the socialist world, Alexander Galich's hero, the ideal Soviet worker, easily proves his point: "When it comes to percentages, you are a hundred years behind us!"[7]

The ideology of the miracle developed from two elements: haste and an obsession with gigantic projects. Stalin opened the era of the first Five-Year Plans with the slogan: Speed decides everything! The leader declared that the race with the capitalist world, which Russia was to "catch up and overtake," was a matter of life or death: "We are lagging behind the advanced countries by 50 to 100 years. We must cover that distance in ten years!"[8] Stalin chose his words carefully and gave clear instructions: 50–100 years in ten years. The speed is stupefying; it doesn't allow people time to look around, to find out what is going on, or to assess the means and ends. The need for speed justifies everything, becomes a powerful psychological instrument of compulsion that deprives people of the will to resist by offering them the hope of a speedy arrival at the goal, and then a chance to relax. The obsession with gigantic projects was the second element in the ideology of the miracle. The works being carried out in the USSR were all on a colossal scale— at least that was what the propaganda said. In the early 1930s gigantic state farms were organized and given possession of tens of thousands of hectares for the production of unprecedented quantities of grain, meat, and other products. The biggest hydroelectric power stations in the world were begun; forest belts that were supposed to change the country's climate were planted; railways linking continents, gas pipelines cutting across Asia and Europe, were built. The gigantic scale of these works was depicted as a miracle possible only under socialism. The ironic observation that Soviet transistor radios are the biggest in the world well expresses the ideologists' gigantomania.

For seven decades the search for the universal key has been going on: first it was world revolution, then tractorization, electrification, planning. Then there was the "opening up of the virgin lands" that turned millions of hectares of land into semi-desert and desert; the planting of corn throughout the USSR; the expanded production and use of chemical fertilizers, and so forth. Each magic key promised in turn to solve all the problems. In Stalin's magic formula, "Speed decides everything!," only the first word was changed. Now it was technology that decided everything, then forest belts, virgin lands, chemistry, and finally Brezhnev's food program. Andropov opened up a new era with an old slogan: Discipline decides everything.

The longing for miracles is cultivated in all the countries of the socialist camp. The search for the magic key goes on everywhere, and everywhere the magic of numbers is used to daze the people. The "hundred million tons of steel" Mao Tse-tung demanded as the "great leap forward" that would carry China into the future; the 100 million tons of sugar the Cubans were to produce during the "great zafra" of 1976; and the "second Poland" Gierek built on Western credits in the 1970s—were all supposed to open the doors to paradise.

The Soviet writer V. Kaverin says that "expectation of a miracle" was given a "long-distance ticket" at the end of the 1920s. New "Shakespeares" were expected to appear miraculously in Soviet literature, and according to Kaverin, the expectation of miracles was carried over into "linguistics, medicine and physiology. Trofim Lysenko is taking care that it should have a truly fantastic development in biology."[9]

Hope for a miracle—and the need for one—opened up vast possibilities for rogues and charlatans who learned the magic words from the ideological dictionary. The biologist Raïsa Berg compares the work of the Academy of Agricultural Science, whose work under Lysenko became world-famous, with the works of the academicians of Laputa described by Swift. The Laputians developed new ways of increasing crop yields; their aim was to make all plants bear fruit at an appointed time, and to give yields a hundred times greater than ever before. The academicians working under Lysenko set the same goals. They failed, as Laputa's academicians failed; but in both places the academicians insisted that their plans could be realized. Failures were put down to enemy intrigues: Lysenko's followers knew for certain that the geneticists, not believing in miracles, "have ganged up with the international reactionary force of bourgeois apologists" and that the people who claimed that "genes do not change" also claimed the "inevitability of the capitalist system."[10]

The attraction of Lysenko's teaching for the Soviet leaders consisted less in the fact that he promised to grow a hundred ears of corn where before one had been grown with difficulty (thus confirming the success of the collective farm system) than its demonstration (or alleged demonstration) that changes in external environment lead to internal changes in the organism that could be handed down genetically. Lysenko provided (or promised to provide) the essential magic key that would open up the possibility of reshaping man and creating the New Man. One of his subordinates, speaking at the famous session of the All-Union Agricultural Academy in August 1948, suggested using this "key" on enemies who expressed doubts about the correctness of "the only correct theory of Marx-Engels-Lenin-Stalin." "As long as we do not increase our 'external pressure' on the minds of our opponents and do not create for them 'appropriate environmental conditions' we shall, of course, not succeed in remaking them."[11] These pseudoscientific terms actually meant a demand for the arrest of biologists and geneticists and their detention in a camp.

Lysenko was the most striking of the scoundrels and rogues produced by the expectation of miracles and the one who did the most harm. But "miracle workers" emerged (and for a while prospered) in various fields in the world of Soviet unreality. One well-publicized story concerned A. Larionov, secretary of the Party's Ryazan regional committee, who in 1959 gave a "firm undertaking" to triple in three years the region's deliveries of meat to the State. The magic device Larionov discovered was striking in its simplicity: all the cattle in the region were slaughtered, and the shortfall was made up by buying meat from neighboring regions. Realizing that he could not repeat the miracle the following year, Larionov shot himself.[12] But Larionov did not invent the "magical device"; similar methods were used regularly by collective farms. For example, collective farmers in the Leningrad region required to produce a rich corn harvest (which did very badly on their soils but was supposed to do well, since Khrushchev had found the "key" to corn growing) transported their potatoes to the Ukraine, sold them, bought corn, and so fulfilled the plan.[13]

Summing up the results of the first Five-Year Plan, which was "completed" in four years, Stalin kept repeating the incantation: "We did not have an iron and steel industry, but now we have one. We did not have an aircraft industry, but now we do. . . . We did not have a tractor industry, but now we do have one. . . ." The Leader presented all these achievements as a miracle, as the creation of a new world on an empty place: it was sufficient for the Leader to wave his magic wand. "How could such colossal changes come about? . . . Is that not a miracle?"[14] Stalin asked, knowing the answer in advance.

It was a miracle to be able to depict life as a miracle, to impart a magical quality to reality. European princes who hired alchemists to seek the philosopher's stone were looking for a miraculous device to relieve them of material worries. The Soviet philosopher's stone really was "philosophical"; it arose from the philosophy of Marxism-Leninism and embraced the country's entire population in its sphere of influence. The very lives of Soviet citizens became miracles; hope for the morrow and expectation of a miracle permeated their way of life. When Ilya Ehrenburg was asked how he managed to survive the Terror, he said, "I don't know," but then added: "If I were a religious person I would probably say that God works in a mysterious way." Not being religious, Ehrenburg reflected in the Soviet way, "I . . . lived at a time when a man's fate recalled not a game of chess but a lottery."[15] He wanted to say that he had survived by a miracle, because to draw the winning ticket in a lottery is a miracle, something that cannot be explained rationally. Ehrenburg was saying that the ways of the Soviet regime are inscrutable. Nadezhda Mandelstam agreed: "It is a miracle that a few witnesses and a handful of manuscripts have survived from those times."[16] Khrushchev was in full agreement with both of them: "Well, I call it a lottery ticket, I drew a ticket in a lottery. And so I remained among the living."[17]

It is a miracle to avoid being arrested or, after standing on line for hours, to obtain some meat or toilet paper. The magical world of "real socialism" differs from the magical world of primitive man only in that the idol everyone must worship is called the Plan; the Science that knows the precise laws of nature and society; the Party. The miracle becomes a rational part of Soviet life. Ehrenburg's and Khrushchev's description of man's fate as a lottery holds true not only for their period, but for subsequent decades of the Soviet system. (Oddly enough, in the magical Soviet world the lottery is known officially as "a game of chess.")

After the first space flights, an antireligious poster was displayed that showed an astronaut in the sky declaring: "There is no God!" Science and technology had disproved convincingly the superstitious faith in religious miracles! But faith in "genuine" scientific miracles and in the magic of science and technology is encouraged. In the late 1960s it became fashionable to try to explain the origins of Christianity on a strictly scientific basis. In an article published in the magazine *Baikal* entitled "Gods Come Out of Space," the philologist V. Zaitsev wrote that according to his calculations, about two thousand years ago a spaceship landed west or northwest of Egypt from which Jesus Christ stepped onto the Earth. Zaitsev based his arguments on the Bible: the star of Bethlehem was the spaceship coming in to land; and Christ's words, "I descended from heaven," "my kingdom is not of this world," "my kingdom is in heaven," were meant literally: heaven meant outer space.[18] Official ideologists considered Zaitsev's hypothesis so dangerous that they gave the job of refuting it first to an astrophysicist who proved that there were no grounds for supposing that any spaceship had visited the Earth, and then to an expert propagandist who declared that Zaitsev was "objectively an ally of the theologians."[19]

Parapsychology became exceptionally popular in the USSR. A Soviet writer has described a parapsychology séance organized in a theatre: "And he remembered where he had seen such faces before—in church. And he realized that those people had not got together to learn but to believe."[20] The longing for something to believe in finds expression in the belief in a "scientific miracle": science becomes the legitimation of faith. Visiting a church can have unpleasant consequences, but attending "scientific" séances at which miracles are produced is encouraged: it is evidence of a progressive outlook on the world. Stories about the miraculous powers of the Georgian faith-healer Dzhuna were treated as scientifically based when it was learned that he had been treating leaders of the Party and government—the priests of the Only and most advanced Science, even the supreme High Priest.

The journal of the Union of Belorussian Writers published a poem in which the poet asserted the right of the Soviet citizen to telephone Lenin: "We have the right—wake up! We have the right—ring up! If you can't bear it, I'll not be silent—We'll all ring Lenin up!"[21] From the Soviet poet's point of view it is perfectly reasonable to make a telephone call to Lenin's tomb: there is nothing mystical about it, because on every wall the Soviet citizen can read the Party's first article of faith: Lenin lived, Lenin lives, and Lenin will live; Lenin lives forever. A telephone call to Lenin is at the same time an appeal to the myth for help[22] and a sign of confidence in the possibility of a miracle. In his remarkable story "I Believe," Vasily Shukshin describes the tragedy of a Soviet man whose soul has been amputated and who is suffering physically from metaphysical emptiness. The protagonist and a priest, both drunk, cry out in an attempt to convince themselves: "I believe! In aviation, in the mechanization of agriculture, in the scientific revolution! In space and weightlessness! For they are objecti-i-ive! . . . I belie-e-eve!"[23]

Mysticism and an unshakable faith in miracles, in the Miracle, are inseparable from the "only true" ideology. The impossibility of achieving the promised Paradise, the daily impossibility of fulfilling the plan, the impossibility of satisfying the population's everyday needs, lead inevitably to mystical explanations of failures and mystical promises of a Miracle. Failures on the way to the inevitable goal are the result of obstacles which can be overcome "by an effort of will." The leaders who are usually—and rightly—accused of cynicism at the same time believe sincerely in the possibility of a miracle that would remove all the obstacles and shorten the road. Alain Besançon has said, They believe that they know. One might add, They firmly believe that they know that a miracle is inevitable.

A science fiction story with the revealing title of "Will Power" sets out in satirical form the essence of the Soviet scientific mystique, or mystical science. A stranger from the future who turns up in a Soviet planning office of the present discovers such disorder that the spare parts he needs cannot be made in time according to the plan. Because the parts are absolutely essential, he resorts to an act of "will power," a way of doing things learned in the future, and miraculously fulfills the plan and earns a quarter's bonus for all the employees.[24] This is the realization of the dream of every Soviet person—the dream of the miracle that helps to fulfill the plan.

Faith in miracles unites leaders and led and creates a mystical link between them that excludes foreigners and strangers. Mystical faith in miracles is the very foundation of Soviet ideology: Soviet ideology is scientific because it cannot be proved; it is true because the miracle that did not happen today may come along tomorrow. It does not demand the "belief" in Marxism-Leninism that people in the West sometimes expect of Soviet citizens. In the story "I Believe" the drunken hero asks the priest who is preaching pantheism directly: "Do you believe in Communism?" and is told "I am not allowed to."[25] That evasive reply expresses the credo of the Soviet ideologists. The new Soviet man is "not allowed" to believe in Communism—in a theory that, like all theories, provokes quarrels and debates and has to be tested. A Soviet person is "allowed" to believe in the Miracle and to expect a Miracle. As a character in Arbuzov's popular 1982 play *Reminiscences* says, "As long as we exist we are waiting for miracles."

What is essential is to observe the ritual, to use the ritual language, to reject other beliefs.

The part played by expectation of and hope for a miracle in shaping the Soviet mentality was tested in the extreme conditions of the prison camps. Varlaam Shalamov, who has provided evidence of how men behaved in the face of death in Kolyma, in the ninth circle of Hell, says firmly: "Hope for a prisoner is always chains. Hope is always the reverse of freedom. A person hoping for something alters his behavior and is more likely to act against his better nature than a person who has lost all hope."[26] Tadeusz Borowski, who survived Auschwitz, produced similar evidence: "Never before in the history of mankind has hope been stronger than man, but never also has it done so much harm as in this war and this camp. We were never taught to abandon hope and consequently we perished in the gas chambers."[27]

Alexander Solzhenitsyn confirms the observations made by Shalamov and Borowski. When, in *The First Circle*, the engineer Bobynin, a prisoner sentenced to twenty-five years, is summoned to appear before the minister for state security, Abakumov, he announces that he cannot be forced to work, because he has nothing. He tells Abakumov: "Just understand one thing and pass it along to anyone at the top who still doesn't know that you are strong only as long as you don't deprive people of *everything*. For a person you've taken *everything* from is no longer in your power. He's free all over again."[28]

The expectation of miracles cultivated in Soviet man becomes a drug that allows him to be content with his situation.

THE MYSTERY

[Russia] is a riddle wrapped in a mystery
inside an enigma.   WINSTON CHURCHILL

The good fairy who was present at the birth of the Bolshevik Party put a present in the cradle: the key to the mystery of world history. Lenin adopted Marxism as a magical key that would open the doors to the future. The custodian of the key, Lenin himself, became the custodian of that mystery, that secret—the High Priest, who immediately established a hierarchy based on degree of access to the secret.

Lenin began at the beginning: "Give us an organization of revolutionaries and we will turn Russia upside down."[29] This famous formula is rather puzzling: Whom is he addressing? Who is to provide the organization of revolutionaries? To whom is the organization to be given? The post-revolutionary history of the Communist Party and the state it created provide the answer to these questions. As early as 1902, when he wrote his most important work, *What Is to Be Done?*, Lenin had no doubts: there were leaders who knew the secret; they had to create a party ("the highest form of organization") that would operate under the leadership of those who "knew"; and the party had to introduce "a socialist consciousness into the spontaneous working-class movement." A pyramid was being built: the leaders, the Party, the working class.

When he said "the revolution is a miracle," Lenin was actually saying: I knew that a miracle could be performed, I knew the secret of the miracle and I performed the miracle. The success of the Revolution introduced an entirely new element into Lenin's concept: the custodians of the secret became the possessors of power. Degree of access to the secret also determined a person's place in the hierarchy of power.

The Revolution transferred power into the hands of the Bolshevik party; at the same time, it swept away whole social strata and broke down social divisions. According to Marxist theory, the proletariat was supposed to constitute the foundation of the new regime. In his analysis of the first Soviet Constitution of 1918, Lenin firmly rejected the idea of "freedom and equality in general," and asked rhetorically: "Freedom—

but for which class and for whose use? Equality—but for whom and with whom?"[30] He was establishing a new form of state: a dictatorship of the workers and the poorest peasantry that would suppress the bourgeoisie. Lenin proclaimed the foundation of the Soviet hierarchy— the division of society into friends and enemies, initiates (of various degrees) and unclean, all clearly identified. He underlined the first paradox of the Revolution: though it had been carried out for the benefit of the majority, it received support from very few. The editor of the first history of the Cheka wrote: "When the new dictator who arrived to take over from the landowners and the bourgeoisie set about building anew he found himself at the outset in a state of marvelous isolation."[31]

The problem arose of how to identify one's own people, how to separate the clean from the unclean who often hide behind a mask. The first task was to guard the secret and expose those who tried to obtain access to it. The most important department of the Cheka ("Lenin's political police,"[32] created on December 7, 1917) was given the title "secret-operational." Vigilance was declared to be a universal duty, along with compulsory suspicion of everyone and everything. The metaphysical mystery turned into the everyday secret. Mystery and secrecy permeated all spheres of Soviet life, performing a pedagogic function and shaping the Soviet mentality.

Orwell knew that without secrecy there could be no totalitarian state. The central character of *1984* suffers because he cannot discover the secret: "I understand how, but I don't understand why."[33] His effort to obtain knowledge not permitted the rank and file inhabitants of Oceania leads Winston Smith to the Ministry of Love, the awe-inspiring Room 101. Soviet citizens are cut off from the secret by a multitude of physical barriers—questionnaires, permits, strictly controlled rations of information that vary according to a person's status, the articles of the Criminal Code—as well as by psychological barriers. Double your vigilance! cried Lenin and Dzerzhinsky in 1918. "The ruinous and subversive espionage work of agents of foreign states . . . has affected . . . all, or practically all, of our organizations; economic, administrative and Party," Stalin asserted in 1937.[34] Primary school children learn that the Czech hero Julius Fucik cried out "Be vigilant!" as he went to his execution. In 1981, the first deputy chairman of the KGB issued a warning about "intrigues of the imperialist intelligence services" that were "trying to get their hands on Soviet secrets."[35]

Everything in the Soviet Union is secret, from the plans of arms factories to the personal lives of Party leaders, from the size of the army or the number of people in prison to last year's *Pravda* and books by Solzhenitsyn. A permit is needed to enter all institutions and a special pass is needed for access to library books in the "closed fund" (this includes the works of N. S. Khrushchev). In 1981, the historian Arseny Roginsky was sentenced to four years in prison camp for having obtained "illegal" entry into the Leningrad scientific library.[36] Party members are brought together at closed Party meetings and the Central Committee informs the rank and file members of important aspects of the Party's activity in sealed letters. It is of no importance that the Party members do not learn any "secrets" either at the meetings or from the letters; what matters is the ritual of secrecy and its pedagogic importance.

The symbol of the KGB is a shield and a sword: its agents protect Soviet secrets with the shield and extract enemy secrets with the sword. The country is blanketed with an unavoidable network of "special departments" that allow the KGB's eyes and ears to protect secrets and catch those who betray them in every office and scientific institution, in the army and the factories. The first law passed by the Supreme Soviet of the USSR after Andropov was made general secretary called for the strengthening of the guard on the USSR's borders, including "the active participation of all Soviet citizens" in the defense of those borders.

The KGB's shield protects the secrets from those who wittingly or unwittingly reveal them. Soviet soldiers who are taken prisoner even for a few hours are declared traitors to their country, and are suspected of giving away secrets—just as the millions of Soviet citizens who found themselves in occupied territory during the war with Germany were suspected.

The sword in the KGB's badge symbolizes its determination to get its hands on other people's secrets. All intelligence services gather information from two sources: legal (military and scientific journals, the press, reports of parliamentary debates, etc.) and illegal (secret agents). The Soviet intelligence service, according to the evidence of one of its top men in Western Europe in the 1930s, "regards as genuine intelligence work only information obtained from secret agents in violation of the laws of the country in which they are operating."[37]

Only that which is truly secret and must be obtained illegally, by the sword, is considered to be of value. The Soviet intelligence officer is depicted as the ideal Soviet man, because he is, according to a book about Richard Sorge, "a person for whom there are no secrets."[38]

The atmosphere of total secrecy in which Soviet people are born, grow up, and die, has become the most important element in their ideological education. The presence of the secret, the effort to get close to it, and the forces repelling them draw them into the Soviet system's magic circle. A particularly revealing example of the effect of the "secrecy factor" on a Soviet person appears in Chingiz Aitmatov's novel *Buranny polustanok (Stormy Halt)*, which was awarded a State prize in 1983 and was well received by both the official critics and the public. An episode in the novel tells of an encounter between a spaceship launched from the Earth as a joint Soviet–United States effort and an alien civilization. Somewhere, far away from the Earth, there is another world, inhabited by beings externally very similar to humans. This other civilization is far ahead of the Earth in development, and offers help and collaboration. After fairly brief reflection, the Soviet-American commission makes what appears to Aitmatov as the only possible decision: to announce to the other planet's inhabitants "our refusal to enter into any kind of contact with them." Moreover, the commission also decides (again, the only decision Aitmatov can see) to surround the Earth with an impenetrable barrier of "robot-laser weapons capable of destroying by means of laser-borne nuclear radiation any objects in outer space approaching the Earth."[39] The Soviet author responded to a message from another civilization by constructing a Berlin Wall in space, and it seemed quite obvious to him that all inhabitants of the Earth would react similarly.

The conviction that so much is secret and the sense of being involved in the secrets produce a sense of "specialness" and superiority in the Soviet person. Soviet emigrants of the 1970s demonstrated this Soviet characteristic: regardless of their attitudes to the Soviet system, they considered themselves the bearer of the secret and its key. The extent of ideology's effect appears not in the extent to which a person does or does not believe in Marxism-Leninism, but in the extent to which he believes that he knows the secret, that he belongs to the magic circle of initiates.

A few years after the revolution, Viktor Shklovsky recalled the legend of the sorcerer's apprentice. The sorcerer performed a miracle; he cut up an old man, threw the pieces into a pot of boiling water, and out of the pot arose a young man. The sorcerer's apprentice did everything according to his teacher's recipe: he cut up an old man, dropped the pieces into boiling water—but there was no miracle, and the old man remained a corpse.

The secret that links Soviet people with the magic circle of initiates and nourishes the Soviet person's sense of superiority is the secret of the miracle that failed, and the hope, as indestructible as life, that it will still occur—which is why the most dangerous of all anti-Soviet books is Hans Christian Andersen's story "The Emperor's New Clothes."

AUTHORITY

Here we have a real leader . . . master and comrade at the same time, one's own brother, who really embraces everyone.
HENRI BARBUSSE, *Stalin*

It is difficult to regard as accidental the fact that the first hagiographic biography of Stalin, deifying the Leader and Benefactor, was written by a Frenchman, Henri Barbusse, a Cartesian, an atheist, and the representative of a free people. Nor can it have been accidental that it was another Frenchman, Boris Souvarine, who wrote the first genuine biography of Stalin at about the same time. Subsequent decades witnessed the birth and decline of worship of the great Communist leader in very different parts of the globe, in China and Cuba, in Albania and Ethiopia. Love for the Leader and Father turned out to be a feeling not unique to the Russian people apparently condemned to slavery by its own history; world history since the Russian Revolution attests to the fact that the Communist system produces worship of the leader as a snake produces poison. The leader's authority embodies the wisdom of the Party that knows the secret of history and the path to paradise, and is an inescapable and essential element of the system. A structure based on the authority of the Party's general secretary is reproduced in Communist parties not yet in power: the Central Committee's general secretary is always considerably "more equal" than other members of the Central Committee and Politburo.

The problem of authority is the problem of the regime's legitimacy. Two weeks after the October Revolution, Gorky declared: "Lenin,

Trotsky and their fellow-travellers have already been affected by the rotten poison of power, as is evidenced by their shameful attitude to freedom of speech and of the individual and to all those rights for the triumph of which the democratic movement fought."[40] For Gorky, the establishment of democracy legitimized the Revolution. But for Lenin, who had carried out the Revolution in order to establish a dictatorship that would put power in his hands, the power that made it possible to build Utopia legitimized the Revolution. Gorky knew Lenin very well: ". . . a very talented man, he possesses all the qualities of a 'leader' as well as the lack of any moral code which is essential for that role and a typically upper-class heartless attitude to the way the ordinary people live."[41] Lenin possessed a quality even more essential to a leader—faith that he knew the answer to the mystery and possessed the magic recipe that would allow him to perform miracles. In March 1919, Lenin set out his philosophy of power: "In a period of fierce fighting . . . we must establish the principle of personal authority, of the moral authority of the individual person whose decisions have to be obeyed without long debates."[42]

The history of the creation of Stalin's "cult of personality" is known in great detail. Everyone who condemned or ventured to criticize the Stalin cult for its lack of moderation contrasted it with Lenin's "modesty" and efforts to establish a collective leadership. But the facts prove that the "cult of the leader" was born immediately after the Bolshevik Party seized power, and that it was the realization of Lenin's "principle of personal authority."

It was essential to build up the cult of the Leader from the very outset, because no one in Russia, apart from a handful of revolutionaries and police officials, had heard of Lenin. But the process did not have to start in a complete vacuum, because the Russian people believed in God, and so they could begin to deify the Leader. Religious associations, symbols, and attributes were used to introduce Lenin to the country where he had seized power. For the 1918 May Day celebrations Demyan Bedny wrote a poem "To the Leader." "You were in a far country, but you were always with us in spirit. Page by page the Holy Bible of Labor has grown."[43] On September 6, 1918, Zinoviev delivered a long report of which 200,000 copies—a fantastic number for that time—were printed. It was the first official (and like all subsequent ones, by no means truthful) biography of Lenin. (For example, Zinoviev claimed that Lenin had been born into a peasant family.) The epithets and images Zinoviev chose leave no doubt about his model: Lenin was the apostle of world Communism; his book *What Is to Be Done?* was the Gospel; throughout the hard years as an émigré (Zinoviev insists that Lenin was an ascetic who led a life of semi-starvation in Paris and Switzerland[44]) Lenin had never lost faith in the imminence of the Revolution whose Coming he accurately forecast. "He was truly chosen from among millions. He is leader by the grace of God. This is the true figure of a leader such as are born only once every 500 years."[45]

Lenin's injury in an assassination attempt acted as a powerful stimulus to the cult of the Leader: Lenin could now be pictured as a martyr whose restoration to health was declared a miracle. Lenin's fiftieth birthday (April 22, 1920) was celebrated on an unprecedented scale. Trotsky depicted Lenin as the embodiment of both the old and the new Russia, a genuine national leader equipped with "the last word in scientific thought." Zinoviev and Kamenev hailed Lenin as the founder and motive force of the Communist Party. It was Zinoviev who first said: "to speak about Lenin is to speak about the Party"; this was later adapted by Mayakovsky, who wrote: "We say Lenin and mean the Party; we say the Party and mean Lenin."[46]

Worship of the leader was cultivated in his presence and with his agreement. Lenin may not have liked the exaggerated praise heaped on him by his colleagues, but he accepted it because he considered it useful. As one writer said, "I believe that Lenin, who could not stand hero worship and who rejected it by every means, understood and forgave us in his last years."[47]

When the Spartans were asked to give their views on Alexander's desire to declare himself a god, they replied with typical terseness, If Alexander wants to be a god, let him be one. Lenin's reply to the insistent wishes of his colleagues was, If the Party needs me to become a god, I agree.

Lenin's death allowed the completion of the process of deification and transformation of the Leader's authority into something beyond human comprehension. The Party's appeal "To the Party, To All Working People" made it clear that the Party considered Lenin's death to have nothing in common with the passing of an ordinary mortal. "Lenin lives on in the heart of every member of our Party. Every member of our Party is a particle of Lenin. . . . Lenin lives on in the heart of every honest worker. Lenin lives in the heart of every poor peasant."[48] Mayakovsky formulated the first precept of the new world:

"Lenin lived, Lenin lives, and Lenin will live." A quarter of a century later, Orwell simply repeated the incantation: "Big Brother cannot die."

The physical expression of the Leader's immortality was the mausoleum where Lenin's embalmed body was placed. Historians usually take the view that it was Stalin who decided to transform the organizer of the Russian Revolution into a "relic." Stalin certainly gave his enthusiastic support to the idea of building a mausoleum, but the idea of embalming Lenin came from one of the oldest Bolsheviks, Leonid Krassin, people's commissar for foreign trade, later a diplomat. Krassin had been connected with the "god-building" movement (Bogostroitelstvo), which aimed to produce a godless "proletarian religion" and which had been popular among Russian Social Democrats in the second decade of the twentieth century, and he was a follower of Nikolai Fedorov, whose amazing philosophy of the "common cause" combined a fervent faith in God with a belief in the unlimited possibilities of science and asserted that following the unification of the whole of humanity the physical resurrection of the dead would become possible.[49] At the funeral of a prominent Party official and engineer, Lev Karpov, Krassin outlined the essence of Fedorov's philosophy: "I am convinced that the time will come when it will be possible to make use of elements of an individual life to reproduce a physical personality. I am also convinced that the time will come when liberated humanity . . . will be capable of resurrecting great historical figures."[50] In 1924, Krassin was made a member of the commission appointed to arrange Lenin's funeral. The American historian Nina Tumarkin quite rightly points to the influence that the 1922 opening of Tutankhamen's tomb may have had on the decision to build the mausoleum and to embalm Lenin's body.[51]

The mausoleum was built in the form of a pyramid at the base of which lay three cubes, as in the Egyptian pyramids. Kazimir Malevich, who drew up a plan of "Lenin worship" with ceremonies including music and singing, saw the cube as an object "symbolizing the point of view that Lenin's death was not death, that he is alive and will live forever." Malevich proposed that every Leninist should keep a cube at home as a "reminder of the eternal lesson of Leninism."[52]

The most important element of the Lenin cult was Leninism—the highest stage of Marxism, the "creative development of Marxism," the very foundation of the authority that legitimized the Party's power. In

February 1924, the *agitprop* department of the Central Committee called a meeting to discuss "propaganda and the study of Leninism" in which Leninism was declared to be a universal science capable of answering all questions: "We must make extensive use of the works of Lenin in the study of all problems (irrespective of the 'themes') for arriving at our own point of view."[53] Leninism became the "only correct teaching" and acquired its opposite, its negation (anti-Leninism) in the form of Trotskyism; the existence of falsehood and evil confirmed the existence of truth and good.

It took Stalin several years and much effort to confirm his authority, but he followed the same path as Lenin. The power struggle of the 1920s was an internal battle to seize "Lenin's mantle,"[54] and its very nature was determined by Lenin, as the strict refusal to tolerate any factions at the 1921 Tenth Congress reduced conflicts between the Party leaders to personal squabbles.

Having seized the legacy, Stalin enlarged it considerably. A perfect system of totalitarian power was created, based on Lenin's authority. The uniqueness of the Stalin model consisted less in the Leader's unlimited power than in its reproduction of the old structure: Absolute power demands absolute obedience at all levels of the *apparat.* Each Party secretary (of a republic, a region, or a district) was a mini-Stalin in the area under his control; Stalin delegated a small part of his authority to each, and required complete subordination in return.

Once he attained the summit of power, Stalin described accurately and succinctly the system he had perfected: "Our Party consists, if we take its leading officials, of 3,000 to 4,000 top leaders. I would call them the generals in our Party. Then there are another 30,000 to 40,000 leaders at the middle level. They are the officer class in our Party. Then there are 100,000 to 150,000 people at the lower level of the Party. They are, so to speak, our non-commissioned officers." Thus there were about 200,000 Party generals, officers and NCOs wielding total power—all dependent on Stalin. To underline the absolute power and (at the same time) the impotence of the people who transmitted Stalin's authority, Stalin demanded that they each "train two Party workers capable of being real deputies."[55] At the height of the Terror this demand had a completely unambiguous meaning, yet it was greeted with delight by the future victims.

The creation of a system of "mini-leaders" at every level of the Party *apparat* was one aspect of the Stalin model. The other was the creation of a network of people to transmit Stalin's authority in all fields of Soviet life, above all, in the world of science and culture. Failure to submit to the authority of Konstantin Stanislavsky in the theatre, Maxim Gorky in literature, or Trofim Lysenko in biology was regarded as a crime against the state and an encroachment on Stalin's authority.

The deification of Lenin was completed after his death. The deification of Stalin took place in his lifetime. Only his death made it possible for the Soviet people to learn what his life had amounted to. In a 1955 poem entitled "God," Boris Slutsky declared: "We all lived in the sight of God, with God at our very side. But he did not dwell in the distant heavens: Sometimes we saw Him Alive on the mausoleum."[56] In the late 1950s, Alexander Tvardovsky gave a very accurate definition of Stalin's place in the Soviet system: "It was simply taken for granted that, without anyone's help, he saw through the smoke from his pipe everything that was going on in the world, and controlled everything like a god."[57] It was taken for granted by everyone that the country was governed by an omnipotent god who saw and knew everything.

After a relatively short period during which the "Stalin cult" was exposed, the attempt to "overthrow god" was abandoned. Stalin's successors quickly realized that destroying the authority of the Leader-God would undermine their own authority and that of the Party. The debate about Stalin's role and significance in the Soviet system continues without a break. Lenin's role has been defined, and no longer interests people; Stalin never ceases to arouse passion. The controversy about Stalin is carried on primarily in literature while Soviet ideologists continue to confirm their inability to offer even a primitive assessment of Stalin's place in Soviet history. They clearly lack the tools for making such an assessment; the only theoretical contribution of the Marxist-Leninists was the introduction of the term "cult of personality," to indicate the period of "mistakes" that began in 1934.

The Stalin era and Stalin's personality have provoked a lively interest among Soviet writers, both those following the official line and those determined to express their own opinions. Soviet writers riding the wave started by Khrushchev's "secret" speech received permission to talk about Stalin's mistakes as a wartime military leader, including his extermination of leading army commanders, one of the causes of the defeats suffered in the first years of the war (novels by Simonov and Bondarev). But the disappearance of the term "cult of personality" from the Party vocabulary signified a change of policy with regard to

Stalin that was reflected immediately in officially sponsored writing. It became fashionable to return to the period of collectivization and to explain away its "excesses" by reference to the "intrigues" of "left-wing" Trotskyists, all identified as Jews (in the works of Sholokhov, Proskurin, Ivanov, and Belov). It was the Trotskyists, according to the official writers, who organized the Terror of the 1930s. The novel *Eternal Summons* reveals the "strategic plan" of Trotskyists working in alliance with the Gestapo: "We shall destroy physically those people who are the most attached to the Bolshevik ideology."[58] And it was only Stalin who saw through that terrible plan! It then became fashionable to depict the defeats of the first years as a brilliant strategic maneuver that ensured victory in 1945. (Chakovsky, Stadnyuk, and Bondarev all wrote in this vein.)

Stalin is portrayed in current Soviet writing less as the brilliant organizer and builder of the Soviet state than as a great military leader and diplomat—and also, as during the Leader's life, as a divine, mythological being. The protagonist of the novel *Thy Name* reflects: "The personality of that man, who concentrated within himself the almost unlimited strength and potentialities of the whole country, will for a long, long time trouble our minds and will be surrounded with the most unlikely and fantastic details and legends." It could not be otherwise, for he was "tireless in resolving the most complicated and sometimes insoluble problems, and his ability never to tire when others appeared to be dropping from fatigue gave his personality in the eyes of those around him a practically mystical force."[59] The poet S. Smirnov rejected the word "practically" on the grounds that it implied some doubt concerning the Leader's divine nature. In 1970, he drew a portrait of the deity: "It was he who in the time of our trials never left his command post. We saw in him our own might. We painted an ikon of him from life and worshipped before it. And when this uniquely supreme figure was struck down by death, it seemed to us, not unreasonably, that the ground was slipping away from beneath our feet."

There is not a single major "unofficial" writer who has not turned to the subject of Stalin with the object of revealing what he was really like. Alexander Solzhenitsyn *(The First Circle)*, Yury Dombrovsky *(The Department of Unwanted Objects)*, Vasily Grossman *(Life and Fate)*, Vladimir Maximov *(An Ark for the Uninvited)*, Fazil Iskander *(Sandro of Chegem)*, Alexander Bek *(The New Appointment)*, Yuz Aleshkovsky *(Kangaroo)*—each has tried in his own way to fathom exactly what Stalin was, to understand his way of thinking, what drove him to act as he did. They all try to destroy the myth, to topple the idol from its pedestal. The writers frequently resort to various forms of satire, from Solzhenitsyn's merciless ridicule, the subtle irony of Dombrovsky, Iskander, and Maximov, to the crude mockery of Aleshkovsky. Laughter is supposed to liberate one from the unbearable burden of worshipping the "authority" of the Leader.

Yet, despite the efforts of the most talented writers, the process of exposing the myth by means of logic and reason, exposing Stalin's crimes and counting up his victims, has not been totally successful; the myth has continued to demonstrate its power. Evidence that it cannot be totally defeated is provided by Alexander Zinoviev's book *Nashei yunosti polyot (The Flight of Our Young People)*. The émigré philosopher now affirms the necessity and the greatness of Stalin, "the embodiment of 'We.' " Zinoviev takes it upon himself to "defend the era" because, in his view, there are no "criminal eras," because Stalin personified the "people's will," and finally because it was the period of "our youth." "Suppose we did commit crimes. But that was the crime of youth, and youth is a wonderful time."[60] Zinoviev has enriched Stalinist mythology by turning the Leader into a symbol of youth. An excellent epigraph for Zinoviev's book would be the words of the Fascist hymn: "Youth, youth, strength and beauty."

The immensity of Stalin's power and the myth of the divine authority of the Leader built around him were a wonderful legacy for Stalin's successors. Stalin's authority and the extent of his power have served as a reference point for succeeding general secretaries, whom the Stalin era has offered the possibility of maneuvering within the limits of the Stalin model. There was no need to return to universal terror: it had already been used, and had done its job, leaving an indelible imprint on the Soviet consciousness. A mere touch-up of the façade could be portrayed as a general overhaul. When Yury Andropov came to power, he immediately hinted at the possibility of a return to some of the measures of the Stalin era, allowing some slogans of the past to recirculate, and awarding state prizes to old novels about Stalin. Thus he announced that his anointment with Stalin's oil was complete—Stalin's authority would now serve him.

And it did. Andropov, fatally ill, became an invisible man, but continued to govern the country. Konstantin Chernenko, also a sick man, attained the magic post after Andropov's death, and held supreme power in his hands, because he was robed in the mantle of authority.

The truth of Orwell's saying was reconfirmed: Big Brother cannot die because the power of the Party is eternal. To this one might add: so long as the power of the Party is eternal Big Brother will live— regardless of the body he assumes. The Leader's authority emanates a magical force upon which the Party, the source of the Leader's strength, rests: they are intertwined, they cannot manage without each other. The ups and downs of the Mao cult in China followed the pattern of changes in the Stalin cult after his death: the instinctive reflex was to destroy the memory of the all-powerful predecessor, but Stalin and Mao were later returned to the pantheon of leaders so that the succeed- ing general secretary would have a direct link with the "divinity"—the laws of history.

The Leader's authority is the Party's authority and the Party's authority is the Leader's. The general secretary's power, while entirely real, at the same time acquires a ritual character. The "Voice from Sinai"—speeches by the general secretary or decrees of the Central Committee—assume the character of magical incantations. They are always ritualistic in form: the first part is a statement about the current situation, always accompanied by an account of successes achieved; the second deals with reported shortcomings, always the result of enemy intrigues, the bad work of the previous leadership, the lower ranks of the *apparat,* the workers, the collective farmers, artists and writers. The third covers measures to be taken to improve, raise, strengthen, and develop the situation. The incantations are always the final definitive word on a given question. They explain, teach and encourage; but above all, they have the power to heal.

It is sufficient for the Leader to name the evil, and to sign the Central Committee decree indicating the ways to remove it, for the evil to disappear. Twelve days after the outbreak of war, Stalin had only to say that Hitler had "deceived us" for the Leader's offenses to vanish, along with his responsibility for the launching of the Second World War and his blind faith in the Führer. It was sufficient for Brezhnev to announce that the deep crisis in Soviet agriculture was the result of bad weather and poor work on the part of some leaders, for the Party to approve the Food Program that was to satisfy all the needs of the Soviet population. Andropov had only to identify the evil ("weak disci- pline") for figures on labor productivity and the fulfillment of produc- tion plans to go shooting upwards.

Faith in the magic effect of the Leader's words is reflected vividly in the stories that grew up around the telephone calls Stalin made to certain writers. The unlimited power enjoyed by the General Secretary who could decide between life and death obviously turned a telephone call from him into an event of exceptional importance. But his contemporaries and the memoirists treat conversations with the Leader like pieces of magic. In 1930, Stalin telephoned Bulgakov, who had complained of being persecuted by the authorities, and he limited himself to offering the writer the right to work as an assistant director in the theatre. Ten years later, when the author of *The Master and Margarita* was dying, three of his friends wrote a letter to Stalin's personal secretary, Poskrebyshev, begging him to ask the Leader to telephone Bulgakov again, saying that "only a powerful and joyful shock . . . can give some hope that his life will be saved."[61] Bulgakov's friends knew very well that Stalin's first phone call had produced nothing beyond permission to live, but they nevertheless appealed to the Leader for a miracle, for they believed the General Secretary's voice could heal the dying man. Bulgakov's biographer cites the letter to Stalin and calls the request for a miracle "an act of blasphemy dictated by sympathy, an act of madness, reflecting the state of public awareness." There is every reason to describe as blasphemy the appeal to a mass murderer for a miracle of mercy. But one cannot describe as madness the Soviet people's faith in the omnipotence of the Leader's authority and his ability to perform miracles, any more than one can call people mad for believing in the magical powers of a shaman. People go to the shaman because he claims to have direct contact with the deity. The direct contact of the Leader and the Party with the deity is proved "scientifically"; Yury Andropov and Konstantin Chernenko could quietly disappear from the Kremlin because the messages they signed that were read over the radio and on television and published in the press made their presence superfluous. The Delphic oracle was never seen—but that did not stop people from believing in its prophecies.

Training people to have faith in miracles and authority and to venerate the secret are the magical tools of the ideological leadership. The ideological training of the Soviet person—"ideological pressure," as the experts call it—is carried out by an army of activists and propagandists. Instructions issued to this ideological army describe the task very precisely: "Ideological work is called upon to assist the transformation of knowledge into a complete scientific philosophy and into the fundamental requirement that everyone should think and act in a Communist way."[62] Ideological pressure is not aimed at the spreading of ideas or opinions, but at training people how to behave. The task is to create a system of automatic reflexes that will arouse in the Soviet person the "need to think and act in a Communist way," i.e., as required by the Leader.

An army of millions of "ideological experts" larger than the Soviet Army itself is employed to carry out this difficult task. The soldiers of this ideological army, executors of the will of the High Priest, must go through a carefully organized system of political instruction that includes schools teaching the fundamentals of Marxism-Leninism, from primary political schools to "the highest level of political education." In 1975, the country had 325 universities of Marxism-Leninism, and about 3,000 town and district schools for Party activists.[63] The titles of the textbooks used in the system of "Party education" indicate the aims and the scope of the training: Marxist-Leninist philosophy; political economy; scientific Communism; scientific atheism; the economic policy of the CPSU; the social policy of the CPSU; party education.[64]

The "ideological experts" or activists trained with the aid of these books have at their disposal political and socioeconomic literature published in enormous quantities to help them to exert "ideological pressure" on the masses. The function of this literature is "to help to train Soviet people in a spirit of high principles and devotion to their motherland."[65] In 1980, there were 220 million political and socioeconomic books issued, more than the number of books on natural science (50.9 million) or technology (160.7 million) combined.[66] One must also bear in mind that, just as the Soviet Army's budget does not consist only of the funds listed as "military expenditure," but is concealed under many other headings, "political literature" is included among the other books and magazines published in the USSR.

By virtue of its very weight and inescapability, the ideological pressure ought to form the New Man and determine his behavior as the blacksmith's hammer shapes a piece of metal. It should create a system of thought and action according to patterns approved by the ideology. If the possibility of independent thought has been excluded and the ability to take a critical view of the world has been erased from the mind, there is no longer any need to believe. Authority reinforced by "science" becomes (as it must become) an insuperable force.

Because psychologists, psychiatrists, and sociologists have failed to research the effect of the ideological steam hammer on the Soviet people, writers have taken on the task. The few Soviet writers who found the courage to tell the truth about themselves and the world around them described people crushed by the weight of the air they breathed. Vasily Grossman hit on the precise words to describe the state of a Soviet person subjected to intensive ideological processing: "under a spell." The principal female character in *Forever Flowing* recalls the collectivization campaign and arrest of the peasants:

> This was more than the GPU could accomplish by itself. All the Party activists were mobilized for the job. They were all people who knew one another well and knew their victims, but in carrying out this task they became dazed, stupefied . . . under a spell. . . . And they kept repeating [these slogans] at meetings and in special party instructions and on the radio; they kept showing them at the movies; writers kept writing them. Stalin himself, too: the kulaks are parasites, they are burning grain; they are killing children. And it was openly proclaimed that the rage and wrath of the masses must be inflamed against them. . . . And I, too, began to fall under the spell of all this.[67]

Dombrovsky describes a town seized by horror as if struck by the plague; he, too, describes people "under a spell":

> Lectures were delivered at which it was said that the organs of the NKVD had exposed an enormous case of wanton destruction. . . . A large number of responsible officials had been arrested and with each day the number of people arrested grew larger and larger. . . . The most severe sentences were handed down. . . . We were gathered together at the end of our lessons to demand executions. . . . Like practically everybody I also believed a great deal.[68]

Pasternak speaks of the political mysticism of the Russian intelligentsia who had fallen sick of "the illness of the century—revolutionary madness." Yury Zhivago, addressing his friend who has returned from exile, reproaches him: "It was painful for me to listen to your story of your exile, of how you grew up in it and how it re-educated you. It's like a horse recounting how it was broken in at the riding school."[69]

The effect of falling under a spell and of agreeing "to have oneself broken in" (and others, too) is achieved with the aid of a tightly laced ideological corset. The tighter the corset is pulled and the more completely the possibility of another point of view, of other thoughts, is eliminated, the more effective the corset is. The ideal is total control.

Freedom is slavery. Two and two make
five. God is power.

GEORGE ORWELL, *1984*

7

Totalitarianization

The history of people's attitudes toward the concepts of
"totalitarianism" and the "totalitarian state" allows us to understand
the meanings of these terms and the reasons for the unending controversy that surrounds them. Benito Mussolini, who in 1932 declared
himself to be a totalitarian and Italy to be a totalitarian state, attached
a positive meaning to the terms; but after Hitler came to power in
Germany, and during the war years, the term "totalitarian" took on a
pejorative sense, and became a synonym for inhuman behavior and
crimes against mankind. Following the victory over German and Italian totalitarianism, yet another totalitarian state was discovered—the
Soviet Union. The "cold war" period saw disputes between those who
considered the Soviet Union a totalitarian state and those who bitterly
disputed the blasphemy of putting Stalin, the victor, on the same foot-
ing as Hitler and Mussolini, the conquered. After Stalin's death, the
majority of Western scholars—Sovietologists, historians, sociologists
and philosophers—demonstrated that to describe the post-Stalin Soviet
Union as a "totalitarian state" was "unscientific."

The word "totalitarianism" does not appear in Soviet dictionaries
and encyclopedias of the 1930s and 1940s. The 1953 *Dictionary of the*

Russian Language defines the word "totalitarian" as "pedantic," i.e., not used colloquially. The definition is short and comprehensive: "Totalitarian: Fascist, applying the methods of Fascism." The *Encyclopedic Dictionary* of 1955 expands the definition somewhat: "A totalitarian state, a bourgeois state with a fascist regime. Characterized by the concentration of state power in the hands of a clique of fascist leaders, by the complete suppression of all democratic freedoms, by a regime of bloody terror against revolutionary and progressive organizations and activists, by the denial of rights to the working people, and by an aggressive foreign policy."

The second edition of the *Great Soviet Encyclopedia* (1956) left this definition unchanged, adding only that the word was derived from the French *totalitaire,* and that Hitler's Germany and Fascist Italy were both totalitarian states. The *Short Political Dictionary* (1969) added Franco's Spain to the list of "totalitarian states," while the third edition of the *Great Soviet Encyclopedia* (1977) charges that "Reactionary bourgeois politicians and ideologists are still trying to make use of the idea of totalitarianism for anti-Communist ends." The 1983 *Short Political Dictionary* is even more specific: "The idea of totalitarianism is used in anti-Communist propaganda for the purpose of creating a false impression of socialist democracy."

The Polish philosopher Leszek Kolakowski points out that the concept of "totalitarianism" frequently is questioned because a perfect model of the totalitarian state does not exist; even in the Soviet Union under Stalin, in China under Mao, or in Germany under Hitler, "the ideal of absolute unity among the leaders and of unlimited power was never achieved."[1] Kolakowski disposes of this objection with the comment that the majority of concepts used to describe large-scale social phenomena do not have their perfect empirical equivalents.

The perfect totalitarian state was described by Evgeny Zamyatin: "Every morning, with six-wheeled precision, at the same hour and the same moment, we—millions of us—get up as one. At the same hour, in million-headed unison, we start work, and in million-headed unison we end it. And, fused into a single million-handed body, at the same second designated in the Tables, we raise our spoons to our mouths. At the same second we come out for our walk and go to the auditorium, to the hall for Taylor exercises, fall asleep. . . ."[2]

Such is the unified state, the world in the thirtieth century. It is an ideal. George Orwell placed the "unified state" a good deal closer to us—in 1984. It is both like and unlike the monstrous world of the future: it is unlike it because it is much more real. Orwell, who for nearly thirty years had been observing the development of the totalitarian world Zamyatin saw soon after its birth, discovered totalitarianism's imperative law: poverty is a form of existence and an obligatory condition of life under "English socialism." In Zamyatin's one state, the problems of chronic shortages of clothing, food, and all essentials did not exist, while for Orwell poverty is a powerful instrument for educating people.

Like Zamyatin, Orwell considers suppression of freedom the main feature of the totalitarian state. "Totalitarianism suppressed freedom of thought on a scale never before experienced." In June 1941, he set forth the fundamental principle of totalitarianism: "It is important to understand that the control of thought is not only a negative feature, but a positive one as well. It not only forbids you to express, or think, certain thoughts; it also dictates what you have to think, it provides you with an ideology, it tries to govern your emotional life and it establishes a code of behaviour."[3] Seven years later, in his novel about the future, Orwell indicated the stages of human history. "The commandment of earlier despotisms was 'Thou shalt not.' The commandment of the totalitarian state is 'You have to.' Our formula is: 'Thou art.' "[4] This is the highest stage of totalitarianism—thou art, therefore thou art not. You exist only to the extent that you submit to the obligatory code of behavior in which you have become a molecule in the "single, million-handed body."

This ideal has not yet been achieved, and this has led, in the words of the American Sovietologist Jerry Hough to "the growth of dissatisfaction with the totalitarian model." Hough has in mind some experts on the Soviet Union. In a book published by the Harvard University Press as a textbook for American students, he writes:

With the death of Stalin fundamental changes occurred in the nature of the Soviet political system . . . the ideology became less rigid and less optimistic about the perfectibility of man; the dictator no longer denominated his subordinates in the way Stalin had, and the party came to assume more of a mass character . . .; the role of the secret police was sharply restricted, and arbitrary terror disappeared . . .; the centrally controlled means of communication became more open to iconoclastic ideas, and the partial raising of the Iron Curtain permitted even more unorthodox ideas to reach many citizens.

Having stated all these "facts" (which exist only in the author's imagination) he can conclude that the Soviet Union is moving in the direction of "institutional pluralism."[5]

Hough's arguments and conclusions deserve attention in that they reflect the stubborn reluctance of many Western experts to take account of Soviet reality and their categorical refusal to use the concept of "totalitarianism." Hough cites examples of other euphemisms: "the administrative state," the "directed state," the "monistic system," and so on.[6]

But a careful reading of the definition of the totalitarian state in the 1977 *Great Soviet Encyclopedia* will erase all doubts and illusions concerning the model of the Soviet state:

> Totalitarian states and regimes are characterized by the transfer to state ownership of all legal organizations; unlimited powers in the hands of the authorities; the banning of democratic organizations; the suppression of constitutional rights and freedoms; the militarization of public life; and the use of repressive measures against progressive forces and dissidents in general.

The accuracy of this description of the Soviet model was so obvious to Soviet ideologists that the 1983 edition of the *Short Political Dictionary*, published after Andropov became general secretary, repeated the *Great Soviet Encyclopedia*'s definition almost word for word; only the reference to the persecution of dissidents was eliminated. Between 1977 and 1983, a new category was added to the list of enemies of the Soviet regime—the dissident. The *Short Political Dictionary*'s inclusion of an article about dissidents, also called "those who have other opinions," forced the authorities to censor the article on the totalitarian state.

The problem of the totalitarian state comes down to the question of power—who exercises the totalitarian power? In the years when Stalin, Hitler, and Mao were in power, the answer seemed very simple. Many historians replied that the power of the party was a necessary condition of totalitarianism, a point of view shared by Orwell. But Leonard Schapiro, the well-known historian of the CPSU, had some doubts: "After all, Stalin destroyed the party as an institution and undermined its monopoly of power."[7]

Despite his excellent knowledge of Soviet history, Schapiro was mistaken. Stalin destroyed members of the Party, but he did not touch the Party as an institution: he could have done so only if he had decided (as was whispered in those days) to have himself crowned emperor. He could not manage without the Party any more than the Party could manage without him.

The first Soviet Constitution of 1918 makes no mention of the Party. But Lenin did not conceal the true state of affairs, and said openly: "We have to know and remember that the whole of the juridical and actual constitution of the Soviet Republic is based on the fact that the Party corrects everything, decides everything and builds everything according to a single principle." It was a very simple principle: power belongs to the Party. Stalin introduced into the 1936 Constitution an article stating that the Party was the "ruling force" in the Soviet state. Lenin's principle was formulated precisely in the Stalin Constitution: "The Party is the ruling element within all organizations, social as well as governmental."[8]

Forty years later, a new constitution extended and supplemented the definition of the Party's place and role in the Soviet system, and the totalitarian nature of the country's administration became evident. It is not without significance that the 1936 Constitution dealt with the question of the Party in article 126, while the 1977 Constitution moved it up to article 6. The constitution now in force declares:

> The ruling and directing force in Soviet society and the core of its political system and of all state and social organizations is the Communist Party of the Soviet Union. The CPSU exists for the people and serves the people. Armed with Marxist-Leninist teaching, the Communist Party lays down the general direction in which society is to advance as well as the line to be followed in domestic and foreign policy, directs the great creative activity of the Soviet people, and gives a planned and scientifically founded character to its struggle for the victory of Communism.[9]

Thus the CPSU declares itself to be the Supreme Authority that knows the Truth, the Goal, and the Way to the Goal. On that basis it assumes total power and gives a firm promise, based on the "teaching," science and the plan, to lead those entrusted to it by History to Paradise. Any attempt to limit the Party's total power is regarded as an attack on Truth and History.

The events of 1980–82 demonstrated the impossibility of limiting the Party's power. The Polish Solidarity movement was doomed because it encroached on certain Party prerogatives in the administration of the economy. In 1956, the Polish Communist leader Wladislaw Gomulka rejected outright a plan for Polish economic expansion drawn up by the best economists of the time, saying: "What do you want to do—limit the role of the Party to organizing May Day demonstrations?"

Only a totalitarian regime can provide the Party with grounds for demanding totalitarian power. The loss of the tiniest particle of complete and absolute power deprives the Party of its legitimacy and makes it into an organization like any other. Once it has lost the power to be the "ruling element," it becomes a mere shell of obsolete and rejected ideas and myths.

The Party's totalitarian power is exercised by taking decisions on all questions of state, social, and cultural life, and putting those decisions into practice under the supervision of millions of Party members. The numerical strength of the CPSU is maintained at a relatively low fixed level. In 1952, the Party consisted of 5,883,000 members in a population of 181.6 million; in 1976 there were 15,058,017 Party members in a population of 255.6 million; in 1981, the year of the twenty-sixth Congress, there were 17,480,000 members out of a population of 266 million. Stalin's Party structure has been preserved: a general staff (the Politburo and the Secretariat of the Central Committee), the generals, and the officers' corps (the *nomenklatura*). This top *apparat* constitutes roughly 3.2 percent of the Party membership. The remaining 96.8 percent of the members work in enterprises, offices, collective farms, etc.[10] Bound together by their proximity to the secrets, the miracles, and the authority, the Party members serve as neurons through which the body of the Soviet organism receives its orders from the "head"—the center of Party power. The author Alexander Yashin described the structure of Soviet society as a system of levers in which each Party member is a lever depressed by the lever above it, and so on, to the very top, where sits the Helmsman.

The advantages of this system are obvious. The personal wishes of a "neuron" or a "lever" cease to be of any importance. The Party member is just a cog in a gigantic machine, and he plays his part so long as he remains in the Party, repeating mechanically the slogans and commands sent down from above. Upon receiving permission to emigrate in 1978, Sergei Polikanov, an atomic physicist and corresponding member of the Soviet Academy of Science, said of his Party membership: "As many others did, I regarded being in the Party like wearing a sort of harness which I had put on voluntarily. Once you've got the harness on you can't take it off without serious losses."[11] The "serious losses" Polikanov mentions are not just a matter of losing a job or having trouble with the authorities; it is also a matter of losing a definite slot in the system, of losing hope and expectations.

The totalitarian character of the Party's power changes the mentality of its members inexorably, and has a decisive effect on the mentality of the country's entire population. The Party attracts the most active, enterprising, and ambitious citizens. In the pre-revolutionary period and the first post-revolutionary period those who joined the Party were enthusiasts, people of principle who believed in the new religion. The conflict between high ideals and the actual practice of revolution, the need to perform dirty, bloody jobs, formed the character of the first post-revolutionary generation of Communists, and had also affected the second generation. Alexander Bek's *The New Appointment,* one of the few Soviet novels to analyze the psychology of the leaders, includes a portrait of a Communist minister utterly devoted to Stalin, one of the organizers of the Soviet economic system, and a man whose proximity to the Leader and skill as an engineer reminds one very much of Albert Speer. Bek's central character, the Stalinist minister Onisimov, falls ill, and his hands begin to tremble badly. The doctor who examines him advises him to "avoid mistakes," and goes on to explain that the word "mistake" was introduced by the famous Russian physiologist Pavlov, who said that when two contradictory impulses or orders leave the cerebral cortex, when an internal signal instructs you to behave in one way and you make yourself behave differently, a conflict arises, a "mistake," and you fall ill. The doctor adds that when a calculating machine is given two contradictory orders it too "falls sick" and begins to shake.[12]

The East German author Stefan Heym, who had not read Bek's novel, repeated this situation, taking as his principal character a famous East German writer, an old Communist who had been forced after the establishment of the Communist regime to lie and lie and lie, whose "mistake" produced a serious heart condition.[13]

A "mistake" can happen only if a man carries in his mind two sets of standards, two ways of looking at the world. Two conflicting impulses or orders can arise in the brain even if one of the systems or points of view is considered incorrect and is rejected; the memory of it is sufficient to produce an impulse.

The Party's totalitarian power makes it possible to eliminate (or at least that is the aim) both the "second system of opinions" and any nostalgia for it. Careful selection brings to the top of the Party hierarchy leaders who have been immunized against "mistakes." These are the third generation of Soviet leaders, who have taken an enormous step in the direction of the ideal Soviet man. The Party's "brain" sends out only one impulse-command. Mayakovsky said proudly: "I feel myself to be a Soviet factory manufacturing happiness." The poet was deceiving himself: a factory could not have committed suicide. In Zamyatin's novel *We*, the Benefactor comes to the conclusion that just a small operation on the brain—the cauterization of the center of imagination—would make a man "perfect, machine-like" and would open up "the road to one hundred per cent happiness."[14] In Orwell's *1984*, Winston Smith finds happiness after frightful torture because his brain then sends out only one impulse-command—to love Big Brother.

The aim of the totalitarian regime is to make extreme measures unnecessary while carefully preserving the memory of them. Striving to create an impassable abyss between the area over which the authority of the totalitarian regime extends and the rest of the world, the regime counts on finally severing the links (with the pre-revolutionary past, with "abroad") which give rise to conflicting impulses.

The totalitarian system is headed by a Leader possessing totalitarian power. The scope of the power exercised by the general secretary of the Communist Party cannot be less than the scope of the power exercised by the Party. The Leader's authority must be the embodiment of the Party's authority. Yury Andropov rearranged some details of the ritual to create the impression of change: he returned to the pre-Stalin practice of publishing a weekly agenda of Politburo meetings. The purpose behind this move was not to reveal the leadership's inner secrets or to "democratize" procedure, but to demonstrate the omnipresence of the Party and its leading body. Judging by the communiqués issued, there are no questions too small for the Politburo to consider—the opening hours of shops and hairdressers and strategic problems connected with the location of new missiles in Europe, ideological work in the theatre and the difficulties of workmen on the Siberian gas pipeline. An incalculable number of problems; and the Politburo provides the only correct solution to them all.

The unending dispute about the nature of the Soviet system is complicated by the emergence of a new type of general secretary. The absolute nature of the power wielded by Stalin and Mao was scarcely questioned (if we except those Western experts who never ceased to regard Stalin as a victim of the "hard-line" members of the Politburo who were forcing the "wonderful Georgian" to do things he found disagreeable), although of course even Stalin could not do absolutely everything he wanted to. Khrushchev recalls that after the war Stalin very much wanted to transport all forty million Ukrainians to Siberia, as he had transported some of the peoples of the Caucasus and the Crimea, but the technical difficulties of exiling forty million people prevented the Father of the peoples from accomplishing his will. But Stalin, just like Mao, could do a great deal. Even Khrushchev, whose power would seem to have been much more limited, carried through (contrary to expert advice) his "willful" dream of "opening up the virgin lands," the catastrophic ecological consequences of which have yet to be fully assessed.

The absolute, tyrannical power of the "brilliant secretaries" makes it possible to define the nature of the Soviet system using the classification devised by Max Weber, who distinguished three "pure types" of regime: those based on law; the traditional; and the charismatic. Leonard Schapiro saw analogies with the Soviet system in both the traditional form of regime and (at times) the charismatic; he emphasized that the decisive factor for both types of regime was the leader's personal authority.[15] The disappearance of charismatic general secretaries may be regarded as evidence that the system has reached maturity. Brezhnev, Andropov, and Chernenko—the leaders in the period of transition—still reflect to some extent the charisma of their "heroic" predecessors. Future general secretaries will probably come off the production line like steel ingots off a rolling mill, and will be forced into shape as they move up the hierarchical ladder, losing all distinguishing personal qualities. The sinister figure of the "new young man" whom Berdyaev saw in 1922, who knows nothing about the past or about other countries, who does not remember the Revolution, the war, the defeats, who knows only of the victories of a mighty army, now stands on the threshold of supreme power.

The charismatic general secretary will disappear, but the charismatic function of the general secretary will remain. Hannah Arendt described in 1951 the point of view of the Nazi leaders to whom the leader was "necessary, not as a person, but as a function, and without that function the movement could not manage."[16] History provides enough examples to allow one to say that a radical, revolutionary "movement" is always in need of a charismatic leader. There can be no doubt that the most surprising revolutionary movement of recent years, the birth of Solidarity in Poland, would have been very different without Lech Walesa. But a system that has ceased to advance has no need of a charismatic leader; such a leader would threaten its composure and its immobility. Such a system does, however, have real need of the charismatic function. And whoever performs that function in the Soviet system possesses considerable power, based solely on the position he occupies.

Maxim Gorky, opening the first Congress of Soviet Writers on August 17, 1934, gave a very accurate definition of the character of the Soviet system: "We are meeting in a country illuminated by the genius of Vladimir Ilyich Lenin, in a country in which the iron will of Joseph Stalin is at work tirelessly performing miracles."[17] No one has succeeded in finding a formula to compare in clarity and vividness with Gorky's definition. The Soviet Union continues to be illuminated by the Sun—the genius of the leader and founder of the state—and Stalin's iron will continues to perform its miracles.

Totalitarianization is the union of all the vectors for the processing of human material into a single direction—aimed at instilling the conviction that the Party (directly or through the bodies it controls) is everywhere, that it is everything, and that without it there is nothing. The ironic little song ("winter's gone and summer's with us, and we thank the Party for it") actually pokes fun at the belief drummed into the mind of Soviet man that it really *is* possible that the winter's departure and summer's arrival depend (if only to a small extent) on the will of the Party. Totalitarianization makes it possible to plan the complete subordination of the individual to the needs of the regime by controlling all aspects of his life, and it makes it possible to mine all exits from the totalitarian system, providing substitutes for the ideas, desires, and very words for patriotism, nationalism, religion, democracy, hopes, noble aspirations—substituted concepts that all lead back to totalitarianism.

> If you can stand the heat of the forge you'll
> be like Marx. If you can't you'd better be on
> your way.   A. DOROGOICHENKO

III

THE INSTRUMENTS

Having chosen the ultimate aim, having sketched out a map of the approaches to it, and having indicated the main lines determining the character of the New Man, his creator selects his tools. The protagonist in Orwell's *1984* did not understand the aims of the totalitarian state he lived in, but he understood, or thought he understood, how it worked, and how it processed the human raw material. Orwell described the operation of the principal instruments with which the "meat of human happiness" was shaped into the requisite New Man: fear; hatred of the enemy selected by the Party; love of Big Brother; power over memory and personal life; controlled poverty; Newspeak. The same instruments, with the exception of poverty, are described in Zamyatin's *We.* Zamyatin saw even then that fear, hatred, love of the Benefactor, manipulation of memory, power over the word and complete control of personal life were bound to change a man's character. He also included literature and art, which Orwell almost completely ignores. And in *We* power belongs to the State-Party, whereas in *1984* the Party is the front-runner.

Zamyatin and Orwell named practically all the principal instruments needed for changing a human being's nature; they did not invent them, for one or another has been used with varying intensity by all rulers. Many a utopian has dreamed of using them all at once.

For the first time in history, and lasting for several decades, a most disparate collection of cutting, piercing, sawing, mincing, drugging, and stimulating instruments has been applied to the task of carrying out a plan whose details have often changed but whose essentials remain unchanged. It is said that in ancient times the Chinese produced grotesque circus freaks by putting newborn infants into special, oddly shaped vases. One of Maupassant's stories describes a woman who wore a special corset during her pregnancy in order to produce circus freaks. According to Victor Hugo, surgery was used for the same purpose. We know that in certain conditions—at exceptionally low temperatures, for example—gases change their structure and become liquids.

The ordinary people of the Russian Empire found themselves, after the Revolution of 1917, living under the most extraordinary conditions.

We are living in an epoch of great fear.
ALEXANDER AFINOGENOV

8

Fear

"We are living in an epoch of great fear" declares the Professor, a physiologist, in Afinogenov's play *Fear,* a great success of 1931, performed in three hundred Soviet theatres. Stalin had no objection to "his" epoch being so described. The need to induce fear as a tool for working on human beings and as an effective means of reeducation was understood and stressed by the leaders of the Revolution, above all by Lenin himself in the very first days after he took power.

Professor Borodin, head of the Institute of Physiological Stimuli, has revealed that a person's behavior is determined by four stimuli: fear, love, hatred, and hunger. The principal character of *Fear* was not original: the discovery of "stimuli" took place a long time ago. Professor Borodin's original contribution is his discovery that stimuli could be used to change a person's behavior; he performs his experiments on rabbits, but assumes that "by analogy, if we find the dominant stimulus in the social environment we shall be able to guess in advance the way along which social behavior will develop," adding, "We are all rabbits."[1] (Describing the events of subsequent years in his *Gulag Archipelago,* Alexander Solzhenitsyn finds only one general word to describe the millions of people in detention: "rabbits."[2]) Borodin decides that his experiments on rabbits mean the arrival of the epoch "when science begins to oust politics." He is seriously mistaken, for it is politics that becomes a science. A student of Borodin's, a Party member who has become a scientist, announces: "They say that politics cannot impose its laws on science! But we will show them that it can. Our policy is remaking people; feelings that were regarded as being in-born are dying out. . . . There is an increase in collective action, of enthusiasm and joy of living, and we are helping these new stimuli to grow."

The almost unlimited possibilities of using fear as a stimulus for dictating people's behavior were known to mankind long before the leaders of the October Revolution were born. Jean Delumeau defines fear in an individual as a shock-emotion, often preceded by something unexpected and produced by awareness of a present, real danger we believe to be threatening our safety. Gustave Le Bon discovered that mass panic and crowd behavior considerably increases, complicates, and transforms an individual's confused behavior.

Delumeau cites numerous examples of "fear in the West," and begins the first chapter of his book with the words: "In Europe from the beginning of our period fear, either camouflaged or openly revealed, is present everywhere." The same can be said of other parts of the globe, as every region has experienced periods of greater and lesser fear: Europe experienced a period of fear of "demons" that reached a state of frenzy in the fifteenth century, as well as fear of the plague that struck the continent periodically for four hundred years.[3]

Following the October Revolution—and perhaps for the first time in history on such a scale—fear was organized deliberately. There had been elements of organization in the false alarms and calls to arms which in 1789 in France evoked the "Great Fear" of the "plot of the aristocrats" who, along with bandits and foreign powers, were threatening the revolutionaries. This was the first "revolutionary fear"; the Bolsheviks later set about organizing fear as both an instrument for defending the Revolution and a means of influencing people's minds.

A new type of police force, the Cheka, was set up on Lenin's initiative to combat enemies and educate the people by means of fear. The Cheka's first deputy chairman, and first historian, Martin Latsis, explained: "We had to set up the Extraordinary Commission [the Cheka] because the Soviet regime had no apparatus for re-educating people's minds."[4] On November 21, 1917, Lenin declared: "We want to organize the use of force in the interests of the working people." On December 17, 1917, Felix Dzerzhinsky, announcing the birth of the Cheka, issued a warning: "Don't get the idea that I'm looking for a form of revolutionary justice . . . I need an instrument of revolutionary vengeance on the counter-revolutionaries."[5] Latsis explained: "The Cheka does not bring the enemy to trial but smites him down. . . . It either destroys him without trial . . . or it isolates him from society by imprisoning him in a concentration camp."[6]

At the height of the Civil War in Russia, Vladimir Korolenko, a well-known writer and convinced democrat, told a representative of the Soviet news agency (Rosta): "The basic mistake made by the Soviet regime is to try to introduce socialism without freedom."[7] Fifty years later, Vasily Grossman wrote: "Lenin's synthesis of socialism and lack of freedom stunned the world more than the discovery of atomic energy."[8] Korolenko, an excellent representative of the Russian intelligentsia with his naive belief in the freedom and democracy that would follow the overthrow of the Tsarist autocracy, regarded the Soviet regime's policy as a mistake. Half a century's experience of Soviet rule convinced Grossman that it was no mistake, but a logical realization of Lenin's discovery.

The Cheka—the "instrument of on-the-spot punishment," as the Chekists proudly called it—was intended to give birth to fear that would paralyze both individuals and society. Trotsky provided the theoretical grounds for the need for fear: "Intimidation is a powerful instrument of policy, both foreign and domestic. War, like revolution, is based on intimidation. A victorious war destroys as a general rule only an inconsiderable part of the defeated army, scaring the others and breaking their will. Revolution works in the same way: it kills a few but frightens thousands."[9]

As far as the October Revolution was concerned, "It kills a few" was rhetorical; according to official figures provided by Latsis, the Cheka executed 9,647 people in the first two years after the Revolution. This figure was cited in a letter sent to France by Pierre Pascal, who analyzed the number of people executed each month to show that the terror was subsiding "as the danger for the Soviet republic was reduced."[10] The first documents on "Red Terror" to be published make it clear that the official figures must be multiplied considerably.[11] Yakov Peters, one of the Cheka's leaders, reported proudly that after Lenin was wounded "the masses themselves . . . showed their appreciation of their beloved leader and avenged the attempt on his life": the number of people shot "certainly does not exceed 600."[12]

Six hundred people executed for an attempt on the life of the Leader (if we are to believe Peters) is not an excessive figure, bearing in mind that the regime's task was to educate the workers and intimidate thousands of people. Throughout the period when he was head of the Party and government, Lenin never ceased to repeat his warning: "Our regime is too soft," and insisted that enemies "must be destroyed without mercy."[13] When the Civil War came to an end, Lenin continued to demand: "With bribery and so on and so forth the OGPU* must wage a battle and punish by shooting after trial." In the decisive manner for which he was noted, the leader of the post-revolutionary state defined the list of crimes that the courts were obliged to punish by shooting— "bribery and so on and so forth." Naturally, Lenin was thinking primarily of political opponents: he insisted on execution by firing squad and even talked of using machine guns in the case of the Mensheviks and Social Revolutionaries in March 1922.[14]

Trotsky was in complete agreement with Lenin, explaining that the firing squad was made necessary by the fact that "in a revolutionary period a party which has been driven from power will not let itself be intimidated by the threat of a prison sentence in the duration of which it does not believe."[15] (Machiavelli, whose works were studied closely by the leaders of the Russian Revolution, pointed out that the Prince was faced with the question of which was better, "to be loved or to evoke fear." Although he recognized that it was "desirable to do both," the great Florentine statesman advised that since it was difficult to do both at the same time, it was safer and therefore better to evoke fear.)

There can be no doubt that in their "brilliant isolation" the Bolsheviks were panic-stricken, afraid of everyone. But the fear they wanted to evoke, and did evoke so successfully, never lost its pedagogic and ideological function. Rafail Abramovich, a Menshevik leader, recalls a conversation with Dzerzhinsky in August 1917, at a time when the two men were not yet deadly enemies. "Do you remember Lassalle's speech about the essence of the constitution?" asked the Cheka's future

---

*In January 1922 the Cheka was replaced by the OGPU, but this was merely a change of name; the political police remained otherwise the same.

chairman. "Of course," replied the Menshevik leader. "Lassalle said that a constitution is determined by the relationship between the actual forces within the country." "And how does this relationship between the political and social forces change?" "In the course of economic and political development, through the evolution of the economy, the emergence of different social classes and so forth, as you very well know." "And would it not be possible," Dzerzhinsky posed the question of principle, "to change that relationship through, let us say, the subjugation or the destruction of some social classes?"[16]

The reflections of the Cheka's future chairman were not a matter of pure theory; following the Revolution of October 1917, the Bolshevik Party, with the aid of the Cheka, set about putting its theories into practice. Latsis translated the reflections on Lassalle's views into the language of the Chekists: "Don't try during the interrogation to dig up material or proof that the person being questioned acted by deed or by word against the Soviet regime. The first question you must put to him is what are his origins, his education and his profession. It is these questions that ought to determine the fate of the accused."[17] The threat of extermination directed at a class, the bourgeoisie (the "impure"), created an atmosphere of all-pervasive general fear. An individual caught up in the extermination machine became just an abstract statistic. Pierre Pascal used the Cheka's official statistics to declare: "The Soviet regime . . . while being obliged to resort to repressive measures, has remained humane, moderate, political and as positive as ever, adjusting the measures it takes to accord precisely with the results expected from them." He stressed: "There was no law about suspects published, as there was during the French Revolution. Only the guilty were subjected to persecution."[18]

But everyone was guilty. And if, after being arrested and interrogated, someone turned out to be innocent, there was the government decree of March 18, 1920, that gave the Cheka the right "to detain such people in a compulsory labour camp for a period of not more than five years"—that is to say, if there were no grounds for handing the case over, not to a court, but to a revolutionary tribunal.

In June 1918, Dzerzhinsky set out for the newspapers his idea of how the Cheka would operate. "We are terrorizing the enemies of the Soviet government so as to suppress crime in the embryo."[19] In the winter of 1921 the Cheka's chairman was able to review the results of his work with satisfaction: "I think our *apparat* is one of the most effective. Its ramifications reach everywhere. The people respect it. The people fear it."[20] Latsis repeated Dzerzhinsky's assessment: "The Extraordinary Commissions have always tried to organize their work and to present themselves in such a way that the mention of a Commission alone would put paid to any desire to engage in sabotage, extortion or organizing plots."[21] In a 1925 novel, Ilya Ehrenburg recalled: "Two syllables, productive of fear and emotion in any citizen who had lived through the years of revolution, two syllables that came before 'mama,' because they were used to frighten children in their cots, as they used to do with the 'bogey man,' and which accompanied the less fortunate after death all the way to the graveside, two very simple syllables which no one can ever forget."[22] The two syllables were *che* and *ka*. The two syllables later became three: *ge-pe-u*. Dzerzhinsky again declared: "This name— GPU—must inspire in our enemies even greater fear than the Cheka."[23] Later there were four syllables: *o-ge-pe-u* (the OGPU) and then *en-ka-ve-de* (the NKVD). Then there were three again: *ka-ge-be* (KGB). But no matter how many syllables they are known by, the descendants of the Cheka will continue to intimidate Soviet citizens and never allow themselves to be forgotten.

The Left Social Revolutionary I. Steinberg, former People's Commissar of Justice, managed to leave Russia and to describe the atmosphere of terror to which he had for a time contributed:

> Simply because you are a former member of the bourgeoisie you are deprived of the ordinary, familiar human rights; you lose your potato ration-card; like a negro in America you are not allowed into public places; your children and family are forced to go and live in an unhealthy corner of the city. Someone from your class or political party opposed the revolutionary regime, and that is sufficient for you, who are yourself innocent, to be made a hostage. You do not wish to admit something or to betray people close to you, so you are subjected to refined or crude, physical or mental torture. You give no obvious reason for being persecuted, you "skilfully" conceal your thoughts from the authorities and you are formally until now in the clear. In that case we will *force* you against your will to reveal yourself through our network of provocateurs.[24]

Steinberg, who had played an active part in the struggle against the Tsarist autocracy and had supported the October Revolution, discovered suddenly that in place of the Russian form of authoritarian rule a system had emerged that had never before existed and that rejected the very idea of the person as an individual.

The atmosphere of fear that grew out of the division of society into a small group of the "pure" and a majority of the "impure," who had to be exterminated but who might be allowed (temporarily) to remain alive, was a powerful means of infantilizing the population; it was no accident that Ilya Ehrenburg used the metaphor of the child who, like Soviet citizens, is scared of the "bogey man."

Long disputes arose over Lenin's "final testament," a letter dictated by the leader of the Revolution in his final minutes of consciousness that included his opinion of his "heirs." For many years the "testament" was not officially recognized; it was finally published in Moscow during the brief period when the "cult of personality" was being condemned. But Lenin's real testament was never concealed, and always remained the basis of Soviet policy. On July 5, 1921, at the third Comintern Congress, Lenin declared: "Dictatorship is a state of intensive warfare. We are in precisely such a state. At the present moment there is no military intervention. But we are isolated . . . until the question is finally resolved the state of terrible warfare will continue. And we say: war is war, we do not promise either freedom or democracy." Lenin subsequently dotted the i's at the All-Russian Congress of Soviets on December 23, 1921: "Without such an institution [as the Cheka] a regime of the working people cannot exist, so long as exploiters continue to exist in the world. . . ."[25]

Lenin gave his final instructions in May 1922 in a letter to Kursky, the People's Commissar of Justice, who was in charge of drawing up the first Soviet Criminal Code: "The courts must not abolish terror; to promise that would be self-deception or just deception; they must provide grounds for it and legalize it in principle, clearly, without any hypocrisy or embellishment. The law must be worded to cover as much as possible."[26] Terror—henceforth and forever—that was Lenin's testament to his successors.

Terror and repression on a mass scale—this is the most powerful means of inspiring fear, and it continued to be used after the conclusion of the Civil War, in the most peaceful period of Soviet history, the NEP years. Whenever situations arose in the Soviet Union that could not be resolved by normal means, the authorities would immediately create a state of tension, alleging that the regime was being threatened by enemies without and within. Such a situation arose suddenly in 1927, as Stalin prepared the country gradually for the next major shock, collectivization, and demonstrations were organized in towns and villages to protest the external imperialist threat. On June 9, it was reported that twenty hostages, prominent officials in the Tsarist regime, had been executed. Then day after day the newspapers published reports "From the Courtroom": on September 12, nine people were sentenced to be shot "for active espionage"; on September 25, four were executed for "terrorism"; on October 22, six were shot for "spying"; and so forth. On each occasion the report ended with the words: "The sentence is final and not open to appeal."

Overtly repressive measures—arrests, executions and concentration camps (in the 1920s, the synonym for a concentration camp was the Solovetsky islands, the "Solovki")—were only the sharpest instruments used to inspire fear; it was also produced by a system of restrictions and bans that became more numerous and more coercive each year. In 1921, a worker made a speech at a meeting in which he expressed the proletariat's feelings following the victorious revolution: "No, we are not trying to get freedom for the capitalists and landowners but freedom for us, workers and peasants, freedom to buy what we need, freedom to travel from one town to another, to move from a factory to the country—that's the sort of freedom we need."[27]

This elementary freedom did not exist. Everything one did—shopping, traveling, changing one's place of work—involved a branch of the law and gave rise to fear. The principal character of Nikolai Erdman's brilliant 1928 play *The Suicide* exclaimed that there were 200 million people in the Soviet Union, all scared, and then, in a state of ecstasy, proclaimed: "But I'm afraid of no one. No one."[28] The secret of the courage of Semyon Podsekalnikov, the only Soviet citizen who feared nothing, was simple: he had made a firm decision to commit suicide before midnight the next day. Erdman's amazing insight became apparent in the fact that his hero, the frightened Soviet citizen who had at last found freedom, used it like a child running away from a strict father—Semyon Podsekalnikov phoned the Kremlin and announced that he had read Marx and that he didn't like him.

From the late 1920s, two simultaneous processes were taking place: repressive measures became more repressive, and the framework within which the Soviet citizen had to live shrank. In Edgar Allan Poe's "The Pit and the Pendulum," a freethinker who finds himself in the cellars of the Inquisition in Toledo sees to his horror that the red-hot walls of his cell are moving closer and threatening to crush him. From 1928 on, for a whole decade, public trials took place in Russia, one after the other. Laws were passed to reduce the area of the prison camp into which the Soviet Union had been turned: a system of passports was introduced that greatly restricted movement inside the Soviet Union (rural dwellers, who were not issued passports, were forced to stay on the land and had no right to leave it); laws were introduced "concerning betrayal of the motherland" that made attempting to escape from the Soviet Union a capital crime; a law was introduced concerning the collective responsibility of family members for "traitors to the country"; labor legislation binding workers to their workplace was made extremely severe.[29]

Fear can't exist without something to be frightened of, without a threat or a temptation that one must escape or reject. The fear that the secret police "organs" were supposed to (and did) inspire was a healing remedy that would protect one from the Enemy. The inventiveness of the Soviet organizers of fear in drawing up a list of enemies is worthy of admiration; the Enemy is generally given a "generic" name—capitalist, landowner, "former" person, government official, counterrevolutionary, enemy of the people. From his very first days in power, Lenin moved the line separating the "pure" from the "impure" (or enemies) far to the left. Explaining the need to introduce a "decree on the press" creating censorship and banning "bourgeois newspapers," the Revolution's leader proclaimed: "We must go forward to the new society and we must treat the bourgeois newspapers in the same way as we treated those published by the Black Hundreds."[30] Before the Revolution the Bolsheviks' enemies were the Black Hundred papers; after the Revolution it was the "bourgeois" ones (though the term was not defined); then it was publications of the Social Democrats and Social Revolutionaries, that is, all those who were not Bolshevik. It was no accident that the first party to be outlawed was the Constitutional Democrats (the Kadets), a liberal-democratic party with a left-of-center platform. Typical of Lenin's decrees in the first years of the Revolution were the lists he drew up of enemies subject to arrest, imprisonment in a camp, or execution, lists which ended with the words "and so on and so forth": the list of enemies always remained open. Individually and as a group, the enemies are depicted as the final obstacle on the road to the Goal, the Last Enemy.

Dzerzhinsky's deputy, Latsis, provided the most revealing definition of terror and fear under Lenin: "When a whole institution, regiment or military school is involved in a conspiracy, what else can we do but arrest everybody so as to avoid making a mistake and in the course of a careful enquiry into the affair pick out and set free those who are innocent?"[31] Latsis's method recognizes that along with the enemies who have to be sought out and liquidated there are also innocent people.

Stalin's method, now well known from the extensive literature on the subject, was based on the principle that there are no innocent people. After the late 1920s the circle of "enemies" was steadily extended until it embraced—after the murder of Kirov on December 1, 1934—the whole country. The physical impossibility of arresting everyone did not prevent their being considered guilty. The list of enemies included many well-known people. The fear bordering on panic that overcame all Soviet citizens was caused in the first place by the conviction that everyone might *turn out to be* an enemy, secondly by the conviction that your closest relative, a member of your family, might also *turn out to be* an enemy; fear prevailed in the basic unit of society.

Speeches, articles, novels, films, and plays demonstrated that a mother, father, husband, wife, or child could be (and could be shown to be) an enemy. The ideologues and commissars of culture produced evidence and proof that there was only one possible way for a Soviet person—the New Man—to behave: to inform on his own father, mother or son if they turned out to be enemies. Sergei Eisenstein worked for a long time on the film *Bezhin Lug* (*Bezhin Meadow*), in which he strove to demonstrate that a son was obliged to betray his natural father to prove devotion to his Spiritual Father. In the screenplay for Part III of *Ivan the Terrible,* which was never shown, the most loyal of Tsar Ivan's men proves his devotion to Ivan by giving his son a knife and demanding that he kill his natural father, and thus reaffirm his love for the Tsar.

Stalin described his technique for handling people with typically shrewd frankness: "The basic . . . method is surveillance, spying on him, getting to know what's in his mind, and mockery."[32] To the German writer Emil Ludwig he mentioned the "methods used by the Jesuits"; but it was actually spying, seeing into their minds, and mockery that Stalin considered the most important tools for shaping Soviet man.

Hatred provides the best environment in which to cultivate fear. The most important feature of the Stalin epoch was the introduction of fear as an obligatory element in the life of every Soviet citizen. It was cultivated not only in the process of ideological education but throughout the course of education, from the very earliest age. People engaged in cultural activities played the most important role in spreading hatred and turning it into a virtue. Having composed the magic formula "If the enemy does not surrender he is destroyed," Maxim Gorky added another aphorism: "If you don't know how to hate you cannot love sincerely." Thus, fifteen years before Orwell, Gorky asserts that hatred is love and insists that what the Chekists do in the prison camps is real humanism, love of humanity.[33]

In a 1966 poem entitled "Fears," Evgeny Evtushenko announced triumphantly: "Fears are dying out in Russia," and assured us: "Today it seems very remote. It seems strange to recall now the secret fear that someone might inform on you, the hidden fear of a knock on your door. But what about the fear of talking to a foreigner? With a foreigner, or even with your wife."[34] Evtushenko was writing those lines at a time when the first show trial after a long interval was taking place—that of the writers Sinyavsky and Daniel, for writing books without the censor's approval and sending them abroad to be published. It was roughly about that time, perhaps a bit later, that Lysenko, captain of a fishing trawler, wrote:

"Everyone who is not with us is our enemy!"—political officers repeated over and over again. There were cases where a young seaman on his maiden voyage, walking through a foreign town, would go in fear, looking fearfully over his shoulder, as though he expected agents to pop out of every side street and approach him and every intelligence service in the world to grab him, bribe him and make him into a spy and a terrorist.[35]

A Soviet person who finds himself abroad, in foreign territory, finds it quite natural to be afraid of the hated enemies around him. What is more, it does not matter which country he is in: if it is not the Soviet Union, it must be enemy country. Captain Lysenko quotes a preliminary lecture delivered to seamen permitted to go ashore in a Swedish port: "As you know, comrades, our relations with Sweden are, of course, not bad. But all the same Sweden is not a good country. It is a bourgeois state with a monarchy. And it makes no difference at all that the Social Democrats are in power there. They are, after all, social traitors and they will be the first to be hanged!"[36]

Hatred generates fear because it is universal. Hatred is cultivated as an essential, obligatory quality in a Soviet person. Training in it is carried on especially intensively in the army. The 1968 law requiring military training of young people prior to their induction into the army specifies its most important task as "ideological and patriotic education." Marshal Ogarkov, former chief of the General Staff, calls "the training of ardent patriots of our native land" the second most important function of the Soviet armed forces. Political officers in the army reveal the essence of this training: "hatred of the enemy is an essential element in the patriotism of Soviet soldiers."[37]

People are trained to hate by all the mass media and means of propaganda, by literature, the cinema, the theatre, and the graphic arts. Hatred is declared an essential aspect of socialist humanism. The contemporary version of Gorky's formula has been turned into a law of Soviet life: "Love of people and hatred of the enemies of humane behaviour are two dialectically interlinked sides of socialist humanism."[38] This definition, provided by a Soviet philosopher, is illustrated by the work of artists and writers. Pyotr Proskurin, a popular Soviet writer,* demonstrates this "dialectic" with disarming simplicity. Describing the same event on two occasions he produces two dialectically differing assessments of it. On the first: "The mind of man . . . has carried out a totally unjustified act of sacrilege, has committed a crime and besmirched the very foundations of life and even of matter itself. The immorality of that act extended so far that it was impossible to take it in, and it will take many long years to grasp what it means." On the second: "It was wonderful." On the first occasion, the hero of the novel is expressing indignation at the dropping of an atomic bomb on Hiroshima, while on the second he is airing his delight as he watches the testing of a Soviet atomic bomb.[39]

The "dialectic" makes it possible to cultivate a substratum of hatred which can be injected into any part indicated by the Supreme Ruler. Zamyatin was the first to describe a festival of hatred—the public execution of an enemy.[40] Orwell called this procedure a "two-minute hate session"; he understood that anyone could serve as the object of hatred. A contemporary of the first decades of Soviet history, he was

---

*A writer's popularity is determined by the size of the printings for his books. Since in the Soviet Union this size is decided by the publishing house, the ideological assessment of a book becomes a factor determining its popularity.

amazed at Stalin's sudden change of policy towards Hitler in 1939. Subsequent decades produced many new examples.

Hatred of Nazism was cultivated assiduously from the moment Hitler came to power. Art played a most important part in this campaign. Bardesh and Brazyak rightly described *Alexander Nevsky* as "the most disturbing of the 'fascist' films" and commented that "Nazi Germany would like to produce a similar film if only it possessed a film genius."[41] But the imagination of French film historians was impressed primarily by Prince Alexander—the blond hero who reminded them of Roland, Siegfried, and Percival. No less important was the part played in the film by the enemies, who evoked irresistible hatred because Sergei Eisenstein depicted them as unpersons, and so fulfilled the first precept for the inculcation of hatred: Deprive the enemy of human features. Two years after producing *Nevsky*, Eisenstein staged Wagner's *Die Walküre* at the Bolshoi Theatre. In June 1941, the Nazi regime and Germans in general again became the object of hatred. Fear of Fascism and Germany arose and disappeared at the wave of a magic wand; hatred and fear were turned on and off like water from a tap.

The second example of how fear and hatred can be whipped up and allowed to subside is to be seen in Soviet–Chinese relations. In the honeymoon years of friendship, when people in the Soviet Union were singing in chorus "Stalin and Mao hear us" and "Moscow–Peking," it seemed as though the alliance between the "great brothers" would last forever. But relations were broken off suddenly by Moscow in 1962, and a conflict developed that led in 1969 to a military clash on the Ussuri River. Soon China became a principal enemy, and fear of the "Yellow Peril" was whipped up by professional propagandists, writers, and artists. Evtushenko wrote a poem entitled "On the Red Snow of the Ussuri," in which he warned people of the threat of an invasion by "new Batys" and called on them to be prepared for "another battle of Kulikovo."[42]* In Nikolai Moskolenko's 1972 film *Russian Field,* a hardworking Soviet collective farmworker laboring for the benefit of her native land loses her son, who is killed by a vicious, treacherous enemy. The film ends with shots from a newsreel showing rows of coffins containing the bodies of victims of the fighting on the Ussuri River and weeping mothers and wives. The enemy is not identified by name; but

*Baty, grandson of Genghis Khan, led the Tatar invasion of the Russian princedoms in 1237–40. In 1380 the Russians defeated the Tatars at Kulikovo.

there is no need to explain anything to an audience which has seen pictures of the funerals on television and documentary films—the hated enemies and murderers are the Chinese. Ten years later, hatred of the Chinese was put on hold, and it was the turn of the Americans and Zionists to be brought to the fore.

The organization of campaigns of fear and hatred requires ready-made history to stimulate the collective memory and mythological threats. Hatred of China was nourished by recalling the invasions of the Tatar and Mongol hordes and the threat of the "Yellow Peril." To develop friendly feelings towards China, people were reminded of the Chinese revolution and the common struggle against imperialism. Hatred of Germany was cultivated by describing the *Drang nach Osten* and the battles with the Teutonic orders in the thirteenth century, while friendlier feelings were cultivated by reference to the common struggle against Napoleon. The history of Russian–American relations, while relatively brief, nevertheless provides sufficient material for switching the machinery of hatred-fear on and off. During the Second World War, when the Soviet Union was receiving weapons, transport and food from the United States under Lend-Lease, Soviet propaganda never tired of recalling the visit of a Russian squadron to New York during the Civil War—the Russia of Alexander II had supported the "progressive" North against Great Britain, which had supported the "reactionary" South. But during the cold war the United States was depicted as the organizer of intervention against the Soviet Republic after the Revolution. The historical traditions of Russian-American friendship were once again recalled during the honeymoon of cooperation in 1975 marked by the joint flights of the spaceships *Apollo* and *Soyuz*.

This exploitation of "history," of selected facts from the past, makes it possible to describe the emotions being aroused at any given moment as lasting and never-changing: hatred and friendship have always existed. The principal goal is to control the emotions and turn them into conditioned reflexes to be switched on at a signal from above. At the time of the confusion produced by the exposure of the "cult of personality" in Khrushchev's speech to the 20th Congress of the CPSU, a Soviet poet told a story about a scientific research institute that had succeeded in making artificial hearts indistinguishable from real ones. The commission that checked the institute's product refused to accept the artificial hearts because they were too much like real ones, declaring: "We need useful hearts, like iron locks, straightforward, convenient to use and able to do everything. . . . To growl or stay silent, to destroy or to love!"[43]

The only enemy against which hatred has been whipped up continuously since the Second World War is the Jews. In the period 1948–53 this enemy was given the name "cosmopolitan"—a neutral word which had had in the 1920s and 1930s rather a favorable connotation,[44] and which suddenly acquired a sinister meaning and became a synonym for the most evil enemy. In the 1960s, the word "Zionism" began to sound ever more sinister and gradually came to signify the Enemy, the very incarnation of Evil, which had to be fought until it was destroyed. In 1975 Soviet propaganda had a remarkable success: the formula that had originated in the USSR, "Zionism is racism," was ratified by the United Nations.

This victory had a double significance: in the first place, the enemy of the Soviet Union was solemnly and officially declared to be the enemy of mankind; in the second place, the word "racism," which had remained in the repertoire of Soviet propaganda with only one out of several meanings, now acquired the ambiguities required of Soviet speech.

Zionism is an ideal enemy, combining as it does all the elements necessary to arouse fear and hatred. From the time under Lenin and Stalin, when all classes were destroyed, as survivals of capitalist society, the "imperialist" enemy took on an abstract character. Only Zionism was at one and the same time an external and an internal enemy, both concrete and abstract, eternal and evocative of concrete historical associations. If there had not been some two million Jews in the Soviet Union,[45] it would scarcely have been possible to think up such an enemy.

In 1974, one of the most prolific opponents of Zionism wrote: "Some five to seven years ago many of us had only a very vague idea of the sort of enemy we faced, the extent of his influence, the length of his tentacles, the nature of his principal strategic goal or of the forms and methods used in his subversive activity."[46] In 1974, when the enemy was better, but still insufficiently known, the Central Committee of the CPSU passed a special resolution "On the strengthening of anti-Zionist propaganda," one of the results of which was the United Nations resolution condemning Zionism as a form of racism.

"Anti-Zionist propaganda" was organized on a scale greatly exceeding the theoretical activities in this field in Hitler's Germany. All means of propaganda were put to use—books, articles in magazines with circulations in the millions, television and radio programs, feature films. Hatred and fear of Jews is instilled from the very earliest age. In the *Pioneers' Pravda* (which has a circulation of eight million and is aimed at children between the ages of nine and fourteen) children were told that "the Zionists penetrate everywhere" and that to carry on their subversive activity they even make use of jeans made by the firm of "Levi." (In an apparent effort to counteract the harmful influence of "Jewish" jeans the Soviet government decided to buy up an Italian factory to produce "anti-Zionist" jeans under the "Jesus" label.)

The creation of an enemy and the organization of hatred are conducted along two lines. The first is handled by scholars: a Permanent Commission was set up in the social science section of the Soviet Academy of Science to coordinate research aimed at exposing and criticizing the history, ideology, and practice of Zionism. The Commission is a center for scholars, and the brain behind the "anti-Zionist" action. Sectors for "combating Zionism" are set up in the humanities institutes of the Academy of Science, in institutes belonging to republican academies, and in Party schools at all levels.

"Scientific" anti-Zionist material is prepared on two levels, theoretical and popular. Theoretical works appear under scientific titles like *International Zionism: Its History and Policy* (Moscow, 1977, a collection of papers written by associates of the Soviet Academy of Science: the Institute of Oriental Studies, the Institute for the Study of the USA, the Institute for the International Working-Class Movement, and the Institute for Latin America); *The Ideology and Practice of International Zionism* (1981, the Academy of Science of the Ukrainian Republic). Works intended for popular consumption consist of mass-circulation literature with self-explanatory eye-catching titles: *Invasion without Weapons, The Zionist Octopus of Spying, The Poisoned Weapon of Zionism.* The "scientific" literature is published in print runs of 3,000–10,000 copies, "for specialists"; popular works in runs of 100,000–200,000, with texts often published in advance in the weekly *Ogonyok,* which in 1983 had a circulation of 1,779,000.

The scientific theory behind Soviet anti-Zionism is the most amazing product of Soviet ideology, a combination of the Protocols of the Elders of Zion and quotations from Marx and Lenin. As their researches intensify, Soviet students of Zionism stress ever more openly the racist nature of their campaign. A book by L. Korneev that purports to sum up the results of many years of work stresses the "ethnic" nature of Jewish capitalism and insists on the need to conduct a battle not only against Zionism but against *"Judentum"* as well. The need for a struggle against "Jewry" is explained by reference to the age-old nature of the Jewish threat to the Russian people and, consequently to the Soviet regime and "real" socialism. Soviet experts on "Zionism" constantly refer to the first "true Jewish pogrom" in 1069 in Kiev and "prove" that according to the latest data, the Tatar yoke was essentially a Jewish yoke, because "many Jews played the part of tax collectors."[47] Developing Lenin's theory of imperialism as the highest stage of capitalism, Soviet Marxist-Leninists assert that in the last quarter of the twentieth century Zionism became the final stage of imperialism.

Zionism is simultaneously an external enemy—Israel is depicted as the center of a worldwide conspiracy against the Soviet Union and progressive humanity—and an internal one, in which Soviet Jews are made out to be agents of Zionism. All of humanity is mobilized in the struggle against Israel, because "by concealed, secret means Zionism penetrates into all the vitally important cells of states the world over, undermines from within everything that is strong, healthy and patriotic and gathers up or seizes all the principal positions in the administrative, economic and intellectual life of a country."[48] All the resources of the Soviet state are mobilized for the struggle against Soviet Jews. "The ideal way of resolving" the Jewish question was, according to Korneev, "set out clearly in Lenin's works."[49] It is complete assimilation. Insofar as Soviet "experts on Zionism" suspect they may meet with some difficulties along that path, and possibly because they would like to resolve the Jewish question "finally," they propose as an alternative the method employed by the former president of Uganda, Idi Amin, as he described it in a long interview published in *Komsomolskaya Pravda:* "There is not a single one of the Israelis who were living here left. I gave an order for them to be turned out because they used their presence in Uganda to establish control over our country."[50]

All references to Judea, the Jewish people and religion, and the Bible have been removed from school texts. Soviet historians want to eliminate the Jews from the past in the hope that they will vanish from the present. Similar instructions are in force in other Socialist countries; all references to the religion of Moses have been cut out of Polish history textbooks.[51]

An active part in the struggle against "Zionism" is played by the graphic arts (drawings from *Der Stürmer* serve as a model for the caricaturists) and literature about art. In Soviet writing, where there is no need to provide a "scholarly" cover for "anti-Zionism," anti-Semitic views are openly expressed. These include explaining the excesses committed by the Soviet regime during the Revolution and the years of the Stalin Terror as due to the activity of Jews eating away at the Revolution from within (for example: Valentin Kataev, "Werther Has Been Written," *Novy Mir,* 1980, No. 6; A. Ivanov, "The Eternal Call," *Roman Gazeta,* 1978), even calling openly for pogroms (Ivan Shevtsov, Valentin Pikul). Books by professional anti-Semites like Shevtsov and Pikul are gradually extending the limits of permitted anti-Semitism; the Party press criticizes them only when they go too far and create such a terrifying idea of the enemy that even the Party, it appears, is unable to cope.

The fear that surrounds the Soviet citizen, circulating about and within him, is at once disturbing and pacifying. Enemies are terrifying, but their presence provides a logical and mystical explanation for all one's difficulties. "Just look around and you see the enemy everywhere," a poet wrote in 1929.[52] The might of the Soviet state has increased immeasurably since then, but the number of enemies has increased even faster. The feeling of being defenders of a "besieged fortress" has been encouraged by the Soviet system since it came into existence. In a besieged fortress it is essential to fear and hate the external enemy who has surrounded the stronghold, who is undermining the walls and threatening your home and your life. The pre-revolutionary population of the Russian Empire did not know this feeling: Russia suffered attacks and herself attacked and had enemies, but she never experienced the feeling of being besieged. That feeling is the result of the challenge hurled at the world by the leaders of the Russian Revolution: having declared its intention of destroying the old world and building a new world, the Communist Party announced that all who stood in the path of that construction were enemies, aliens.

These enemies became the justification for everything done by the regime, the only force defending the walls of the fortress against the aliens. Enemies were to blame for the difficulties of everyday life; it was they who poisoned people's minds and who threatened another war. The 1968 invasion of Czechoslovakia was easily explained as a response to the emergence of a new threat on the Soviet frontier. The same explanation was offered for the 1980 invasion of Afghanistan and the 1983 shooting down of a South Korean airliner. War, which the Soviet leaders alone are capable of averting, is a terrible danger that prompts people to forget their grievances and problems. Fear of aliens produces a feeling of comradeship, of the collective, a desire to close ranks.

The feeling of being in a besieged fortress produces fear and distrust of other people who may turn out to be on the other side, or be seduced by the enemy. If at one time children or parents, husbands or wives, turned out to be enemies (and the achievements of informers are still glorified to this day), then it was perfectly natural to believe that anyone could be an enemy or a covert agent of the KGB. The state of total distrust, well known in the countries of Western Europe during the German occupation, has existed in a considerably more intensive form in the Soviet Union since 1917. As one would expect, Stalin expressed better than anyone else the atmosphere of total suspicion in which all Soviet people lived. Khrushchev recalled that on one occasion, for no special reason (that was what struck the members of the Politburo particularly), Stalin suddenly declared: "I'm a hopeless case. I don't trust anyone. I don't even trust myself."[53]

Alexander Zinoviev called his book on Soviet man *Homo Sovieticus;* he might have called it *He Who Is Scared.* Transferring Soviet man outside his "fortress" and describing *Homo sovieticus* in emigration, Zinoviev depicts a stranger from another planet, afraid of everyone and everything, hating everyone and everything, and firmly convinced that it is precisely because he is afraid of and hates everyone that he is a "superman."[54] Fearing the KGB most of all, he attributes to that organization a magical omnipotence equal to the panic-stricken fear he is experiencing.

Zinoviev is a patient who describes with the precision and typical limitations of the invalid an illness cultivated assiduously among the Soviet populace. The atmosphere of fear has turned them into frightened children scared to leave the dark room in which they have been shut because they are convinced that they can't live anywhere else. Their dark room is crammed full of weapons, and that makes them even more scared. Their only consolations are the other occupants of that dark room, and the guards. The paralyzing effect of fear has given birth to one of the most important qualities of Soviet man—the firm conviction, a mystical belief, that nothing must be changed, that the system will continue to exist forever, and that, as Zinoviev asserts, it is the fate of all humanity.

The anonymous Soviet author of the first serious study of the Polish events of 1980–82 (which circulated in *samizdat*) thinks the Polish revolution became possible because Gomulka was "the first person in history to try out 'socialism without the threat of prison.' " The cessation of arrests and a considerable reduction in the extent of repressive measures "led in Poland to a reduction in the level of fear."[55]

The Russian historian Vasily Klyuchevsky, recounting the struggle of the Russians against the Tatar yoke, wrote that it took two generations of people who had grown up not knowing what it was to fear the Tatars to produce the people who went into battle in 1380 at Kulikovo and routed Mamai.

Every system of production relationships forms, in accordance with its essential nature, a special social type of person as an economic operative, and in the first place a specific type of worker.   KARL MARX

The state exercises control over the extent of labor and consumption.
CONSTITUTION OF THE USSR

9

Labor

The present Soviet Constitution limits itself to stating the obvious: the state controls labor and consumption as it controls everything else. The preceding "Stalin" Constitution of 1936 described the relationship of the state to the performance of labor by its citizens more colorfully and expressively: "In the USSR labor is an obligation and a matter of honor for every citizen capable of working." This formula expresses precisely how labor is regarded in the Soviet Union: as an inescapable duty and a "matter of honor." The Constitution was actually making use of one of Stalin's most famous sayings: "Labor in the USSR is a matter of honor, a matter of valor and heroism." Part of this was included in the country's basic law; the complete form became part of the decoration on the gateways into Soviet prison camps.

These two aspects of labor in the Soviet Union found full expression in the combination of Stalin's formula and the place where it was displayed. In the post-Stalin period, the late leader's words were no longer quoted; breaking with the glorious past, the authorities even changed the wording of the Constitution. But the slogans that adorn the post-Stalin camps continue to insist on the magical qualities of Soviet labor: "Honest labor is the way to shorten your sentence." Labor and freedom, i.e., life outside the camp, are indissolubly linked, just as they were in the famous slogan that adorned Hitler's camps: *Arbeit macht frei.*

The Revolution's ultimate aim, its super-task, was the creation of a New Man, and from the first days of Bolshevik power, this determined their attitude to labor. Work was regarded simultaneously as a creative function (the construction of a new world) and as a pedagogic one (the construction of a New Man for the new world). It followed, therefore, that anyone who worked badly was interfering with the construction of communism, of heaven on earth. Labor became an ethical category, since, in Lenin's words, everything that contributed to the building of communism was moral, anyone who worked well for communism was a good person, a moral person, and anyone who did not wish to work was a bad and immoral person, an enemy.

The biggest surprise for the new regime in the first months after the Revolution was the proletariat's lack of desire to work. Theory taught that it would be natural for the proletarian revolution to be opposed by its natural enemies, members of the bourgeoisie. But all the theoretical forecasts were proved wrong because it was the working class, in whose name and for whose benefit the Party had carried out the Revolution, that refused to work.

All sorts of words were invented to describe the unexpected behavior of the working people. The word "strike" was considered suitable for describing the behavior of former civil servants who refused to work for the Soviet regime and even of teachers infected by "petit-bourgeois" ideas. But the proletariat could not go on strike in a proletarian state, so they were said to be troublemakers, to be carrying out sabotage, or to have "deserted from the labor front." All these terms simply meant that the factories had come to a halt and that there was a sharp drop in labor productivity in those enterprises that were still operating. By 1919, industrial production had fallen to a sixth of what it had been in 1913, and the number of people employed in industry had been halved.[1] Labor productivity began to decline rapidly in 1917; by 1920 it was only 27.1 percent of the 1913 level.[2] Workers were simply quitting their jobs and going elsewhere. The obvious reason for the nation's economic ruin and the justification for its collapse was the civil war that broke out in the summer of 1918, but the real reason was the Revolution, which had destroyed the economic and social foundations of the old regime.

Three slogans had permitted the Bolsheviks to seize power in October 1917: Peace for the people; Land to the peasants; Workers' control of production. The first two were straightforward and easily understood. The third slogan was abstract and theoretical, and it made clear that the Party that had seized power in haste had no idea what to do with the proletariat or the economy. Very little thought had been given to this question, because for Lenin the only serious problem was how to seize power. The work of administering the state could (he believed for some time) be carried out by a cook.

Workers' control very soon "disorganized completely the work of the factories, mills and mines,"[3] since the workers quite clearly were unprepared to "control" production. Indeed, the new leaders themselves had no idea what "control over production" meant—but they did know that the workers had to "control" or "manage" on behalf of the state and in the interests of the vanguard of the working class, the Party. Immediately after the Revolution the Party started a campaign against workers' trade unions, depriving them of the rights and prerogatives they had won in battles with the Tsarist government. There was a sudden increase in the number of trade-union members, because all workers in an enterprise now had to belong to a union, and membership dues were deducted automatically from wages. The trade unions were transformed from organizations of class-conscious active workers who knew their rights and were ready to fight for them into an appendage of the state. In the new trade union rule books the word "strike" was obliterated and the task of the trade unions was said to have changed from the struggle for better economic conditions to organization and management of industry under the state's guidance. P. N. Kolokolnikov, one of the founders of the Russian trade union movement, wrote in February 1919: "The trade unions are steadily losing their militancy and are being turned gradually into government institutions. They are becoming more like part of the administration every day, and seem to be ever more ready to abandon the interests of the workers in favour of ensuring the rights of the regime as entrepreneur."[4]

The disorganization produced by "control over production" and the reluctance to turn it into a real system of self-management prompted Lenin to turn to nationalization of all means of production, which resulted in a revolution whose significance was appreciated only decades later. The authors of this experiment could not foresee its outcome. Gorky wrote: "For people like Lenin the working class is what iron-ore is for a metal worker. Is it possible in all the given circumstances to cast a socialist state from this ore? It is apparently impossible, but why not try? What does Lenin risk if the experiment doesn't succeed?"[5] The answer to Gorky's second question is easy: Lenin was risking nothing. The answer to the first question—whether he could "cast a socialist state from this ore"—was not so simple. In the first place, it required a definition of what was meant by "a socialist state." In 1917, Gorky undoubtedly had in mind something different from Lenin. What is certain is that "from this ore"—that is, from the Russian working class, later from the peasantry—a state was "cast" of a hitherto unheard-of type, that called itself socialist. Soviet history also bears witness to the fact that in the process of "casting" from the available "ore" a new material was created. Nationalization of the means of production played the most important role in this process (later to be called "re-forging"). Public or state ownership of factories, mills, railways, small businesses, and trade produced a new attitude to labor. Theoretically, everything became "ours": "common property." As Lenin put it: "The greatest change in the history of mankind is taking place—of forced labour for labour for oneself."[6] In practice, everything belonged to the state.

A conflict developed between the workers who expected the state to improve their conditions, and the state, which instead demanded sacrifices and even greater efforts from them, since they were working for socialism, i.e., for themselves. Both parties were disappointed: the workers because their conditions had changed sharply for the worse since the Revolution; the state because the workers had not come up to expectations. Lenin knew what he wanted: "Labour under Communism is unpaid labour for the benefit of society . . . voluntary labour, labour beyond what is demanded, labour performed with no account taken of reward."[7] But, as Lenin soon realized, Russian workers turned out to be insufficiently mature and class-conscious, and they refused to work for nothing. The leader of the Revolution concluded that the workers did not want to work, didn't know how to work.

Various "scholarly" explanations were offered for the lack of willingness to work. According to Lenin, a significant factor, along with the proletariat's lack of class-consciousness and maturity, was the famous "Russian laziness": "The Russian is a bad worker compared with those in the advanced countries."[8] According to Trotsky, "as a rule a man tries to avoid work. Zeal is not a natural quality."[9]

In the course of the Five-Year Plans a new formula developed that expressed remarkably well the relationship between the leaders and the led: if you can't do it, we'll teach you; if you won't do it, we'll make you. The discovery of force as a means of resolving problems had already taken place—on the first day of the Revolution. In March–April 1918, Lenin came to the conclusion that they would have to use force against the working class, that people would have to be forced to work and taught to work. "Discipline" became the magic word, the miracle-working key. The leader of the Party and state spoke in the spring of 1918 of "iron discipline" and of "unquestioning submission to the will of one person, the Soviet leader, in work time."[10] Education in the "new discipline" was declared to be "a new form of class struggle in the transition period"[11]—that is, a "class struggle" with the proletariat who were unwilling to work in the new conditions. The ideologist of the "workers' revolution," V. Makhaisky, was a merciless critic of "Lenin's socialism," which he declared to be a deception of the proletariat, and he pointed out that "without compulsion it is impossible to force a slave to work diligently for his exploiter. A hungry man will not voluntarily carry well-fed parasites on his back."[12] The Communist Party leaders knew this very well, and appeals for discipline, given legal form in April 1918 in the decree on labor discipline, became the basis for developing the theoretical justification of the need for forced labor.

Convinced that unpaid communist labor was not to be achieved for the time being, Lenin produced a new conception of labor in the transition period under socialism: "Socialism presupposes work without capitalists, work performed for society with the strictest accounting, control and supervision by the organized avant-garde. . . . Moreover, both the amount of work and how much is paid for it must be determined."[13] The Party, the "organized vanguard," had to control, supervise and determine the amount of work and what was paid for it. Trotsky, in full agreement with Lenin's idea, completed it with a frank definition of forced labor. "We are moving towards a type of labor, under public control on the basis of an economic plan which is obligatory for the whole country, i.e., it is compulsory for every worker. That is the basis of socialism."[14] Nikolai Bukharin agreed completely with Lenin and Trotsky:

From the point of view of the proletariat, in the interests of the real and not the fictitious freedom of the working class, *it is essential to abolish the so-called "freedom of labour"* [my emphasis] because that freedom cannot be reconciled with a properly organized "planned" economy and distribution of the work force. Consequently a system of labour conscription and state distribution of workers under the dictatorship of the proletariat is an expression of a relatively high degree of organization of the whole *apparat* and of the stability of the proletarian regime as a whole.[15]

The leaders of the Revolution correctly assessed the significance of forced labor and its connection with planning and the stability of the regime. Half a century later, Soviet lawyers named the most important elements in the "socialist organization of labor." They were "the planned direction of citizens to their work and their distribution between the various branches and different enterprises, the training of skilled workers, the fixing of wage levels, and ensuring the socialist organization of production, and of safety measures and labour discipline."[16]

In the early days of the Revolution, Party leaders concluded that forced labor based on iron discipline was a temporary measure made necessary by the exceptional circumstances brought about by the Revolution, but that it was in accordance with the laws of socialist construction. The anonymous author of a 1919 article in the government newspaper *Izvestia* voiced views then current in the Party leadership, insisting, "The political dictatorship of the proletariat also demands an economic dictatorship. . . . It is essential to bring discipline into every enterprise and to appoint a dictator. . . . Without such measures as piece-work, bonuses, fines, dismissals and dictatorial measures by specialist administrators the country's economy . . . will not be rebuilt."[17] In the 1980s, when the Soviet state considered itself to be a superpower and demanded parity with the United States, Soviet economic dictionaries put emphasis on the word "discipline" as the main foundation of the socialist system. In addition to the basic entry for the word "discipline," dictionaries have entries on state discipline, planning discipline, production discipline, technological discipline, and labor discipline; the political dictionary completes the collection, with an entry on moral discipline.[18]

The apt formula defining the relationship to labor as an ideological category combining socially useful activity with the pedagogic function was proposed by Dzerzhinsky. In 1919, explaining the purpose behind the concentration camps that had already been in operation for six months, Dzerzhinsky proposed "to keep these concentration camps so as to make use of the labor of people under arrest, for the gentlemen who get by without doing a job of work, and for those who can't work without some compulsion being applied . . . for a slapdash attitude to the job, for negligence, for lateness and so forth." He coined a formula: "It is proposed that we set up a school of labor."[19] The concentration camp—the highest form of forced labor—was intended to strike fear into those who had not been arrested and to teach those who had been arrested how to work. Stalin's hymn "to labor in the USSR" on the gates of the Soviet camps, and the praise for the pedagogic virtues of labor in Soviet prison camps today, bear witness to the unchanging attitude to labor in the Soviet Union.

The law included in the very first Soviet constitution, "he who does not work shall not eat," was not so simple as it might appear. The Revolution that had upended Russia's social pyramid had legitimized a new hierarchy in labor as well. All work was no longer the same. It was essential to work, but the kind of work one did defined one's position in the new world. The Constitution began by putting peasant labor into a lower category of human activity than labor in industry, because the former was individual work that gave rise to a petty bourgeoisie, while the latter was a collective effort that produced the class to which the future was supposed to belong. The hierarchical arrangement of labor was reflected in the list of constitutional rights: in elections to the Soviets the vote of one worker equalled five peasant votes, and a considerable number of peasants "who employed hired labor" were deprived altogether of the right to vote. Trade was declared unproductive labor, an unnecessary and harmful activity and a survival of capitalist social relations. Private trade was abolished, merchants lost the right to vote, and preparations were made for state trade (which in the period of War Communism had existed only on paper) to be replaced by a system of socialist distribution.

Although private trade had been permitted in the NEP years, it remained a little-admired occupation, a "bourgeois" element indulgently allowed to persist in the socialist system out of kindness. The criminal code drew a very vague distinction between permitted "trade" and "speculation" (profiteering), which was severely punished. The word "Nepman," used to describe all representatives of the private sector, was a synonym for a concealed enemy who inevitably would be exposed. Nearly seventy years have elapsed since the Revolution, but the trade and service sectors of the economy are still considered work of a lower category, inevitably associated with deceit, robbery and corruption.

The NEP period was a time of experimentation, a time for comparing the two systems—the state and the private sector. In spite of all the administrative and financial obstacles put in the way of developing private enterprises (primarily in agriculture, but also in the case of small factories, foreign concessions, shops, and so on), there was no doubting their success—which contributed to a considerable extent to the country's recovery. The economic success of the private sector only served to underline its potential for ideological harm: by preserving and expanding capitalist relations in a state just entering upon the construction of socialism, the private merchants were delaying the approach to the goal and interfering with the education of the New Man.

A return to the system of War Communism (in a considerably improved form) became inevitable. Stalin gave the signal for the second "great leap forward" at the end of the 1920s. The period of "reconstruction," as the years of the first Five-Year Plans and the collectivization of agriculture were called, created favorable conditions for developing the Soviet economic model with the special Soviet attitude to labor. Gigantic armies of largely or totally unskilled workers (the majority of them former peasants) were used to erect huge industrial complexes, factories, dams, and railways—large-scale work that made it possible to employ successfully the strategy of the "big battalions." Industrialization became a kind of warfare in which the masses, the crowd, under the leadership of commissars and making use (with strict controls) of technical experts, performed deeds of valor and kept advancing; every factory built, every cubic meter of concrete produced, every kilometer of railroad track laid was treated as a battle won, in a war in which victory was inevitable.

Trotsky had called for the militarization of labor in 1920; it was not carried out until the late 1920s. Stalin rejected some surface details of Trotsky's model, but he preserved its essence and confirmed the correctness of Trotsky's formula: "The militarization of labor . . . is the inevitable and fundamental method for organizing our work force . . . in accordance with the needs of socialism in the period of transition from the supremacy of capitalism to a communist state."[20]

The army became the model for the working class. In a country portrayed as a fortress under siege, the Red Army was there to defend the borders against the external enemy while the working class and the peasants on collective farms waged war against nature, technology, and internal enemies obstructing the building of socialism. Discipline and enthusiasm were demanded from the troops on the "labor front" just as they were from soldiers in the Red Army. Discipline was ensured by the extremely tough provisions introduced into labor legislation in the period 1929–34. *The History of the Soviet State and Law* states: "The laws relating to labor in the period of the first Five-Year Plan raised the degree of responsibility of the worker for the fulfillment of his duties as an employee."[21] That meant criminal responsibility. For example, "the delivery of poor quality or unfinished goods" was to be punished by "deprivation of freedom for a period of no less than five years." For the first time the "deliberate violation of labor discipline was also to be treated as a criminal offence." "Rules concerning discipline" very similar to the army regulations on discipline[22] were issued for workers in different branches of industry. The concept of having a single individual responsible for the running of an enterprise *(edinonachalie),* of giving the manager of an enterprise dictatorial rights, including the right to dismiss workers and hand them over to the courts, was put into practice. In 1933, the trade unions, which long had defended only management interests, were nevertheless considered superfluous and were abolished by being absorbed into the commissariat for labor; they were later revived during the war.

Severely repressive administrative measures were never the only means used to "mobilize the masses"; along with the "stick," the authorities also exploited faith in the possibility of a real improvement in the standard of living, and the hope that "temporary" difficulties would disappear. The enthusiasm that undoubtedly inspired a portion of the population in the first post-revolutionary years was an important factor in constructing the "Stalin" model. But the Party, which was in charge of the process, never allowed the feelings of the working people, even the most orthodox, to develop spontaneously. Enthusiasm was kept under strict control and was directed where and to the extent the Party considered necessary.

The idea of "socialist competition" (i.e., "competition between large sections of the working people, aimed at improving and raising the rate of socialist construction"[23]) was first put forward by Lenin. In April 1929, a Communist Party conference passed a resolution on the organization of socialist competition, and in May the Central Committee approved a special resolution laying down the rules for displays of "mass enthusiasm." Thus was born a superior way for the laboring masses to "demonstrate their enthusiasm and readiness to work," known as "shock work."

A shock worker was an outstanding employee who produced more than the economic plan demanded. The emergence of this idea did more than enrich the growing vocabulary of the Soviet language; it also signified a turning point in the development of a policy towards the proletariat, and marked the beginning of a new stage in the formation of Soviet man. The birth of "shock work" was accompanied by the introduction of piece work, which had been abolished after the Revolution on the grounds that it was an especially repellent form of exploitation. "Shock work" served as an excellent argument in the campaign Stalin had begun to suppress the obsolete idea of "equality." "Equality" was declared to be a middle-class concept and given the pejorative synonym "egalitarianism" (uravnilovka).

The word udarnik (shock worker) originally referred to the part of the breech of a rifle or gun that detonates the cartridge's percussion cap when the weapon is fired. During the First World War, the idea of "shock" military units to carry out special operations and inflict concentrated "shocks" on the enemy was developed. This use of a term from the military lexicon was no accident, since labor was being depicted as a war for socialism. But the emergence of the "shock worker" meant a division of the work force into a "vanguard" and "laggards" who not only were not in the front line but were preventing the front from advancing. Antagonism developed, and was encouraged, between the vanguard and the laggards. "Light cavalry units" were set up among the shock workers, mostly Young Communists, whose job was to supervise the work of the "laggards" in an enterprise, and to descend on the places where they lived to check up on their way of life. In a story entitled "The First Wave," V. Veresaev describes how Yurka, a young shock worker, comes to realize the need to spur his fellow workers on, and overcomes his outdated, harmful feelings of working-class solidarity:

For the first time he felt deep within himself that these workers [the laggards] were not comrades but enemies against whom he was going to wage a ceaseless battle. And it was very pleasant suddenly to become aware of his right not to suppress his indignation but to go at them openly, to put real pressure on them and beat them mercilessly until they learnt to respect labor![24]

On the night of August 30, 1935, a young miner named Alexei Stakhanov managed in the course of a single shift to extract, instead of the seven tons of coal demanded by the Plan, 102 tons, thus exceeding the Plan fourteen times over, by 1,400 percent. This marked the birth of a higher form of shock work: the Stakhanov movement. Instead of the shock worker, the hero was now the Stakhanovite *(Stakhanovets)*. The Stakhanov movement was declared to be a specifically "Soviet, socialist form of labor," and Alexei Stakhanov told newsmen that he and his comrades had made a remarkable discovery: work went better if one member of a brigade worked the coal face while the others performed auxiliary functions. In this way, "rationalization" (with which miners the world over had long been familiar) was combined with enthusiasm: by urging each other on they made it possible to overfulfill the Plan many times over. The two elements of the "new form of labor" were supplemented by material incentives, and a new social hierarchy, defined by the percentage by which the plan was overfulfilled, was given a material basis—the hierarchy was determined by the level of wages. On January 20, 1936, the newspaper *Trud* reported that in one mine in the Donets basin sixty workers were earning between 1,000 and 2,500 rubles per man—they were the Stakhanovite vanguard. Seventy-five miners earned 800–1,000 rubles; 400 earned 500–800 rubles, and the rest earned an average of 125 rubles.

But it was not these officially recognized elements—rationalization, enthusiasm, and material incentives—that made the Stakhanov movement a specifically "socialist form of labor": to exceed the production target several times over, sometimes several tens of times over, required careful preparation and organization of the work, possible only with the agreement and participation of the management—the people in control of production, the people who decided who was going to be a *Stakhanovets*. The "vanguard," the *Stakhanovtsy*, were rewarded with the money, privileged medals, and decorations that became the visible sign of a man's place in Soviet society. The concept of "distinguished people" again became current, this time referring not to the aristocracy but to the *Stakhanovtsy*. At the same time, similar ideas were being employed in Nazi Germany, where the slogan "work ennobles a man" *(Arbeit adelt)* acquired extensive popularity. All these benefits were given to the new "nobility" by the regime on whose good will the selection of the "nobles" depended. It was up to the regime to decide whether they should be knocked off their pedestal. Appealing to people to increase their "vigilance," Stalin stressed: ". . . The real wrecker must from time to time demonstrate his success at work because that is the only way he can preserve his position as a wrecker."[25]

In the 1930s, during the second revolution—very much more radical than the October Revolution—the Soviet regime carried out the nationalization of human labor. Work ceased to be measured by results; the criterion was now the regime's attitude to the worker, of whom it demanded devotion to the Party, or *ideinost*—total acceptance of communist ideology. Several decades later, this essential principle of the Soviet model remains in force: "The foundation of a truly socialist way of working is a high level of ideological conviction and competence."[26] In the beginning comes the ideology and only later competence, i.e., professional training.

In the first years after the Revolution, before the new regime had its own specialists, the "ideological" element in the production process was provided by "red managers"—Party members who lacked the necessary professional training but who had given a guarantee of devotion to the cause of Revolution. They fulfilled the role of commissars attached to the "specialists" *(spetsy)*—survivors of a cursed past. As the number of "red specialists" increased, the task of bringing ideology into an enterprise was transferred to the secretary of the Party organization. The secretary was more important than any other representative of the management, because he alone was concerned with the fulfillment of the plan and the training of workers. It was only thanks to him that what a Soviet sociologist called a "miracle of transformation" took place "through association with labor."[27]

One of the first Soviet sound films, *Vstrechny* (1932, F. Ermler and S. Yutkevich), gives a picture of the way the secretary of a Party committee should go about his work: only the reshaping of a man makes it possible to overfulfill the plan, and only the overfulfillment of the plan makes it possible to reeducate a man—to perform a miracle!

The nationalization of labor, a previously unheard-of idea, included all forms of activity, including Party work. The Party secretary, representative of the supreme authority, was important only to the extent that he was a product of that authority. Having underlined the fragility of the position occupied by the *Stakhanovtsy,* Stalin dispelled all hopes that Party members might have had about their own immunity: "The present wreckers and saboteurs . . . are for the most part Party people, with a Party card in their pocket. . . . The strength of the wreckers today . . . consists of their Party card."[28]

A film called *The Party Card* (1936, screenplay by K. Vinogradskaya, director I. Pyrev) convincingly illustrated Stalin's words. Power and privilege belonged to the Party card, not to the person who held it. Power belonged to the Party, not to its members. The censor and critic O. Litovsky called the film "a genuine, moving poem about a Party card."[29] The Party card, like the title of *Stakhanovets,* was given and taken away at the will of the supreme authority.

The collectivization of the countryside completed the process of nationalizing labor—the business of managing the cultivation of the land was transferred into the hands of the Party. Farm labor became an impersonal activity carried out on orders from above. Long before the arrival of the agricultural machinery (Lenin's magic "hundred thousand tractors"), the Soviet countryside saw the arrival of the Plan, Discipline, and Ideology. Outstanding collective farmers, whose successes were organized by the same methods as the successes of the *Stakhanovtsy,* were decorated with orders and medals, rewarded with privileges and cash bonuses, and entered the category of "distinguished people."

The Soviet attitude to labor was to a large extent influenced by the way labor was organized in the prison camps. The "school of labor," as Dzerzhinsky called the concentration camps in the early days, entered a period of unrestrained growth towards the end of the 1920s. Little islands of camps metastatized throughout the country; a camp empire was organized on a historically unprecedented scale in terms of both size and number of prisoners.

Soviet camps were known officially as concentration camps until the mid-1930s, when disloyal competition on the part of the Nazis, who adopted the same name, made it necessary to put the term "corrective labor camp" into the Soviet legal vocabulary. That name for the Soviet camps expresses exactly their dual function: while remaining the most important instrument for engendering fear and terror, the camp becomes also a model of "socialist labor."

Trotsky and the other Bolshevik theorists who claimed that slave labor could be productive were right, assuming that they were talking in terms of the new criteria of "productivity." Soviet slaves—the prisoners in the camps—worked badly, because slaves usually try to work badly, and because the Soviet slaves were starving and had to live in monstrously inhuman conditions. But the slaves' low output was compensated for by their number. They were prodded into working harder by issuing bread to them in direct proportion to the degree to which they fulfilled the plan. Failure to fulfill the plan meant reduction in the bread ration to the minimum—which spelled death.

The camps were organized so as to try out the possibilities of "socialist labor": millions of prisoners became the "army of labor" of which the Bolsheviks had dreamed after the Revolution. Huge detachments of prisoners were easily transported from one end of the Soviet Union to the other, and they worked according to the plan under strict supervision, carrying out tasks set by the Center. Labor became extremely collective, because the human being, as a personality or an individual, ceased to exist, and was transformed into "human material."

Lenin's firm conviction that communism would be built out of "masses of human material, spoilt by hundreds and thousands of years of slavery, serfdom and capitalism"[30] underlay both practice and theory. It was not by chance that a "genuinely scientific system for producing a communist personality" was developed in the 1930s by Anton Makarenko, a teacher who for many years had been in charge of colonies for juvenile delinquents. Makarenko based his "genuinely scientific system" on his conviction that if he had succeeded in his colonies in reforming young criminals, the worst sort of human material, there could be no doubt about the possibility of remolding every other kind of human material "in the new social conditions." In his *Pedagogical Poem* and his theoretical works, Makarenko explained his discovery: the way to reform a human being and produce a communist personality was to enclose the individual in a collective. According to Makarenko, "A collective is a freely associated group of workers, united by a single aim and a single action, organized and supplied by the organs of the administration, discipline and responsibility."[31] The "freedom" of the worker (a term which included, according to Makarenko, schoolchildren, students, everyone engaged in "socially useful activity") depended on the extent to which he understood the "necessity" of belonging to the collective. For Makarenko, the ideal collectives were the army and the camp, and he introduced into his colonies for juvenile delinquents elements of army discipline and ritual (uniforms, route marches, flags, and so on).

The success of the campaign for "socialist labor" was given legislative form in a government decree introducing the "labor book" as of January 15, 1939.[32] The book was a document without which it was impossible to obtain work; it recorded the reasons the holder had left his previous job and any penalties imposed or bonuses received. In an article headed "Socialist Labor Discipline," *Pravda* welcomed the government's move: "The introduction of labor books and of awards for self-sacrificing work, and outstanding efforts, the institution of the highest award—the title of Hero of Socialist Labor—and the other measures aimed at regulating labor discipline have been welcomed with great joy by the Soviet people. It signifies a new page in the glorious history of the campaign for socialist labor discipline."[33]

That remarkable formula, "the glorious history of the campaign for socialist labor discipline," expresses precisely the special nature of "socialist labor": the unceasing campaign for discipline takes priority over work. A government decree of September 6, 1973, introduced a new version of the labor book and repeated the 1938 formula: ". . . with the aim of increasing their educative importance in the matter of strengthening labor discipline." Andropov's first words after having been elected general secretary were about the campaign for discipline. In his first major speech after being appointed to the same position in 1984, Chernenko spoke of the problem of "improving public order, organization and discipline."[34]

The "glorious history" of the campaign to "strengthen" discipline and "raise" the labor productivity has gone on, is still going on, and will continue to go on, because it is the history of the nationalization of man's productive and creative efforts—the corruption of labor.

Even the Party's most secret archives are hardly likely to contain a plan for the corruption of labor and perversion of a natural and normal human function, but everything the Communist Party has done since the Revolution, despite superficial changes and apparent departures from original ideas and replacement of leaders, has been directed at the transformation of human beings. The blow struck at labor was aimed at destroying the essence of the "old" person. Trotsky asserted that human beings did not want to work—"as a rule a man tries to avoid work." His words were echoed nearly seventy years later by

Chernenko: "To labor is laborious, and that's all there is to say."[35] The conclusion was, and remains, very simple: without control by the Party, without compulsion, people will not work. The measures taken by the Party under whose leadership the Soviet economic model was created have led inevitably to the demoralization of labor.

Centralization and planning have killed enthusiasm, creative initiative, and belief in the need to work. The process of demoralizing labor, which took several decades in the Soviet Union, was repeated more rapidly in the other socialist countries. Andrzej Wajda's film *Man of Marble* (screenplay by Alexander Scibor-Rylski) depicts this process well, telling the story of a young Polish worker inspired by an ardent desire to be a builder, to become an outstanding laborer—a shock worker, a *Stakhanovets*—who discovers that he has been tricked and that the Party has stolen his enthusiasm to use it for its own purposes.

The socialist attitude to labor developed among manual laborers, among factory and farm workers, when they saw how "shock work" was organized, how norms were raised and earnings fell. A saying emerged that all socialist countries claim as their own (and that might well have been first heard in any of them): They pretend to pay us, and we pretend to work.

Manual labor finally lost its attraction and prestige. The socialist ideology that talked of unbroken progress and advance towards the Goal condemned "manual laborers" to a low social status, as Makhaisky pointed out. A diploma in higher education and "brain-work" (including all work in the state bureaucracy) became the signs of success in society.

For a "manual laborer" to do a job badly became a form of working-class self-defense. But collective farm workers did not have such a weapon; their only way of expressing their dissatisfaction was to escape from the countryside. The factory worker had the possibility of black-mailing his immediate superior, who was responsible for fulfilling the plan, by demanding, for example, an increase in wages.

By far the best of the relatively small number of works by Soviet writers that discuss the difficulties that arise when politically backward workers work badly (or not well enough) and demand pay beyond that prescribed by law is Vladimir Voinovich's story "I Want to Be Honest" (in English, "What I Might Have Been"—Voinovich's original title for the story), about a construction foreman who simply wants to do "an honest day's work: "In the end, for better or worse, this is my work.

And if I can't do it the way I want to, to the best of my ability, then why drag all this out?"[36] But he is unable to work as he would like—the working conditions don't permit it. "I want to be honest," he tells his boss, and gets the reply, "Who needs your honesty?"[37] It is not only not necessary, it is harmful, because it casts doubt on the system and the socialist model of the economy and society.

In his passionate account of the Stalin system, *The Flight of Our Young People,* Alexander Zinoviev cites as an example of the "Stalin style of leadership" the story of a major construction site that involved the sacrifice of many lives and which was "senseless from the economic and any practical point of view." "The great historical sense of the project" consisted, in the author's opinion, in the fact that it was "primarily a way of organizing people's lives." The senseless labor of tens of thousands of people, their sufferings and sacrifices, consequently had an ideological purpose. As the central character in the book put it: "Our severity, immorality, demagoguery and other well-known bad qualities were highly moral from the historical point of view."[38]

Morality of the "Stalin type," which the book declares to be "historically necessary," rejects the "honesty" of the central character in Voinovich's story. It is typical that the character should declare the "morality" of the Stalin period to be on a high level; i.e., of a higher type, much above the "lower morality" that existed previously.

This "maximum morality" creates a special link between the governors and the governed—complicity in an act of deception and in the destruction of the "lower" morality. Yury Orlov, a physicist and founder of the Moscow Helsinki Watch Committee, who spent many years in prison, wrote an article entitled "Is It Possible to Have Socialism of a Non-Totalitarian Kind?" (circulated in samizdat) in which he discussed the question of the "right to work" granted in exchange for unquestioning loyalty to the state. Orlov wrote that on condition of his absolute loyalty the Soviet person obtains "liberation from a substantial share of the responsibility for the effectiveness of his work," and the right "to work worse, sometimes very much worse, than he could." The state falls in with this, Orlov says, because "the dictatorship finds it useful if the average citizen has a certain complex of guilt and gratitude for being treated leniently."

The unspoken acceptance of bad work (not recorded in any government document, but nonetheless obvious) demoralized the workers and developed in them the conviction that they really needed people to take

care of them, to control and supervise them. The testing period the
Soviet system went through after Stalin's death, the history of the
post-Stalin years, demonstrates the impossibility of transforming the
Soviet system: it apparently is like an egg, ideally suited for its particular function—but it cannot be changed, only broken.

The Soviet system withstood and overcame two principal tests,
economic reform and the scientific-technological revolution. In his efforts to improve on the Stalin model, Khrushchev made use of Stalin's
favorite device, the amalgamation of various ministries followed by
their redivision into smaller parts and the creation of new administrative units. Khrushchev transferred the "egg" from one place to another,
touching it up where the paint had peeled off. In the heat of his "reforms" he managed to bring about the single genuine reform of the
Soviet system: the egg was to be cut in two, and the Communist Party
was to be divided into two parties, one for industry, the other for
agriculture. After that, Khrushchev's fall from grace was only a matter
of time. The late 1960s, the beginning of the Brezhnev era, was a time
of much animated discussion of economic reforms and all sorts of
articles on the subject in magazines, newspapers and books. Many
distinguished Soviet economists proposed what came to the same thing:
the introduction of elements of a market economy, a reduction in the
pressure exerted by "planning by directive," abandonment of excessive
centralization. They pointed out that the reforms would have a decisive
effect on the Soviet people's psychology and their attitude to work.

In 1983 we learned of the Novosibirsk Document, a "confidential"
report read at a special seminar organized by the economics department
of the Party's Central Committee, the Academy of Science, and the
Soviet State Planning Commission. According to some sources, the
report had been prepared by members of the staff of the Institute of
Economics and the Organization of Industrial Production in the Siberian branch of the Academy of Science under the leadership of
Academician Tatyana Zaslavskaya. When it reached the West the report gave rise to numerous commentaries, because Zaslavskaya discussed frankly the "shortcomings" in the Soviet economic system and
the signs of decline in the growth rate of the national income, "which
is not sufficient to ensure either the necessary increase in the people's
standard of living or the intensive technical reequipment of industry."
But the report devoted most attention to the "producers," as could be
seen from the heading "Concerning the necessity for a deeper study in

the USSR of the social mechanism of development." The main "short-coming" in the Soviet "system for managing the economy" was, according to Zaslavskaya, its "inability to provide the necessary forms of behavior in workers in the social-economic sphere."

The fundamental problem is obvious to everyone: the "producers" produce and work very badly. It is therefore necessary "to change their behavior," and the ways to solve the problem are obvious; as Academician Zaslavskaya says: "Administrative methods of management are ineffective here."[39] Most obvious of all, however, is the reluctance—the Party's reluctance—to change anything at all in the system's mechanism.

Zaslavskaya's report produced something of a sensation in the West by its frankness about the shortcomings of the Soviet economy, but it bore witness only to the fact that the characteristics of the Soviet model are very well known in the USSR itself. From time to time we learn of critical comments by specialists who propose ways of "improving the egg": in 1965, for example, A. G. Aganbegian, a specialist in econometrics who later became a corresponding member of the Academy of Science, said (in lectures delivered to specialists) the same things Zaslavskaya was to say eighteen years later. Zaslavskaya spoke of the signs of a slowing down of the Soviet economy "over the last twelve to fifteen years." Aganbegian had gone even further: "In the last six years the rate of growth of our economy has dropped roughly by two-thirds."[40] In 1982, V. Trapeznikov, director of the Institute for Automatic Systems and Management, voiced some sharp criticism of the system of central planning; the same shortcomings were criticized in 1965 and again in 1983, and the same panaceas were proposed.[41]

Even more convincing proof of the impossibility of changing the economic system is provided by the rejection of the magic wand offered by the "scientific-technical revolution." As far back as 1954 the *Short Philosophic Dictionary* was quite categorical on the subject: "Cybernetics is a reactionary pseudoscience which emerged in the USA after the Second World War. . . . Cybernetics throws a sharp light on one of the main features of the bourgeois outlook—its inhumanity and its determination to turn working people into appendages of machines, into an instrument of production and a weapon of war."[42] Less than ten years later, the Party completely rehabilitated the former pseudoscience: "Cybernetics is the science dealing with the common features in the processes and systems of management." There was even reference to the "real prospects" of applying the methods of cybernetics in various fields.[43] Cybernetics became fashionable, since it promised a way of solving all difficulties. Marxism-Leninism, the only scientific method for understanding the world, acquired the only scientific technique for applying that method—cybernetics. The new formula defining Communism became: Soviet power plus the computerization of the whole country. In 1984, the Soviet deputy minister for foreign trade complained: "First of all they called cybernetics a pseudoscience; now we are paying out millions of rubles for imported computers. And this is not just a matter of purely technological or material losses."[44] The deputy minister was in fact referring to the psychological "price of one mistake." In the 1960s they tried to correct the "mistake."

Loren Graham, the American historian of science, recalls that in Moscow in the early 1970s he was shown plans for a gigantic system of computers that the Russians intended to set up for the "scientific management" of their economy.[45] In the late 1970s, the Soviet leaders were convinced of the fundamental incompatibility of computers and communism. Electronic machines are used, naturally, where it is impossible to manage without them, primarily in the arms industry. But the principle of "computerization of the country" as a method of perfecting the system and realizing the Soviet model has been rejected. The Soviet leaders realized that the computerization of the economy would amount to a real reform of Soviet society; the danger consisted not only in the need to provide the computer system with truthful information, the monopoly over which Andropov confirmed with yet another law about "the protection of state secrets," not only in the release of the computer operator from supervision; the principal danger was that computerization deprived labor of its ideological function. In G. Bochkarev's popular 1970s play, *The Steel Workers,* the "positive hero" declares: "The man who makes good steel is a good man." But only the management of an enterprise decided who was going to make good steel and fulfill and overfulfill the plan—that is, who was to be a "good man."

In the late 1970s, the "computer danger" became apparent to the leaders of the CPSU. It was then that Brezhnev "delivered a report of theoretical importance concerning the proper way to increase the role of the Party in the expansion of the economy" in which he declared that only the Party, "armed with the teachings of Marxism-Leninism and its experience of organizing the masses politically, is competent to determine the main directions in which society is to develop." The qualities required of a Soviet person at work were "a high level of ideological understanding and competence." There was no disputing the fact that professional competence took second place to ideology. This was true not only of industrial production, but of science as well. The Soviet Union had entered the 1980s with "the largest army of scientists in the world,"[46] but a Central Committee decree reviewing the work of the scientific center of the Soviet Academy of Science in the Urals said: "The Party committees are not devoting sufficient efforts to raising the effectiveness of scientific research . . . and have not yet organized the sort of campaign that is needed to strengthen discipline and improve the organization of labor and to raise the efficacy of ideological education and mass political work."[47]

The priority attached to ideology in the role allotted to labor and its use as an instrument for training the human being determines the unique nature of Soviet society, and of the economy in particular. Having subjected the Soviet economic system to a thoughtful analysis that identified many of its faults, the American economist Marshall Goldman nevertheless concluded that "the Soviet Union appears, though perhaps with some hesitation, to be developing into a part of society worldwide"—perhaps because "the Soviet leaders have practically no choice. Modern technology has forced the world to come closer together. Today you can get from New York to Moscow more quickly than you could get to Chicago forty years ago. Moreover the telephone makes it possible in theory to speak to Moscow just as quickly as to Chicago."[48]

Goldman's arguments could not be more logical, but his logic has no relationship to the Soviet system. At the time he was writing his book (1982) he knew, of course, that the real distance between Moscow and New York—despite new technology—has increased many times over since the beginning of the twentieth century. He probably knew as well that the automatic telephone lines linking the USSR with the Western world were replaced in 1979 by operator-controlled lines. Professional economists (this applies not only to Western economists but also to Soviet ones, including those who have emigrated) are not willing (even if they could) to abandon the standard economic criteria in analyzing the Soviet model. Having accepted the geometry of Euclid, they do not want to learn about the geometry of Lobachevsky.

But only Lobachevsky's geometry enables us to understand the specific nature of a model never before encountered. Since 1930 the

Soviet Union has been having "temporary difficulties" with the supply of foodstuffs, including bread. In 1981–82 the Soviet Union bought 46 million tons of grain abroad, and it has apparently decided to purchase about 35 million tons each year. A campaign was organized to encourage people to be "more careful in their use of bread," and it was proposed that instead of the standard weight of 1–1.3 kilograms, loaves of bread should in the future weigh no more than 900 grams, since the bread was of such poor quality that if it was not eaten straightaway it went stale and became inedible.[49] But the bakeries refused to reduce the weight of the loaf because that would affect their fulfillment of the plan. A typically Soviet solution of the problem was found: a network of collection points was organized where stale bread would be bought from the population.[50] The *avoski* (string bags) which the Soviet citizen is never without, in the hope of coming across the miraculous appearance of some goods in the shops, used to be 70 centimeters long; in 1980 the standard length was reduced to 45 centimeters, in 1981 to 30 centimeters. The food problem was solved—a loaf of bread and a head of cabbage now filled an *avoska* to the top. In response to the demands of angry Soviet citizens, the standard size was again altered: double *avoski* 60 centimeters long are now being produced—for twice the price. In the end the state was the gainer (for the time being) of 10 centimeters per *avoska*.[51] At the same time, an American senator was protesting the "new inequality" in the United States: 70 percent of the schools in well-off sections of one city had microcomputers, while only 40 percent had them in the poorer sections.[52]

Hopes of a new kind of "magic wand" ("reforms," the "scientific and technological revolution") drifted in and were dispersed like mist. The one trusted and reliable "wand" was that discovered by Lenin: "accounting, control and supervision by the organized vanguard." Since the early 1980s there has been less talk in the USSR of the scientific and technological revolution, and much more about "detachments of people's controllers"—i.e., vigilantes. Evidence of the extent of "people's control" is provided by a report made by the first secretary of the Party's Grodno (Belorussia) regional committee that the region had "50,000 vigilantes"; and "schools for people's controllers" had been set up in enterprises and organizations where lectures were given on such subjects as "the campaign to increase the effectiveness of publicly owned industry, to improve the quality of the product and to protect socialist property."

According to the 1979 census there were 1,140,000 people living in the Grodno region, of whom 48 percent lived in urban areas. (Vigilantes work in the cities; collective farms have their own controllers.) It may be assumed that the ratio of vigilantes to working people was roughly the same everywhere; the Soviet Union thus has at its disposal a many-million-strong army of vigilantes, who make it possible to do without "reforms" and to ignore the "scientific-technological revolution."

A 1983 film called *A Train Has Stopped*[53] provides an excellent picture of the situation in the Soviet Union at that time. A passenger train has been brought to a halt by a collision with a freight truck caused by a failure to observe elementary instructions and a working style aimed only at fulfilling the plan. The investigator who arrives to inquire into the affair quickly identifies the guilty persons—the head of the depot, the signalman and the engine driver who was killed in the accident. He has no doubt that the way to deal with the problem of bad work is to introduce severe new laws and to tighten discipline, but the local leaders solve the problem by turning the accident into an act of heroism on the part of the engine driver, a Communist who died to save his passengers: his death becomes a pedagogic tool. For the authors of the film there were only two solutions—to make the law more severe, and to increase the ideological work.

A comparative analysis of Soviet and non-Soviet economies leaves no doubt: the train has come to a halt—a conclusion that is at the same time correct and quite incorrect. The Soviet economy represents a very special model; its goal has never been to satisfy its population's needs, but always to satisfy the needs of the state. The Soviet economic system guarantees the needs of the Soviet military machine; in fact, the Soviet military machine is the Soviet Union itself. There is no point in looking for the "military-industrial complex," so easy to find in the United States, in the Soviet military machine. The entire Soviet state, the entire population, exists for war, mobilized and called to the colors. Eloquent evidence of this feature of the Soviet economic model can be seen in the fact that the successes registered by Soviet military-space technology have not been reflected in any way in the field of consumer goods.

The demands made by the war the Soviet leaders have declared on the entire non-Soviet world determines the nature of the economic system, and of all aspects of life in the Soviet Union. War demands above all else a stable society behind it and the population's loyalty—

which explains the paradoxes of the Soviet economy. The concentration of the nation's resources on the task of satisfying military demands leaves a minimum of resources to satisfying the population's everyday needs.

The Soviet economy is one of controlled poverty. As compensation for the absence of consumer goods, the state gives the people the opportunity to do bad work. Everyone knows the existence of such an opportunity obviously is contrary to the law: a Soviet journalist inquiring about the reasons for the bad work, "the reality and outward appearance of things," quoted a conversation with a rather tipsy workman, who said: "I make you a television set which will break down almost as soon as you buy it, and you are making me a child's pram which will collapse tomorrow. Why do we work so badly?" the workman asked, and replied: "Because we pretend that we are working well."[54]

Everybody pretends. The workers pretend they are doing good work when they know that their work is badly done, but they consider it their privilege to do bad work, since they are paid very little; moreover, they can't buy anything with what they earn, and even if they do come across something by chance it will be of poor quality. The "bosses" pretend because they are concerned only about the fulfilment of the plan, though they know the plan is a fiction and that the goods they produce are of low quality. The country's leaders pretend because they are convinced that they can obtain what they need for military purposes by repeatedly raising the degree of control in the armaments industry and can ensure the loyalty of the Soviet population by agreeing to let them do bad work.

A popular Soviet witticism advises: If vodka interferes with your work, give up work. In the late 1970s, the Soviet leaders realized, first, that the USSR was lagging hopelessly behind in the race to acquire the revolutionary new technology; and, second, that, even if they were successful in introducing that technology into the USSR, it would completely destroy the stability of the country's social relationships.

The leaders recognized the threat the new revolution represented to a system that had come into being after the "last revolution": the switch from an industrial society to one based on information technology would mean that the Party would lose its monopoly over time and information, and its legitimacy as a regime. At the same time the leaders understood that without the new technology it would be impossible to preserve the Soviet Union's status as a superpower, i.e., parity in the arms race.

It was decided that new technology would be introduced under strict control in certain defined sectors of the national economy. Plans were drawn up for the introduction of new computers, automated production lines, robots to replace workers, and so forth. A new department of information, computer technology, and automation was set up in the Academy of Science in 1983. But limits to this process were laid down immediately: computerization was necessary, but personal computers were unnecessary, even harmful. Evgeny Velikhov, the Academy's vice president, explained that ordinary people in the Soviet Union had no need of personal computers, since they would have access to a sufficient number of publicly owned ones.[55] A Novosti press agency correspondent wrote to an American newspaper to refute a report on Soviet backwardness in the computer field and remarked that "there is no demand in the Soviet Union for personal computers because we have no private enterprise."[56]

Evidence of the absence of a need for personal computers (from the point of view of the Soviet leaders) can be seen in the number of telephones in the USSR, compared with the size of the population. In 1982, there was one telephone for every ten people; while in Great Britain, for example, there was one for every two or three people.[57]

The lack of telephones cannot be explained solely by the failure of the industry to produce them, or the authorities' lack of interest in satisfying the population's needs; it is also a deliberate act of policy. Telecommunication experts reckon that there is a saturation point for telephones of roughly one telephone to every three people: once this level has been achieved, additional problems arise for authorities who wish to impose their will on a population. The example of Poland, where the saturation point is still far from being reached, is instructive: the introduction of martial law in December 1982 was accompanied by the interruption of all telephone contacts throughout the country. It is easy to imagine the extent to which communications possibilities would increase if people had private computers.

Soviet leaders have decided to allow the scientific-technological revolution to enter the Soviet Union along a narrow channel and under strict control. The task of welcoming the new technology has been entrusted to the most advanced branch of Soviet industry—spying. A powerful apparatus has been created to acquire and steal the necessary technology. According to a book by John Barron about the KGB: "The Soviet Union has succeeded, primarily through the KGB, in turning American research work, development, inventiveness and industrial genius into an important reserve of the Soviet state."[58] Barron may exaggerate the part played by the KGB, which is only a part of an enormous apparatus for extracting information that would be inconceivable in any other state. French experts have drawn up a diagram of the "extractors," which include the KGB, the GRU (military intelligence), the State Committee for Science and Technology, the Academy of Science, the Ministry of Foreign Trade, and the State Committee for Economic Contacts. The "extractors" receive orders to purchase or steal from the Military-Industrial Committee attached to the Council of Ministers, which in turn is directed by certain departments of the CPSU Central Committee.[59] Even this carefully channelled revolution is causing and will continue to cause the Soviet system a lot of trouble, because the machines that are bought, stolen or copied will have to be serviced and provided with spare parts, which will also have to be bought or stolen, and the abundance of foreign technology will require additional sets of instructions. A Soviet journalist admitted that he was embarrassed that "in our factories and on our building sites you see all kinds of machines called 'Magirus,' 'Caterpillar,' 'Olivetti.' "[60]

The principal conflict is, however, between the revolutionary foreign technology and Soviet man. Even the most perfected technology cannot operate (until now at any rate) entirely without people: in the Soviet Union, technology cannot operate without Soviet people. Why should a Soviet person do good work with the new technology if doing bad work has become a natural quality of the New Man?

The special nature of the Soviet person's attitude to labor and technology, including the new technology, can be explained by the fact that the terms "technology," "mechanization," "robotization" and "computerization" have a special meaning in the Soviet Union. In the summer of 1984, *Pravda* published a letter that described the "complete mechanization" of potato fields in the Pskov region. The farm was using potato-harvesting machines behind each of which fifteen or twenty people gathered the potatoes as they were dug.[61] Workers in city offices and factories are mobilized for the potato harvest, and a distaste for the work is cultivated in the collective farm workers, who know that the town-dwellers will harvest the potato crop, and in the town-dwellers who know they are performing a senseless task and are being taken away from their proper duties.

The Soviet Constitution now in force has codified the rights and duties of "labor collectives," defined as "the basic cells in the socialist society." In June 1983, the Supreme Soviet of the USSR approved a "Law on labor collectives" that was in fact a reaction to the events in Poland aimed at erecting a barrier against the ideas about workers' self-management that had been given currency by Solidarity. The Poles' "anarcho-syndicalist" interpretation of self-management was rejected, and the law offered in its place "socialist self-management" built "on the basis of the tested principle of democratic centralism."[62]

The law defined a labor collective as "an association, duly registered as an organization and juridical body, of working people employed jointly in enterprises and organizations in various branches engaged in production or not," and so extended the rights of the collective. The individual has rights only insofar as he is a member of a collective and becomes, according to the law, a "cog." This is the realization of "the great principle of collectivism." Heading the collective, according to the law, "stands the party organization," with the right to supervise the management work and "to expose shortcomings in good time and remove them." The collective is allotted the duty of raising labor productivity, carrying out the plan, dealing with people violating discipline, and concerning itself with the ideological and political education of its members. The "collective," i.e., the Party organization, the management, and the trade unions, must assume responsibility for maintaining discipline and ensuring the important right to do bad work. The education of Soviet man thus becomes a duty of Soviet man himself, under the guidance of the Communist Party.

Nikita Khrushchev, in his usual direct and outspoken manner, forecast the Soviet future in 1963: "Do you really think there's going to be complete freedom under Communism? Communism is an orderly, well-organized society. There will be automatic systems and cybernetics. But there will also be trusted people who will tell people what to do. Someone has to keep an eye on the cogs. Who will that be? It will be the man whom we trust."[63] A quarter-century has passed since then, and the accuracy of Khrushchev's forecast has been fully confirmed. The future has nowhere to hide—Soviet lawgivers are watching.

> Oh, we shall allow them to sin; they are
> weak and helpless and they will love us
> like children for letting them sin.
>   DOSTOEVSKY

10

Corruption

A British journalist reviewing Konstantin Simes' book *The USSR: Secrets of a Corrupt Society* came to a familiar conclusion: "The Russians are human and they have changed very little in the course of the centuries," and recalled (inevitably) the "Potemkin villages" of Catherine the Great and *The Inspector General,* Gogol's play about the reign of Nicholas I.[1]

Whales live in water, but it would be a mistake to regard them as fish. Bribery has always been practiced on a large scale in Russia, but it would be an unforgiveable mistake to compare Russian bribery with the total corruption that distinguishes the Soviet system. Leaving aside the fact that the situation in Russia began to change after the judicial reforms of the 1860s, there is a difference in *principle* between the Russian and the Soviet state. The practice of bribery, of giving "baksheesh," existed and continues to exist in many countries. But nowhere has it become a way of life or entered into the very pores of the state and social organism as it has in the USSR. In the totalitarian state to which everything belongs, corruption has assumed a totalitarian character and acquired an additional, unique, ideological function: the education of the New Man. For example, low prices for consumer goods which are in fact not on sale are fixed with a view to "creating the illusion that these goods are available," the illusion that they can be acquired even by someone with a small income on condition that he is ready to wait in a long queue.[2]

The bribe, "baksheesh," is a means of overcoming the barriers raised by the bureaucratic *apparat*. Before the Revolution and the birth of the Soviet state there were no such barriers anywhere, because such an all-powerful and omnipresent *apparat* performing such functions did not exist. Bribery and theft—corruption—spread as the Soviet state swallowed up new fields of activity: the most important stages of corruption's triumphant advance were collectivization and state planning.

A planned economy and a system of chronic shortages result in the emergence of "grey" (semi-legal and illegal) markets that allow the plan to be carried out. As one economist explained, the Soviet system of planning "is based on the principle of the 'trial of strength.' From top to bottom, starting with Gosplan and ending up with the worker on the shop floor, a struggle goes on between the managers and the managed for setting the plan's targets."[3] In setting targets, the "interests of the state" take second place, and the plan figures are fixed in the first place by the "trial of strength"—the people who have to carry the plan out try to be given as low as possible a target figure for output and as high a figure as possible for the use of resources. A low target makes it possible to fulfill and overfulfill the set task and to get a bonus, while possession of a large quantity of resources (raw material, for example) makes it possible to exchange some of it for needed machinery, tools and supplies.

Consequently, "the corruption of higher-ranking officials takes place on a mass scale and is more or less harmless."[4] The existence of the all-important plan, whose fulfillment is the first duty of all Soviet officials, means that corruption at all levels of the Soviet economy is essential—and consequently, a virtue. Failure to fulfill the plan is a much more serious crime than bribery or making use of the "grey" market. Bribery of employees at higher and lower levels and other forms of corruption become the only possible way of getting the system to work; and since the entire Soviet economy is embraced by the plan, all Soviet people are involved in the system of corruption in the course of their work. Corruption acts as a lubricant that makes possible the operation of a machine that combines "total and permanent control and permanent falsification."[5]

The system of permanent shortages exposes every aspect of a Soviet person's life to corruption. Shortages engender universal theft in workplaces; the Russian language has marked this phenomenon by the invention of a special word—*nesun*. In the Soviet understanding of the word, a *nesun* is not a thief, because he takes at work what he cannot find or buy in the state-owned shops. The criminal code classifies the *nesun* as a person who steals socialist property, and provides for severe punishment whenever the periodic "campaign against corruption" is started up. The universality of this form of theft is well illustrated in the following anecdote. A woman working in a children's nursery brings home a child, whom her husband agrees to adopt. She then brings home another, then a third. When her husband at last objects, his wife replies that there is nothing apart from children that she can take from her workplace.

The great achievement of the Soviet workingman, the right not to work, can be won only for a bribe in cash or in kind (for carrying out work not permitted by the law) to the foreman, who fixes the amount to be paid. The worker depends on the foreman to whom he pays the bribe, and the foreman depends on the worker to fulfill the plan and give him the bribe.

The result of all this is a vicious circle from which there is no escape: the necessities of life must be obtained either by stealing, by "taking home," or by giving bribes. Shortages have made foodstuffs into a means of exchange in the hands of sales clerks who will release them in exchange for a cash bribe or for something else in short supply. The free health service has resulted in terrible overworking of doctors and poor service on the part of the "free doctors"; only a bribe will guarantee a doctor's attention or the doctor of one's choice. Only illegally can you buy (on the "black" market) the book you want, a theatre ticket, the right to travel to a city where you might find things for sale that never reach the provinces or villages. Yury Alexandrov, a driver who decided to break away from a group of Soviet tourists and stay in Paris, described conditions in a Siberian village at the end of 1983: "We had not seen any sausage for three years. . . . We had even forgotten what a sausage looked like. . . . As for meat, we had already forgotten when we last ate it."[6]

Rural areas as well as cities participate in the vicious circle of planning, shortages, and corruption. A samizdat author who is a most attentive observer of Soviet village life says: "For the peasant, thieving is a continuation of his struggle to have his share of necessities. . . . A peasant farm cannot be run without farm machinery, without farm buildings, or without a thousand small things—a roll of wire . . . lubricating oil . . . wheels, nails."[7] None of this can be bought in the shops.

A correspondent of *Literaturnaya Gazeta* (than which nothing could be more official) wrote about this situation, quoting a conversation with an honest Soviet person, an institute professor who in the course of redecorating his flat found that he needed some skirting boards not for sale in the shops. He gave some money to an acquaintance, who produced the skirting boards and said he had bought them off the watchman at the shop where they were supposed to be sold. The professor complained, We keep on ass-licking and deceiving ourselves, saying we "obtained" or "bought from a private source"; nobody says outright "I stole" or "I bought stolen goods."[8]

The demoralizing effect of such Soviet corruption lies in its creation of a new scale of values, a new scale of prestige. In capitalist society, the possession of money and the prestige that accompanies it is a natural attribute of that society. In the Soviet Union, having money is an unnatural phenomenon. An assistant in a butcher's shop at the time of a meat shortage acquires an importance far greater than that of an academician. But everyone from the butcher to the academician knows that the newly acquired prestige contravenes the officially declared foundations of Soviet society. The stigma attached to trade since the days of the Revolution has not been removed: it is camouflaged by the conditions of life, and silently acknowledged as a lie essential to existence.

The collective-farm market, which is permitted but strictly controlled, has become in Soviet terms "a phenomenon of perplexing complexity"—a Soviet journalist has compared it with "the atom as understood by modern physicists." The complexity of the market—the natural business of buying and selling known to mankind for millennia—derives from the fact that it cannot be completely controlled; hence the "shamefulness" of the business itself. "To engage in trade became something shameful—more shameful than getting drunk or stealing," a publicist wrote.[9] In a novel called *Univermag,* a Soviet bestseller in 1982, I. Shtemler shows convincingly that in the Soviet system "to trade" and "to steal" are synonyms.

Soviet trade practices eloquently demonstrate the limits of the scientific-technological revolution in the USSR. Employees in the trade network have successfully prevented the penetration of automatic cash registers into self-service shops, cafés, and so forth. Since 1964, Leningrad has had an association to service automatic registers in 102 cafés and shops selling wine, ice cream, cigarettes and tobacco, but in 1976 not one of those shops actually had a register.[10] The situation is similar in other cities and other shops.

Automatic cash registers destroy the living contact between the person selling and the purchaser—that is, they make it harder to steal. As Alexander Galich pointed out, the trouble with an automatic machine is that it doesn't know how to cheat.

A planned economy with constant shortages of goods creates a situation that becomes a source of wealth for those who show enterprise, energy and initiative. Operations conducted on the fringes of what is legal under Soviet law, and even beyond the law (what is sometimes called the "second economy"), are evidence of the strength of the commercial instincts upon which the socialist system has declared war. The state makes use of the surviving entrepreneurial instincts not only to keep the wheels of the Soviet machine turning but also to satisfy consumer demands that Soviet industry cannot and does not wish to satisfy. Arkady Adamov, a popular author of detective stories, has written many books about crimes that include, for example, organizing underground factories for the manufacture of knitted garments. In the words of the investigator in one of these stories, "There was an empty space which the state either did not wish or was not able to occupy."[11] That space is occupied by the "underground entrepreneur."

Additional resources obtained by bribing planning authorities can provide means to organize production of goods not covered by the plan that find their way onto the black market. Additional resources—machines, tools, raw material—can be acquired on the black market, or stolen. Evgenia Evelson, who for many years worked as a lawyer, wrote a detailed account of forty-two trials involving economic matters. On the basis of these and other legal cases she concluded that the "left" or "second" economy exists in the USSR primarily at the expense of "stocks of raw materials and of heavy and light machinery which is siphoned off from the State's reserves."[12]

The scale of this phenomenon is such that the term "left economy" has been legalized by use in official court sentences and directives issued by the Supreme Soviet.[13] It is quite obvious that the "left economy" could exist only with the cooperation of authorities in planning departments, the administration, and the Party. It is equally obvious that agreement to the "siphoning off of stocks" is given in exchange for bribes. The "left economy" is essential to the system, but it is criminal, since it exists in violation of the law—and the law is violated with the knowledge of the people who made it and protect it.

There is much convincing evidence in newspaper reports of trials (when a campaign to "combat corruption" is taking place), in Soviet literature, and in the reminiscences of émigrés of the demoralization both of the population and of the power *apparat*—Party bodies, state organs, the legal system, the police, and the KGB. The twenty-sixth Congress of the CPSU (1981) confirmed a list of offenses that had to be combated: "It is necessary by all organizational, financial and juridical means to close all the cracks that permit parasitism, bribery, profiteering, allow people to make money without working and commit abuses of socialist property."[14] Chernenko called for an "energetic campaign against profiteering and the theft of socialist property and money-making," and he was echoed by the minister for internal affairs: "The education of the New Man is closely interconnected with the task of overcoming such anti-social behavior as drunkenness, hooliganism, parasitism, bribery, profiteering and the theft of socialist property."[15]

Total power is the first incentive to corruption and the "bribery and money-making" Chernenko talked about. Konstantin Simes has described in detail the "tribute" system that Party secretaries extract in their own bailiwicks, where they are absolute masters. The second incentive is uncertainty about the regime's legitimacy. Boris Bazhanov, Stalin's secretary in 1923, spoke of finding information in the Politburo archives about a special "Politburo diamond stock" set up to cover the possibility of members of the Politburo losing power, which would provide them with a livelihood and means of carrying on their revolutionary struggle. Bazhanov said this stock of jewels still existed in the mid-1920s, and was taken care of by the widow of Yakov Sverdlov, who had kept her maiden name and was not employed anywhere.[16] Lydia Shatunovskaya, wife of an Old Bolshevik, lived for some time in the Kremlin and later in the Government House in Moscow that had been built for the regime's elite. In her memoirs she quotes a conversation she had just after the Revolution with Klavdia Baibakova, who also lived in Government House and was the wife of the minister for the oil industry (he later became first deputy to the chairman of the Council of Ministers and chairman of Gosplan*). Shatunovskaya asked the minister's wife, who traded on the black market:

> "Why do you go in for black-marketeering in this way? . . . After all, you've got everything anyway." The minister's wife retorted: "You don't understand our position. Your husband is a professor and will still be a professor tomorrow. . . . But we are kings for a day. Today my husband is a minister and we have everything, but tomorrow he might turn up at the ministry and find them all turning their backs on him. And when he gets to his office he may read in the paper that he is no longer a minister—that he is a nobody."[17]

Evgenia Evelson was present as a lawyer in 1965 at the closed trial of a man named Galushko, first secretary of the Bauman district Party committee. This unchallenged master of a central district of the nation's capital, a man living entirely at the expense of the state as though under communism, had been caught in the act of accepting a 35,000-ruble bribe for his efforts to quash a case involving an illegal knitwear factory. To the question put by the judge, What reasons prompted you to commit this offense? the defendant Galushko replied, Uncertainty about the morrow.[18] After the death of the chairman of the Leningrad city soviet, Nikolai Smirnov (a close friend of the Politburo member Frol Kozlov), his official safe was opened; in it were found jewels and large sums of money belonging to Smirnov and Kozlov; but until his death Kozlov remained a Politburo member and a contender for the post of general secretary.[19]

The last months of the Brezhnev era were marked by a scandal connected with the arrest of a group of thieves, bribe-takers, and smugglers linked, in ways never officially explained, with Galina Brezhneva, daughter of the General Secretary of the CPSU.

Awareness of the illegal nature of existence, of the fact that only outside the law can you obtain everything from basic essentials to luxury goods, is an important factor in the education of Soviet man. Total corruption is supplemented by a state system of informing on

*He was dismissed by Gorbachev in 1986.

people that makes a virtue of keeping an eye on what other people are doing, to atone for your own sins.

The scale assumed by corruption and its recognition by the state are illustrated by the special questionnaires for informing on people in use since the early 1980s. A "card for reporting on a person who has committed a breach of the law" distributed in 1984 in Lithuania allows one to name a lawbreaker, underline the applicable offense in a prepared list, and send the card in to the police. The questionnaire says: "The person initiating this card is not obliged to sign it"; so the informer—the "initiator"—can remain anonymous. The list of offenses that can be reported is interesting: "is living on casual earnings, has an income without working, refuses to pay alimony or debts arising from civil cases, avoids summons by the police or the courts, has no job, has been previously in trouble, does not pay attention to his children's education, drinks too much, uses drugs, commits offenses and other breaches of the rules governing public order and socialist community life."[20]

The vast majority of the Soviet Union's citizens could well be the subject of such a "report card"—or, if they wished, could become "initiators" reporting on neighbors. The practice of using "report cards" increases the number of "people's controllers" many times over and sometimes produces unexpected results that exceed what was intended. The *Baku Worker* was obliged to complain about the stream of reports that swamped the police and the KGB, especially since, as the paper complained, "many of the denunciations had nothing in common with 'vigilance,' being simply a matter of settling personal accounts."[21]

The Novosibirsk Document—composed by employees of the Institute of Economics and the Organization of Industrial Production of the Siberian branch of the Academy of Science and made public in 1983— says that "the social type of worker" being formed "at the present time in the USSR" does not correspond with "either the strategic aims of an advanced socialist state or the technological demands of modern industry." The document lists the qualities of today's Soviet workers:

... slack labor and production discipline, attitude of indifference to the work being done, low quality of work, social inertia, a poor opinion of work as a means of self-realization, very marked interest in the acquisition of goods, a relatively low moral level. It is sufficient to recall the vast scale of operation of the so-called *nesuny,* the prevalence of various "shady" deals at the expense of society, the growth of small manufacturing "on the left," dishonest accounting and the payment of wages irrespective of the work done.[22]

The document stresses that the qualities it lists, the standard sins of Soviet man, are found in workers whose character was formed "in the most recent Five-Year Plans," i.e., in the Brezhnev period, which covered nearly four Five-Year Plans. The conclusion drawn by the document's authors may be regarded as a denunciation of the work of the late General Secretary to the benefit of the new one. But this accurate, pitiless assessment of the product of the "Soviet social machine"—Soviet man—should not mislead us: the authors reveal in their "confidential document" their high professional level and they propose to "perfect the social machine" by the tried methods of strengthening discipline, raising the degree of "social activity," and restricting "consumer orientation."[23] Soviet economists know perfectly well that the faults of the Soviet economy are the virtues of the Soviet political system.

The circle closes: a special form of corruption allows people to speak freely—in a narrow circle, among people who can be trusted—about shortcomings, including corruption.

Why do they have to be training people? What kind of devilish arrogance they must have to impose themselves as educators! . . . Efforts to educate the people have been replaced by the slogan about training them.   NADEZHDA MANDELSTAM

11

Education

The first Five-Year Plan was approved in 1927 and came into force officially in 1928. On October 13, 1928, *Izvestia* reported:

In our system of scientific planning one of the most important issues is the planned training of the new people—the builders of socialism. The People's Commissariat for Education has set up a special commission for this purpose which will coordinate the now uncoordinated work of the pedagogical, psychological, reflexological, physiological and clinical institutes and laboratories, combine in a single plan their research on human development, and direct the results of their efforts into the mainstream of practical work in socialist education and socialist culture.

It was only natural that the most important object of "socialist education" should be the child. Speaking at the thirteenth Party Congress (1924), Bukharin declared: "The fate of the Revolution now depends upon the extent to which we of the younger generation will be able to train the human material capable of building the socialist economy of a Communist society."

THE SCHOOL

The first stage in processing "human material" was the school. One of the Soviet government's first moves was to abolish the old educational system; in order to build a new school system, wrote V. Lebedev-Polyansky, a high official of the Commissariat for Education, the old school had to be done away with. The radical nature of the "Regulations governing the single labor school," passed in November 1918, was no less radical than the Revolution itself. All the "attributes of the old school" were eliminated—examinations, lessons, homework, Latin, school uniforms. The administration of each school was handed over to a "school collective" that included all the pupils and the entire school staff, from teachers to caretakers. The word "teacher" was abolished and replaced by "school worker," or *shkrab* (from *"shk*olny *rab*otnik, "school worker"). Everyday management of the school was carried out by a "school soviet" comprised of the *shkraby* and representatives of pupils over twelve years of age, of the working population, and of the department of education.

The "new school" rejected completely the old methods of teaching and adopted up-to-date pedagogical theories, both Russian and foreign. The books of the American philosopher John Dewey were translated into Russian and published widely, enjoying a special success. The Soviet school of the 1920s was the most advanced in the world in both teaching methods and its self-management. The teacher-revolutionaries forecast imminent victory: "The state is dying away. We are moving out of the kingdom of compulsion into the kingdom of freedom. . . . In accordance with this the importance of the teaching profession also changes. . . . Knowledge of a person and the ability to educate him acquire decisive significance."[1] According to Marxist theoreticians, the school arose along with the state and would disappear along with it, becoming instead a place for playing games, a club. It would be replaced by the Communist Party, the soviets, trade unions, factories, political meetings, and the courts. The authors of Russia's revolutionary pedagogical theories were convinced that the words "new" and "revolutionary" were synonymous, that "revolutionary" was identical with "new" and *vice versa.*

At the end of the 1920s they discovered they were wrong. The state was not preparing to die away; it was getting stronger every day—Stalin spared no effort in that direction. At the same time, attitudes toward the schools were changing. In the 1930s the attributes of the "scholastic feudal school" were restored, and the experiments with teaching methods and programs were declared to be "Left deviations" and "covert Trotskyism." A clear sign of the breach with the policy of building the "new school" was the replacement of education commissar Anatoly Lunacharsky (who had held the post since November 1917) by Andrei Bubnov, a Party official who had for many years been head of the political directorate of the Red Army.

It was a 180-degree turn: self-management was replaced by the exclusive authority of the director (the principal) and "firm discipline"; instead of the "collective" mode of teaching (the "brigade method") there were traditional classes, lessons, and timetables. In 1934, "stable" curricula and textbooks were introduced, so that throughout the Soviet Union all the schools would be teaching the same subject with the same textbooks at any given time. For each subject there was one textbook, approved by the Party Central Committee.

Yet this 180-degree turn did not signify any change in the ultimate goal. Both Lunacharsky and Bubnov were Old Bolsheviks who knew what they wanted. The dispute over the schools was concerned not with principles but with methods and techniques for processing human material. The basic problem arose from the need to combine the formation of the New Man with his education. In the first years after the Revolution, the revolutionary school was necessary as a means of making a complete break with the past and destroying pre-revolutionary social connections. At a 1918 congress of educational workers it was stated clearly and unambiguously:

> We must create out of the younger generation a generation of Communists. We must turn children, who can be shaped like wax, into real, good Communists. . . . We must remove the children from the crude influence of their families. We must take them over and, to speak frankly, nationalize them. From the first days of their lives they will be under the healthy influence of Communist children's nurseries and schools. There they will grow up to be real Communists.[2]

As the Soviet system matured, in the Stalin period, when the new world was modelled by force, the image of the school changed. The interests of the state and the school, according to one Soviet historian, merged, and the idea of school autonomy was therefore seen as counterrevolutionary.[3] Parents had changed: the Soviet family had come into being, and the state would employ its services to help bring up the younger generation. But the goal remained the same: E. N. Medynsky, one of the most active pedagogues of the Stalin period, repeated the 1918 formula in 1952 with virtually no alteration: "The Soviet school, including the primary school, brings its pupils up in the spirit of Communist morality."[4] A quarter of a century passed, and again: "The central task in educational work is to provide young people with a Communist moral outlook."[5] This unchanging formula is supplemented by a quotation from Lenin: "At the foundations of Communist morality lies a struggle to strengthen and complete Communism. That is the basis of Communist upbringing, education and learning."[6] The preamble to the Central Committee's outline of the directions to be taken by the reform of the Soviet school system published in January 1984 and confirmed by the Central Committee and government in April of the same year, quoted Andropov: "The Party aims to achieve a situation in which a person is educated here not simply to be the possessor of a certain quantity of knowledge but primarily to be a citizen of a socialist society and an active builder of Communism."[7] The school law that confirmed the Central Committee's project ends with the instruction "to raise the vanguard role and sense of responsibility of teacher-Communists in bringing about a radical improvement in the quality of the teaching and of the Communist upbringing of the rising generation."[8]

The Soviet school system, once the world's most revolutionary, became its most reactionary and conservative. But the Party never for a minute lost sight of its goal—the creation of the New Man. Throughout Soviet history, the school has remained a powerful instrument for achieving that end. In the 1920s, when the teaching profession was making use of advanced (mainly Western) pedagogical theories, Soviet pedagogues asserted that without communism literacy was not needed.

The need to acquire "a certain quantity of knowledge," as Andropov put it, was not denied—the practical need for such knowledge was obvious. But the imparting of "knowledge" was always secondary, as though it were a necessary evil, an additional element in the process of training, persuading, and shaping. The history of the Soviet school system may be regarded as the history of efforts to find the best combination of upbringing (character training) and education, to develop techniques to turn education into a means of character building and at the same time to infuse all teaching materials with "ideology."

The author of a book on "methods of teaching political literacy" that was obligatory reading in the early 1920s stressed the possibilities offered, for example, by arithmetic, and suggested that teachers should compose questions like this: "The proletariat of Paris rose up and seized power on March 18, 1871, and the Paris Commune fell on May 27 of the same year. How long did it exist?" The author adds: "Naturally, in this case arithmetic ceases to serve as a weapon in the hands of bourgeois ideologists."[9] In 1955 a scholarly work on folktales indicated how they should be "interpreted correctly" in work with children. "Tales about animals give a correct idea of the age-long class hostility between the oppressors and the oppressed people. . . . 'Baba-yaga,' the 'mistress' of the forest and the animals, is depicted as a real exploiter oppressing her servant-beasts."[10] Two decades later, Academician I. Kikoin produced a book on teaching methods in which he stressed the importance of the theory of relativity by saying that "although Lenin was not a physicist, he had a deeper understanding of the importance for physics of Einstein's theory of relativity than did many leading scholars of the day."[11]

This bolstering of Einstein's authority with the all-powerful authority of Lenin is a striking example of the subordination of knowledge to ideology. It is not just that *Materialism and Empiriocriticism,* the work in which Lenin is supposed to have "understood the importance of the theory of relativity," was written in 1908 and published in 1909, while Einstein's first article was published in 1905 and his theory set out in its final form only in 1915; and it is not just that Lenin does not refer to Einstein, because he did not know of him in 1908: in 1953 Einstein's theory was considered to be "anti-scientific,"[12] and in 1954 he was reproached for having "under the influence of Machist philosophy" given his theory "a distorted, idealistic interpretation." Only in 1963, ten years after the death of Stalin, did the *Soviet Philosophical Dictionary* announce that "the theory of relativity entirely confirms the ideas of dialectical materialism and the assessments of the development of modern physics which Lenin gave in *Materialism and Empiriocriticism.* "* In 1978 it was announced that the principal confirmation of the

*Einstein's name does not appear in Lenin's book, and Lenin makes no reference in it to the relativity theory.

importance of Einstein's theory was the fact that Lenin had been the first to reveal its significance.

The task set for the Soviet school system explains the lively interest displayed from the early 1920s in physiology and psychology as means of training and persuasion. Insofar as the "main practical problem" raised by the new structure of society was "the problem of bringing about changes in the nature of man on a mass scale in the process of exerting a socialist influence on him," the problem was said to be "pedological": "It is precisely in childhood, in the period of development of a person's growth, that the environment is the most powerful and decisive factor . . . determining all the later stages in a person's further development." In their efforts to bring about "a vigorous speeding up of our creative mutability" the "pedologues" turned first to the work of the physiologist Ivan Pavlov about conditioned reflexes because "these teachings concentrate on the external environment and its stimulants."[13]

The teachers dreamed of making use of the latest achievements of Soviet science, which in the 1920s and 1930s was actively engaged in studying the possibility of changing a person's psychology and physiology. Scholars and pseudoscholars reported marvelous discoveries that made it possible to restore a person's youth and to set about the production—on a conveyor belt—of socialist man. Mikhail Bulgakov's 1925 novel *Heart of a Dog,* never published in the USSR, gives an excellent idea of the atmosphere prevailing at the time—the expectation of miracles, of the elixir of youth and of eternal life. Alexander Bogdanov, a philosopher and doctor and one of the founders of the Russian Social-Democratic Party, died in 1928 as a result of an unsuccessful experiment in blood transfusion carried out to prove the possibility of rejuvenating people and the theory of the universal brotherhood of man. A research institute was put at the disposal of Professor Kazakov, who announced that he had discovered a miraculous medicament—*lizaty.*[14] Kazakov was arrested in 1938 in connection with the Bukharin affair, accused of being responsible for the murder of Menzhinsky, chairman of the OGPU, and executed. From statements he made it emerged that he had used his miracle-working *lizaty* mainly to treat Soviet leaders. In 1937, the commissariat for health established in Leningrad a fifty-bed hospital for oriental medicine that was capable of handling 200–300 patients a month.[15] Perhaps the best indication of the extent to which miracles were expected was the name of the man put in charge: a specialist in

Tibetan medicine, Dr. Badmaev; one of Rasputin's predecessors at the Tsar's court had been the Mongol-Buryat healer Badmaev. The difference between Zhamsaryn Badmaev, who treated the Tsar's family with miraculous grasses, and Dr. N. N. Badmaev, the Soviet doctor who treated the "working people of the USSR," was that the latter worked "according to plan" and on the basis of a "materialist philosophy."

Conditioned reflexes, *lizaty,* Tibetan grasses, the study of the "brain barrier"—genuine science and charlatanism got along fine so long as they all started with an assertion of the direct connection between environment and psyche, and promised to transform people's psyches by acting on the environment. In such an atmosphere, the emergence of the greatest charlatan of the twentieth century, Trofim Lysenko, was inevitable. If the wonderful idea of transforming nature on the basis of Stalin's teachings had not occurred to this charlatan agronomist, it would certainly have occurred to someone else. The idea hung in the air; it was exactly what was wanted; and it expressed the spirit of the age, the essence of the "rational" Soviet ideology.

The gifted psychologist A. S. Vygotsky explained the role of the teacher in society by developing Pavlov's theory of a second system of signals, an intermediate structure, that filters the stimuli or signals coming from the physical world. The brain of a child or of a person who has only just become literate, Vygotsky explained, is conditioned by the interaction of elemental and non-elemental concepts. An authoritarian educational system, supplying a person's mind with organized concepts, makes it possible to shape and control the elemental factors.[16]

The conclusion to be drawn from all these theories was obvious: the possibility of processing human material had been demonstrated scientifically; the thing was to get on with it as quickly as possible. Dr. Zalkind stated in the late 1920s that the USSR had "revealed absolutely new and extremely rich pedagogical possibilities at nursery-school age—possibilities that were unknown in Western nursery practice," and continued: "A no less rich and no less promising material on the problem of mutability was obtained by Soviet pedology from children at the pre-school age. . . . Under our pedagogical system a new pre-school child has emerged."[17] Lunacharsky stated categorically: "We know that the development of a child's body, including his nervous system and his brain, is the real object of our work. . . . Man is a machine which functions in such a way as to produce what we call correct mental phenomena. . . . Man . . . is a piece of organized material that thinks, feels, sees and acts."[18]

In the following decades a number of external changes took place: in 1936 pedology was abolished and declared to be a "bourgeois anti-science"; many names of top people in pedagogy, psychology, physiology, and biology—men who had been the standard-bearers of science—were suppressed, and the candor with which they voiced their dream of a miracle in the early post-revolutionary period disappeared. But the determination to begin the work of forming the child remained, and they wanted to bring their influence to bear as soon as possible. The rules governing the running of nursery schools approved in 1934 described the school's function thus: "To instill love for the Soviet Motherland, for their own people, its leaders, the Soviet Army, making use of the richness of their native land, national creativity and striking events in the life of the country, accessible to a child's mind."[19] The 1969 New Program of preschool education in the nursery school suggested that attention should be directed to "the formation from early years of such important moral feelings as love of the Motherland, of the Soviet people and of Vladimir Lenin, the founder of the Soviet state, and respect for the working people of various nationalities."[20]

Intensive "psycho-physiological researches" were continued into the behavior of very young children, and were said to have produced evidence of "the great cognitive possibilities of children in the first two years of life" and of the role of "position-finding reflexes." And The Institute of Preschool Education of the Academy of Pedagogical Science carried out special research into the growth of emotional processes at the preschool age and into "their importance for the formation of socially motivated behavior."[21]

The external changes in education in the early 1930s reflected precisely the process of building the socialist utopia, and marked a switch to new techniques for processing human material. The main objective now was not to change the environment, which in due course would result in changes in people, but to train the children—training which, Zalkind complained, "our worst enemies call training children to perform like animals." But the "enemies" were correct: Soviet pedagogy indeed was employing, as well, "methods involving hypnotic and terroristic pressure on children."[22] From the early 1930s on, the technique gradually was perfected, and the attitude to ideology changed: it ceased to be a system of views based on certain unalterable concepts and became instead a system of signals emanating from a higher authority. The need to "believe" disappeared—the extermination of the "ideological Marxists" in the days of the Terror was a sign that a new era had begun.

An excellent illustration of the limitless possibilities that opened up for pedagogy is provided by a little song sung by children who have hardly learned to speak. For two decades Soviet children sang: "I am a little girl, I play and sing; I don't know Stalin, but I do love him." In the mid-1950s the words were changed: "I am a little girl, I play and I sing; I don't know Lenin, but I do love him." What is important is the expression of love for a remote divinity; his name doesn't matter.

The training method demands rote repetition of movements or words, as well as a model to demonstrate the correct movements and to say, Do as I do! The generation trained on the Stalin model was followed by a generation trained on the Lenin model. The signal "Lenin" enters the mind of a Soviet child immediately after birth: no sooner does he open his eyes than he sees portraits of the Leader; among the first sounds he hears is the Leader's name; and among his first words, after "Mama," is "Lenin." "When he enters the first class in school as a simple, freckled boy he reads that word for the first time in his very first book."[23] It is absolutely true, as the poet M. Dudin states, that the first word read by a Soviet child is "Lenin." The recommended reading list for schoolchildren in the first eight grades is headed: "Lenin—Party—People—Revolution," and the first book on the list is *The Life of Lenin: Selected pages of prose and poetry in ten volumes.* The seventy-eight pages of the list contain dozens of books about Lenin—verses, prose, plays and reminiscences.

The thousands of popular jokes ridiculing the Leader's deification are ordinary people's attempt to escape from the hypnotic dream into which Soviet man is plunged. The Lenin jokes have Lenin as their subject, but the cult model makes it possible to create a ritual of worship that remains unchanged into which the names of Lenin's successors can be inserted, as one changes worn-out parts of a machine. The nineteenth Komsomol Congress (1982) assured the Party that it would

cultivate convinced fighters for Communist ideals and educate the young people to follow the example of the life and work of the great Lenin. . . . A striking example of selfless service to the cause of the Communist renewal of the world for us is the career of that faithful continuer of the cause of the great Lenin, the outstanding politician and statesman of modern times, the tireless fighter for peace and social progress, the wise mentor of the young, Comrade Leonid Ilyich Brezhnev.[24]

Just two years later, a young worker from a Moscow factory assured the new general secretary: "We have someone whose example we can follow and from whom we can learn. . . . We have before us your brilliant career, Konstantin Ustinovich."[25] To call Chernenko's career "brilliant" was perhaps the greatest piece of hyperbole since the time when Stalin was called the greatest genius of all times and all peoples. But the young worker was not seeking hyperbole or comparisons; he was not expressing his own feelings—he was simply taking part in the ritual.

The Leader is the basic model, the basic pattern. "Cultural workers," writers, filmmakers, artists, and so forth, create smaller-scale models—positive heroes—in his image and likeness. One of the periodic decrees ("concerning the creative links between literary magazines and the practice of communist construction") of the Central Committee gave the same instruction: "New generations of Soviet people are in need of positive heroes close to them in spirit and time."[26]

A special place in the gallery of positive models is reserved for the heroes of children's literature. Children's writers sing the praises of boys and girls ready for adventure who perform heroic deeds and sacrifice themselves for the Motherland; children have drummed into them the need to destroy the enemy and to be ready to die. An author of essays on the history of Soviet children's literature stresses the exceptional merits of the work of Arkady Gaidar, a classic writer of literature for children: "For the first time in children's literature Gaidar introduces into a book about a Soviet childhood the concept of 'treason.' "[27] Pavlik Morozov was the first positive hero in Soviet children's literature because he exposed his father's "treason" and perished, having done his duty. In marking the fiftieth anniversary of the death of the young parricide, *Komsomolskaya Pravda* stressed the importance of the "legendary deed of heroism" for the education of Soviet children and adults.[28] Half a century after the birth of the "legend" of Pavlik Morozov, the magazine *Yunost* published a story called "The Sunflower" which tells of a young, talented artist serving as a border guard who from his watchtower catches sight of someone crossing the border. Deciding it is an enemy (nobody else would dare to "violate" the border), the Soviet guard jumps him: "He jumped on to the hated back, feeling he had a hundred horsepower within him. He heard the uneven breathing of the other man and dug his teeth into the man's neck." The young border guard suffers fatal injuries, but he has carried out his duty. In the hospital before he dies he comes to the conclusion that he has behaved absolutely correctly, that a Soviet man could not act differently. The woman doctor attending the dying man expresses the general feeling: "What he did merits the highest praise."[29]

In Brecht's play Galileo says: Unfortunate the country that has need of heroes. If we accept this, we can have no doubt that the Soviet Union is the most unfortunate country in the world; and not only because it has need of innumerable heroes (a popular song says: if the country needs us to be heroes every one of us can be one): the country's misfortune is the sort of heroes it wants to have. Soviet children and young people have held up to them examples of soldier-heroes and police-heroes. In 1933, Gorky pointed out with satisfaction: "We are starting to create Red Army literature that has never existed before that we don't yet have today."[30] Today, millions of copies of books are published about war, spies, policemen and people employed by the secret police. There are stories about them in movies, on television, and on the stage, as well as in songs, pictures, and sculpture. The Central Museum of the Ministry of Internal Affairs has a special exhibit devoted to A. M. Gorky, head of both the regular and the secret police. Inspired by these heroes, schoolchildren regularly take part in organized war games known as "The Eaglet" and "Lightning." The bodies that organize and run these games include the Central Committee of the Komsomol, the Ministry of Defense, the Ministry of Education, the Ministry of Higher and Secondary Special Education, the State Committee for Professional and Technical Education, the Central Committee of the DOSAAF Organization (which assists the Army in providing military and ideological training for civilians), the Soviet Committee for Sport, and the Joint Society of the Red Cross and Red Crescent.

"Lightning" embraces schoolchildren (both boys and girls) in the lower grades (first to seventh); "Eaglet" takes students from the upper grades (eighth to tenth). In 1984, 13 million schoolchildren took part in "Eaglet,"[31] competing in rifle shooting, grenade throwing, obstacle courses, dealing with an area exposed to an atomic explosion (in special protective clothing), and in military route-marches. According to a Soviet journalist who wrote a delighted account of these "games," the

"Eaglets" study the history of the Soviet Armed Forces and engage in tactical training.

Since 1973, the officers in command of the war games, professional soldiers with the rank of general, have organized national games in addition to "Eaglet" and "Lightning": in October, the junior army triathlon; in November–December, a competition called "Together and Strong"; in January–February, an operation called "In the path of the heroes"; in March, an operation called "Defense"; in April, operation "Sniper"; and in May, "Dolphin."

"Military-patriotic education," which begins in the nursery school and continues through kindergarten and primary school, constitutes the most important element in the Soviet educational system. A book by employees of the Soviet Academy of Pedagogic Science says: "The basic educational task of the Soviet school system is to develop in the younger generation a Marxist-Leninist philosophy and to train convinced materialists and staunch fighters for peace." The teachers' greatest responsibility is to infuse every subject taught with "a system of the basic philosophic ideas," and it is their duty to keep in mind the need to "train character in the process of learning" and to stress the "ideological purpose" behind every subject taught.[32]

Comparison of methodological instructions given a quarter of a century apart makes their continuity clear. In 1952: "The history course is of great educational value—it introduces the pupils to the Marxist-Leninist interpretation of history." In 1977: "History, the social sciences and the humanitarian sciences are especially important for education in school. It is in the school that are laid down the foundations of a scientific understanding of the way society develops, and of Marxism-Leninism." It is obvious that the humanities are particularly suitable for infusion with "ideological content," but Soviet teaching experts do not ignore the natural sciences. In 1952 it was pointed out, "Since 1949 the teaching of anatomy and physiology has been to a considerable extent restructured on the basis of the teachings of the great Russian physiologist I. P. Pavlov, and the teaching of the fundamentals of Darwinism on the teachings on I. V. Michurin." In 1977: "Taking a course in biology leads to a conviction that there is no divine origin in nature and encourages the formation of a firm atheistic position." In 1952, among the most important tasks for a course in chemistry was: "to familiarize students with the scientific bases of chemical products and with the role played by chemistry in warfare; to help students to develop a materialistic understanding of the world." In 1977: the school must teach the foundations of nuclear physics and chemistry, which enable the schoolchild "who has thought seriously about these matters not to resort to the hypothesis about God. . . . Physics and mathematics . . . are not just technical subjects; they are also part of economics and the productivity of labour; consequently it is also a social category which is related directly to the building of Communism."[33]

In 1984, after the new school law had been enacted, it was emphasized: "The whole process must have a much greater ideological content. This task is dealt with in the process of teaching practically all the subjects both in the humanities and in the natural sciences." The special nature of the Soviet education system, which is concerned primarily with character training, determines the "new psychological and didactical approach to the study of the teaching program." It uses a deductive method of reasoning to explain each subject, since Soviet pedagogical science has established that "an earlier theoretical generalization of information acquired makes the teaching more effective." All "generalizations" and all basic theoretical data "are based on Marxism-Leninism"; the teaching method consists in setting out material from the "known" to the "known"—from Marxist-Leninist generalizations to Marxist-Leninist facts. In this way, the possibility of children having independent thoughts, questions, and doubts is removed. Soviet schoolchildren are required, "in order to raise the theoretical level of the education," to study "the works of the classics of Marxism-Leninism, the most important documents relating to the CPSU and the Soviet state, the international Communist and working-class movement in lessons teaching history, social science, literature and other subjects."[34] This list of "theoretical texts" actually refers to speeches made by the current general secretary and resolutions issued by the Central Committee. "Raising the theoretical level" amounts in the end to learning by heart the current political vocabulary.

An analysis of Polish school textbooks carried out in 1980 showed that the methods used for shaping Soviet man have been applied in other Communist countries as well. He identified four interrelated ideological tasks performed by Polish textbooks: the formation of a Marxist view of the world, man, society, culture, economics, and various historical and contemporary social problems; the inculcation of atheism; the subordination of historical and current information to Russian and Soviet interests; and the general presentation of the present

Polish state as a socialist nation and the only unquestionably worthy object of genuine patriotic feelings.[35]

The British historian Hugh Seton-Watson said with indomitable optimism in 1975: "The growth of material well-being [in the USSR] . . . was accompanied by a rapid expansion of education at all levels. . . . Successive generations of young people learned to think."[36] Seton-Watson did not realize that Soviet teaching methods were aimed at preventing schoolchildren from thinking.

Since the Party controls the school system, the Central Committee drew up the plan for the reform of Soviet schools that was enacted in April 1984. But even the CPSU cannot run schools without teachers, "the sculptors of the intellectual world of the young person," as the school law says. The part played by the teacher as the means of putting across Party policy and as the "sculptor" of the Soviet person explains his position in society. "Sociological research shows that the prestige of the teaching profession among young people is impermissibly low," a Soviet teacher declared bitterly in 1976.[37] In Veniamin Kaverin's 1984 novel *Zagadka (The Riddle),* a woman teacher complains: "I, for example, in unfamiliar company, on a beach somewhere, am ashamed to admit that I'm a teacher. There are professions that enjoy prestige— manager of a shop selling footwear or food, an artist, a market researcher, an actor or someone in charge of a garage. But teaching is a profession which, alas, has not gained respect." The teacher knows the reasons for this lack of respect: "People have no faith in teachers." There are other reasons: the low pay, the very heavy workload, and the lack of authority over the schoolchildren. But the most important is the lack of faith in the teacher, which results primarily from the fact that the children understand that the teacher is not telling them the truth. The teacher is well aware of this; as the teacher in Kaverin's story says: "I would be doing the honest thing if I quit teaching, which I love, because the first thing you ought to teach is the truth, and only afterward geography or physics."[38] The impossibility of "teaching the truth" obliges people to lie, to be hypocritical, and to deceive. The way their teachers deceive them is obvious to schoolchildren, from the very earliest grades, since the assessment of a pupil's progress is based not on his knowledge but on the need to fulfill the progress plan. The work of a class, a school, a district, a region, or a republic is assessed in the same way; in the words of a Moscow teacher, G. Nikanorov, "The principle of measuring results in quantitative terms is implanted in us from top to bottom."[39] A French minister of education, visiting Moscow, was delighted to discover that "there were practically no cases in the Soviet school system of pupils repeating a year over again. It is not more than one percent."[40] His observation was quite correct, but the minister did not understand that he was observing the effect of planning. At the beginning of each school year, according to a Moscow teacher, "the percentage of successful students is often set at over 99 percent."[41] Consequently, the teacher is obliged to give "satisfactory" or even "good marks" even to pupils who know nothing, so as not to upset the fulfillment of the plan by the class, the school, the district, or the republic.

Making the fulfillment of the plan the first "pedagogic" task ensures a deliberate lowering of the teaching level for the benefit not of the good pupils, but of the backward ones. Behind this policy there lies not only the "planification" of the whole country, but also a pedagogic idea formulated by Makarenko: "The purpose of pedagogical work consists not in discovering some tendency in a child, determined by individual, including biological needs, but in the general process of organizing the child's life and of the social and collective relationships, in the course of which the child's personality is formed."[42] Soviet teachers have to explain to their pupils that "there is still a need for such kinds of work as cannot be called interesting or creative, but which are absolutely essential."[43] They also have to explain that it is the state which decides who will carry out the "interesting" work and who will have to do the "essential" jobs.

The lack of respect for teaching is, as I've said, also the result of very low pay. In Maria Glushko's novel *Vozvrashchenie (The Return),* a teacher jokes bitterly: "Since we are not paid very much and there's nothing for us to steal, we . . . are forced to live a rich intellectual life. Of course, we could take bribes, but no one offers them."[44] This last remark must bring a smile to the face of the Soviet teacher, who knows very well that bribery does not halt at the school threshold and that teachers are also included in the magic circle of those who give and take bribes.

Going to school for the first time—the first step he takes out of the family and into the outside world—the child comes face to face with the realities of the Soviet system. More than the knowledge that the teacher conveys, it is the teacher's behavior that becomes the most important factor in the child's training, for it is here that the disciplin-

ing of the Soviet person begins. The teacher's personal qualities—
honesty, love of the profession, ability and desire to do the job well—
cannot have any serious effect on the way the system works. If the
system senses the slightest resistance, it will expel the obstacle. Vladimir Tendryakov, a writer who has followed events in the Soviet school
system closely, devoted his novel *Chrezvychainoe (The Emergency)* to
a scandal that takes place in a small provincial town when it is discovered that a mathematics teacher believes in God. He has never uttered
a word about religion to his pupils, and his subject appears to have no
connection with religion, but he is forced to leave the school because
his presence upsets the "system" and is evidence of the possibility of
choice—he is interfering with the training process.[45]

Whatever the teacher's personal wishes, the pupil regards him as a
knife in the hands of the state, as someone carrying out orders that
require him be a liar and a hypocrite. The children see that the teacher
receives a pitiful reward for painfully hard work and he has no authority in society. And that is the way life begins.

Children inevitably grow older. University students remember
school very well, and their attitude toward their professors is colored
by their attitude to their teachers. There are many stories and novels
about students at the center of a conflict—the problem of betraying a
professor. Students betray their professors by reporting on them and
exposing them at meetings under pressure from the Party, having discovered that this offers the only possibility of making a career. For
Soviet writers like D. Granin, Yury Trifonov, I. Grekova, V. Tendryakov and Vasily Grossman, the betrayal of a professor symbolizes
the system's pressure on the individual. In this conflict there is also an
element of revenge on the teachers who have betrayed the pupils from
the very first schooldays.

The word "reform" is rarely used in Soviet parlance regarding the
Soviet system; decrees of the Central Committee and the government
dealing with various kinds of change use only optimistic expressions;
they speak of "raising," "improving," "extending," "strengthening,"
and so on. The importance of the changes made in April 1984 was
underscored by the fact that they were called "a reform of the general
and professional school system." The April reform brought into being
"the school in conditions of the perfecting of advanced socialism," the
school of the twenty-first century: "It is a question of enabling the
Soviet school to develop, teach and train the younger generations to

have a more accurate idea of the conditions in which they will be living and working fifteen or twenty years ahead and more—in the approaching twenty-first century."[46]

The 1984 school law records precisely the state of the Soviet system after seven decades of existence, and its leaders' dreams of the future. Its general drift shows an intention to enter the twenty-first century back to front, totally cut off from everything new that might destroy the entropy of the Soviet system and the total power of the Party. With striking obstinacy, it confirms the strategic goal: "The unchanging foundation of the Communist upbringing of pupils is the development in them of a Marxist-Leninist outlook on the world."[47] It defines new tactical directions for achieving the goal, bearing in mind the approaching twenty-first century—and it also records the fact that the Soviet system of education has achieved something less than complete success.

The principal task facing the school system consists of "developing in the rising generation an awareness of the need to work." To carry out this task—a surprising one in a state born of a proletarian revolution and ruled by a party of the working class—the law requires the school to "ensure a close interconnection between studying the fundamentals of the sciences and the direct participation of the schoolchildren in systematic, organized, feasible, socially useful and productive labor."[48]

Changes have been made in the structure of the school system. Schooling now starts at the age of six instead of seven, the lower age undoubtedly connected with a desire to begin working on the child as soon as possible. With this aim in mind, a new structure is introduced with a primary school (first to fourth grades), "incomplete" secondary school (fifth to ninth grades), and the "complete" secondary school (tenth and eleventh). Instead of the compulsory ten-year program which hitherto existed, this nine-year program adds on a further two-year course for those able to continue in an institute of higher education. The ninth grade becomes the threshold at which selection takes place—the majority to enter the work force, the minority to enter college or university. As a result of the reform, the number of schoolchildren entering professional and technical institutes or going straight into the work force will double.[49] The number of candidates for entry into institutes of higher education has accordingly dropped by half. In 1950, roughly 80 percent of the children finishing secondary school entered an institute of higher education; in the late 1970s, the figure was not more than 18 percent.[50] Apparently even this is too high; on the threshold of the twenty-first century the Soviet state has discovered that its greatest need is for workers. The selection of schoolchildren is to be carried out "in accordance with the needs of the national economy and taking account of the interests and abilities of the children, the wishes of the parents and recommendations by the schools' pedagogical councils."[51]

In order that, after completing nine grades, fifteen-year-old boys and girls can work productively, the law requires schools to see that students acquire a trade in the course of their schooling, and also provides for "the compulsory participation of schoolchildren in socially useful and productive labor"[52] during their summer vacations. The leading journal of the Ministry of Education commented with satisfaction: "The experience of 1981 has shown that there has been an increase in the scale on which schoolchildren of the fourth to sixth classes, and even of the first to third classes, are being drawn into socially useful labor in the summer holidays. This tendency must be encouraged and extended."[53] The school law has made the "tendency" compulsory.

Pravda underlined the fact that the schools were to devote "special attention to inculcating in people a sense of the need to work."[54] It follows that the school not only must teach a trade: before all else, it must instill a sense of the need to work wherever the Party or the government decrees. Thus two tasks—training as a Communist and the acquisition of a trade—merge.

The third principal task—the Soviet school system of the twenty-first century stands on three pillars—is the development of "military-patriotic training." Not satisfied with all that has already been done in this field, the authors of the new law included a paragraph from the 1968 law on compulsory military service, and required schools "to place at the foundation of the military-patriotic training of the pupils the task of training them for service in the armed forces of the USSR, teaching them to love the Soviet Army, and the development in them of a strong sense of pride in belonging to a socialist society and its constant defense. To raise the level and effectiveness of military training in the general and professional schools."[55]

No school system in the world, with the possible exception of that of Khomeini's Iran, goes in for military training from the earliest age. "Military-patriotic training" is intended to train future soldiers for service in the army, but a no less important task is to instill into schoolchildren from the very first grade (from the age of six, according to the new law) military virtues: discipline and unquestioning submission to an order, hatred of the enemy, who is named by the teacher.

The teacher of military subjects has an increasingly important role to play in the school, and "military-patriotic training" colors the teaching of all subjects. The new law devotes special attention to the teaching of Russian in the non-Russian republics, demanding that "additional steps should be taken to improve the conditions for studying, along with the local language, the Russian language, which has been accepted voluntarily by the Soviet people as a means of communication between peoples," and stating that "a fluent mastery of Russian must become the norm for young people completing secondary school."[56] Special attention is devoted to the Russian language not only because it is used as a powerful vehicle for Soviet ideas, and as a means of Sovietizing the population, but also because the army demands it. The law's article regarding the Russian language is, in fact, a reply to the complaint of Marshal Ogarkov (former Chief of the General Staff): "Unfortunately there are still quite a lot of young people coming into the army today with a poor knowledge of the Russian language, which makes their military training much more difficult."[57]

The text of the Soviet school law is noteworthy not only for what it includes, but also for what it leaves out. In particular, it passes silent approval on the tendency visible in recent years to reduce the amount of time devoted to teaching of foreign languages. In the 1980–81 school year, the upper grades were allotted one hour a week for a foreign language. Bearing in mind that only one foreign language is taught, this is obviously a deliberate move aimed at isolating ordinary Soviet citizens from the non-Soviet world; the necessary number of foreign language specialists will be produced in special schools. But the most important silence concerns the scientific-technological revolution: the school law gives detailed instructions on how to increase ideological influence on young people, how to train them for work in industry, how to turn them into soldiers, but deals only in one obscure sentence with the need "to equip pupils with the knowledge and experience necessary for handling modern calculating technology and to ensure the extensive use of computers in the teaching process."[58] The legislators talk about the need to "arm" people with a knowledge of the latest technology in the conditional tense—"when there will be computers."

In September 1984, the *Uchitelskaya Gazeta (Teacher's Newspaper)* reported that "the computerization of the Soviet economy will take place in fifteen years," by which time the schools will every year be turning out one million boys and girls who have mastered computer technology. In 1985, according to the plan, the schools should receive 1,131 "Agat" personal computers made in the USSR.

The rejection of the idea of "computerizing" schools is based on reasons of principle and ideology: to make information accessible to a large number of people, and to inculcate the special habits of analytic and independent thinking essential for work with the new technology, goes against the whole Soviet system of training and education. The Soviet journalist who asserted that in a country of "mature socialism," there was no need for "personal computers," only of big machines, was admitting that the emergence of the computer could be compared only with the discovery of fire or the invention of the alphabet.[59] But he considers it perfectly natural that in the Soviet Union, fire, the alphabet, and computers should be at the disposal of the state, that distributes and controls matches, letters of the alphabet, and cybernetic technology. The necessary number of programmers and of people knowing foreign languages can always be produced in special institutes.

The new school curriculum mentions—apart from Marx, Engels, and Lenin—the names of two pedagogues, N. K. Krupskaya and A. S. Makarenko. These names underline how little the model of the Soviet school has changed. The task of education formulated nearly half a century ago by Makarenko, founder of a "genuinely scientific system for educating the Communist personality"[60] and father of Soviet pedagogy, remains the principal goal for the future: "We want to educate the cultured Soviet worker. Consequently we must give him an education, preferably secondary, we must provide him with qualifications, we must discipline him, and he must be a politically advanced and devoted member of the working class, a Young Communist and a Bolshevik."[61]

Makarenko never tired of asserting that the Army—the army collective, as he put it—represented the ideal model of the school that would produce the "cultured Soviet worker." The Soviet school of the twenty-first century should, on the basis of the 1984 law, achieve that ideal: to train worker-soldiers who accept a hierarchical system and discipline, who receive the knowledge that they must have in a form that does not require thought or discussion, and who are firmly convinced of the inevitability of the victory of communism. A similar ideal occurred to Hitler. Speaking at a 1937 May Day celebration in Berlin, he set out his own program:

> We have begun in the first place with the youth. You will never manage to do anything with the old idiots [laughter in the hall]. We take their children away from them. We make out of them Germans of a different kind. When a child is seven it knows nothing yet about its birth or origin. One child is like another. At that age we take them into a collective to the age of eighteen. Later they enter the Party, the SA, the SS and other organizations, or they go into the factories. . . . And later they are sent for two years into the Army.[62]

The ancient Romans asserted that he who wished for peace should prepare for war; and, following this precept, built a world empire. Clausewitz explained the paradox: war is always started by the one who defends himself. If the state attacked by an aggressor does not defend itself, there will be no war.

The school system has made its new task the improvement of schoolchildren's preparation for peace by stepping up their training for war, and it is beginning with the six-year-olds.

THE FAMILY

> The family is under the protection of the State. CONSTITUTION OF THE USSR

"The Red Triangle"—it is the title of a ballad by Alexander Galich—is a laconic yet exhaustive definition of the Party's policy with regard to the family as it has been from the first day of the Revolution. The triangle of love is a concept that emerged, apparently, along with the monogamous family: he, she, and a third person (male or female). The constant presence of Lenin (the Party) and the third angle in the triangle determines the special nature of the "red triangle." In 1970, when celebrations of the centenary of Lenin's birth reached a state of frenzy, hundreds of jokes were told as an antidote to the excitement. One of them alleged that the Soviet Union had organized the manufacture of triple beds because "Lenin is always with us."

The Revolution, which aimed at remaking not only society but—in the first place—man himself, could not fail to regard the family as the most important target. Penetration into the basic cell of society and into its genetic structure was the condition for achieving the goal.

In advancing on the "bourgeois family," tactics were employed that had been used in the war on the school—legislative measures and an ideological attack. Among the first acts of the new Soviet regime (December 18 and 19, 1917) were laws concerning civil marriage (replacing marriage in church) and divorce. It was no accident that the first legal codes concerned the family and the school (September 16 and 30, 1918).

In the decade after the Revolution, the family in the USSR experienced its first shock. A legal code on the family and marriage that was promulgated in 1926 extended the provisions of the 1918 code to the limit; for example, divorce could be obtained at the request of only one of the parties, who was not obliged to inform the other (it was sufficient to send a postcard to the registrar's office), and gave legislative form to the revolutionary breakup of the family and social customs. The code of 1926 was, in the minds of those who drew it up, the last step on the path to the final disappearance of the family as a social institution. In 1930, the *Small Soviet Encyclopedia* quoted P. Stuchka, one of the first Bolshevik lawyers, who declared that "the family is the basic form of slavery," and promised that the family would die out in the near future, along with private property and the state.[63]

Knowing it was impossible to abolish the family immediately by law, the creators of the new world set about destroying it from within. "The family has not yet been destroyed," A. Zalkind said in 1924. "A destitute proletarian state does not yet have the resources, either educational or economic, to replace the family completely, and therefore it must be revolutionized and proletarianized. The part to be played in this matter by the younger generation is tremendous."[64] The attack on the family was conducted on a broad front. The main targets were young people, children and women—the "weak links" in the family chain.

The emancipation of women is an age-old theme of utopians. In his *What Is to Be Done?* Chernyshevsky argued that the liberation of women was an indispensable condition for the liberation of society. For him, as for many other utopians, the liberation of women meant, firstly, putting women on the same level as men and, secondly, destroying the monogamous family that enslaved women. Soviet revolutionary law "liberated" women, giving them equal rights with men—in the family. At the same time an active campaign was launched to spread new attitudes about sexual relations that would lead to the emancipation of women. Wide publicity was given to appeals for "free love" made by Alexandra Kollontai, a Communist, the first woman minister (people's commissar for the social services), and in her free time a writer. Kollontai's views acquired considerable popularity and became the model for the new morality. Lenin himself bore witness to the success of the battle with the family. In a conversation with the German Communist Klara Zetkin, the leader of the October Revolution complained:

> Although I am by no means a dreary ascetic, the so-called "new sexual life" practised by young people and often by adults as well seems to me quite often to be a variation on the good old bourgeois brothel. . . . You are, of course, aware of the famous theory that in a Communist society the satisfaction of sexual desires and the demands of love will be as simple and of as little consequence as drinking a glass of water. Because of this "glass of water theory" our young people have gone out of their minds. . . . This has got nothing to do with free love as we Communists understand it.[65]

The founder of the Soviet state did not go on to explain what the Communists understand by "free love," nor did he publish anything on the subject over his signature during his lifetime. Zetkin's reminiscences, which became a lasting basis for Soviet sexual morality, were published only after his death.

The clash between the two conceptions—Lenin's and Kollontai's—reflected tactical differences. Lenin considered that "the Revolution demands a concentration of effort by the masses and by individuals." Kollontai assumed that the Revolution had already triumphed and that one ought therefore to make use of the "winged Eros . . . for the benefit of the collective."[66] Lenin remained silent—in his lifetime—realizing that the "winged Eros" and "free love" were contributing to the destruction of the bourgeois family.

Kollontai ended her novel about free love with an appeal: "Love and work, work and fight, live and love life, like the bees in the lilac, like the birds at the bottom of the garden, like the crickets in the grass!"[67] The absence of any literary talent in *Love of the Worker Bees* did not prevent the "free love theory" from gaining extensive popularity (perhaps it even helped?). It contained the most important components of the "new": liberation of men and women from the ties of the bourgeois family, and a class hierarchy in the field of sexual relations. The dialectic approach to freedom was revealed especially clearly with regard to free love: the theorists of the "glass of water" preached complete freedom, but insisted on the necessity for class "selection." Kollontai subjected the hero of her novel to severe criticism—he was a Communist who abandoned a proletarian girl in favor of a bourgeois woman.

The emergent proletarian literature made the conflict between "mind" and "body" one of its principal themes. In A. Tarasova-Rodionova's novel *Chocolate* a secret policeman perishes because he cannot resist the charms of a woman from a hostile class. In *Natalya Tarpova*, a novel by S. Semyonov that was very popular in the 1920s, the heroine after much painful hesitation chooses a Communist. Harmony of class and sex find poetic expression:

> *I throw kisses ever fiercer and noisier.*
> *Lines from Marx fall on the bed from pockets,*
> *Big ideas about the equality of all people . . .*
> *My caresses carry them off in a moment, stupefying,*
> *To float away again ever clearer.* [68]

The author of a catechism on the sexual life of the proletariat *(The Revolutionary Norms of Sexual Behavior),* pointing out that "the sexual life of the greater part of people today is characterized by an even sharper conflict between a person's social inclinations and his sensual sexual attractions," demanded: "Sexual selection should be based on class, revolutionary-proletarian expediency."[69]

The literature of the 1920s accurately reflects the confusion of minds and feeling caused by the revolutionary slogans and appeals to build a "new life" and fight against the "old family." Dasha Chumalova, the first "liberated woman" in Soviet literature, stood up for her right to be on terms of equality with her husband at work and in private life. She tells her jealous husband: "There has to be in us a merciless civil war. There is nothing stronger or more difficult to suppress than our habits, feelings and prejudices. Jealousy is raging within you—that I know. It is worse than a despotism. It is a kind of exploitation of man by man that can be compared only with cannibalism."[70] But she was a rare example of a woman's use of her right to "free love." Dozens of novels depicted the tragic reality: unfortunate girls and women completely baffled by the revolutionary slogans. Lunacharsky was obliged to come to their defense. He quoted a typical dialogue between young people in the 1920s:

> *The Man:* Sex and the satisfaction of sexual feelings is a simple thing and one must stop dithering about it.
> *The Woman:* Perhaps that's right, maybe it's also scientific, but all the same, what will happen: if you throw me over and I have a baby, what will I do?
> *The Man:* What a narrow-minded way to think! What middle-class caution! How deeply entrenched you are in bourgeois prejudices! I just can't look on you as a comrade!

Lunacharsky summarized: "So the frightened girl thinks she's behaving in a Marxist and a Leninist way if she refuses nobody."[71] A character in Lev Gumilev's *Sobachi pereulok (Dog's Lane),* the young Communist Khorokhorin, a Chekist and later a student, tries to persuade a girl on the same course: "I have regarded you and still regard you as a good comrade! After all, if I came up to you and said I was hungry and had to go and work, surely you would share a crust of bread with me like a good comrade?"[72] The most popular novel of the 1920s, Sergei Malashkin's *Luna s pravoi storony (The Right Side of the Moon),* describes the fate of Tanya, a country girl who joins the Young Communist League and, after she has been persuaded of the revolutionary nature of "free love," becomes the wife of twenty-six men. How typical the picture of Tanya was is confirmed in autobiographical books by young Communist writers.[73]

The Old Bolshevik P. Lepeshinsky admitted how powerful a force the notion of "free love" was: "What can you set against this theory? Parental authority? There is none. The authority of the Church? It doesn't exist. Traditions? There are none. Moral feelings? But the old morality is dead and a new one has not been born." He summed up the situation: "The old type of family has been absolutely destroyed and there is no new one yet."[74]

Yet Russia, having become Soviet, still remained a peasant country: more than 80 percent of the population lived in villages. The destruction of the family and the breakdown of morality was clear: the Revolution followed on the heels of war, first with Germany and then the cruel and merciless Civil War which began this breakup of the family and decline of morality. The wartime loss of life, and above all the number of men killed, gave rise to a situation that was recorded in the first population census after the war in 1926. According to the previous census of 1897 the proportion of men and women in Russia was practically the same—49.7 percent and 50.3 percent. But in 1926 there were 5 million fewer men than women. This imbalance between the sexes was to increase, so that by 1959 there were 20 million more women than men, and in 1981 the figure was 17.5 million. This plays a large part in determining the character of the Soviet family, the state of morality, and relations between the sexes.

At the start, however, revolutionary ideas met with resistance, especially in the country districts. They were opposed by religion, by centuries-old habits, and by the economics of farming. So the revolutionary war against religion was carried out by means of administrative methods—blows against the Church and ideological campaign against the "old way of life." These administrative methods—which closed down churches and organized schisms within the Church—allowed the authorities to hope for positive results in the future. The ideological work was supposed to have immediate results, changing the way of life of millions of citizens of the Soviet republic. Trotsky, who took an active interest in the "new way of life," commented in 1923 that "the way of life is much more resistant to change than the economy," and consequently "in the field of family relationships we find ourselves, so to speak, still in 1920–21 and not in 1923."[75] Recognizing the extent of the resistance put up by the "way of life" compared with the economy which it was still easy to nationalize, the people's commissar for military and naval affairs measured changes in the former in months or, at worst, in years.

The working-class regime had, according to Trotsky, "explained to the citizens that they had the right to be born, to enter into marriage and to die without having resort to any magical gestures and psalm-singing by people in cassocks or other priestly garb." But Trotsky himself knew very well that it was not enough to give people the right to do without religion—you had either to force or to persuade them to stop believing. The campaign of persuasion included creating an "atheistic substitute" for religion. Lenin believed that the theatre could replace religion. Trotsky suggested some practical steps for making use of the theatre for anti-religious propaganda. In a book about the "new way of life," he reported proudly that "the workers' state has its own feast-days, its own parades, its own symbolic spectacles and its own theatricality."[76]

The first step toward creating a "Communist ritual" was to make use of religious rituals: the authorities organized "red" baptisms, "red" weddings, "red" Easters and so forth. A great deal of publicity was given to thinking up new names for children, to mark a new arrival in the new world. Registry offices displayed lists of names recommended for infants that had nothing in common with the liturgical calendar. In the town of Ivanovo, for example, people were urged to call a newly born daughter Atlantida, Industria, Izida or Traviata, or, in the case of a boy, Izumrud, Genii, Singapur.[77] Trotsky spoke approvingly of the popularity of such names as Oktyabrina, Ninel ("Lenin" backwards), REM (Revolution, Energy, Peace).[78]

The destruction of the "old" family and "old" way of life, so closely associated with the "religious survival" in all its forms, was conducted under the slogan of the "new morality." A character in a novel—a young proletarian who becomes a student—reflects: "College has provided me with grounds for the law that the masses discovered by instinct—'Everything is moral that serves the world revolution, and everything is immoral that serves to split the ranks of the proletariat, to disorganize and weaken it.' Like a cold shower, this concise law opened my eyes, to all that happened in the revolution, to myself and to my place in the new society that is being constructed."[79] In a book designed for young people a theoretician of the new morality announces: "The old morality is dead, decomposing and rotting." The principal mark of the new morality was its relativism. "Thou shalt not steal," the commandment in what was called the "exploiters'" Bible, was replaced by the marvelous "ethical formula" of Comrade Lenin: "Steal the stolen goods." That did not mean, the moralist explains, that "the robber who attacks a citizen and seizes his property, even if he's an NEP-man, is also behaving ethically. The only 'thefts' that are ethical and moral are those that contribute to the well-being of the proletarian collective." In exactly the same way one is expected to reject the commandment that says "Honor thy father and thy mother": "The proletariat recommends that you should honor only a father who has adopted a revolutionary-proletarian standpoint and who brings his children up in a spirit of devotion to the struggle of the proletariat." In the framework of the proletarian ethic, the commandment "Thou shalt not commit adultery" no longer relates to the traditional concern for marital fidelity but is relevant only because the "search for a new sexual partner" is "a very complicated business" that takes too much time and energy and is a "theft of creative class strength."[80]

Alexander Voronsky, one of the organizers of Soviet literature and a very influential literary critic, while explaining the harm that could be caused by Zamyatin's novel *We* (banned by the censor), asked the questions: "Can one accept and defend the murder of a bound man? Can one have recourse to spying?" And he replied: "One can and one must." He produced an irrefutable argument: "We Communists . . . now ought to live like fanatics. . . . In this great social struggle one needs to be a fanatic. That means to suppress mercilessly everything that springs from the heart, from personal feelings, because this can, from time to time, cause harm, interfering with the struggle and hindering the victory."[81]

Questions concerning the family, sexual freedom, the new morality, and the campaign against the old way of life evoked considerable discussion in the 1920s, and various views were expressed concerning the tactics to be adopted. Half a century later many people might find views surprising for their frankness and for the freedom with which people expressed ideas that were later spoken only in code. Theorists and practitioners of socialism (that is, of the construction of the New Man) agreed with the need for the state to control the private life of its citizens. None of them doubted that the state should determine all aspects of life. In the 1920s the first blow struck against the family, morality, and the old way of life marked the beginning of a process, the results of which are described convincingly sixty years later in a textbook of "scientific Communism": "The socialist way of life differs radically from the bourgeois way of life, where it is each person's private affair. In conditions of socialism concern for the way a person's life is organized, for the growth of his intellectual demands and the rational organization of his free time becomes a matter of state policy." Since the textbook defines "way of life" as "the non-productive part of human life which is connected with the satisfaction of people's material and intellectual needs (for food, housing, clothes, communal services, medical treatment, holidays, and mental and cultural service)," it is obvious that a person's entire life has "become a matter of state policy," because the "productive part" of a man's activity—his employment—is wholly in the hands of the state. Man becomes totalitarian man—the totality of his activity is determined by the state.[82]

The shock of the Revolution and the post-revolutionary incursion into people's private lives produced results. In Trotsky's words, the family fell apart.[83] The decisive blow was struck in the early 1930s, during the collectivization of agriculture. Abolition of individual peasant small-holdings led to the destruction of the "bourgeois" family. Collectiviza-tion, which Stalin described quite accurately as a "great breakthrough," was total war against Russia's entire population and above all against the peasantry which, ten years after the Revolution, still preserved a certain independence of the state. The war was conducted on a broad front, making use of administrative, legislative, and ideological weapons, and the family and morality were among the most important targets under attack. According to official figures, in 1931–32 "240,757 *kulak* families were expropriated and transported to the northern and eastern regions of the Union."[84] Even this unsubstantiated figure reveals, when deci-phered, the nature of the war. Peasant families in Russia had as a rule many children, between four and eight. Families exiled "to the north and east"—i.e., to Siberia and Kazakhstan—were sent together, including adult children living separately and their families. Thus the average family consisted of two old people, six grown children with their spouses, each couple having four children: a total of thirty-eight people. Some of the expropriated kulaks were exiled to remote regions, while others were uprooted from the villages where they had been born and lived their entire lives. Finally, a certain number of kulaks, never officially stated, suffered physical extermination (according to calculations by historians and demographers, not less than 15 million).

The campaign against the kulaks had an important educational function. Decades later, when the state exposed the "cult of personal-ity," S. Pavlov, First Secretary of the Central Committee of the Kom-somol, reported that in the 1930s Stalin had instructed the Komsomol: "It was brought right to the forefront—and it's down there in black and white—that the Komsomol's most important task in all its educational work was to spy out and identify the enemy, who then had to be removed by force through economic pressure, organizational and politi-cal isolation, and physical extermination."[85]

In the course of the first post-revolutionary campaign against the family, women and young people were used for destroying intimate personal relations. During the second campaign the main instrument became, as Pavlov confirmed, young people. Analyzing the aims of the "great terror," Robert Conquest has come to the conclusion that "the disintegration of family loyalty was a conscious Stalinist aim . . . Stalin's idea of a good young Communist demanded not this sort of political training, but the qualities of an enthusiastic young nark."[86] To which one must add only that the training of an enthusiastic nark was just what the political training was.

The early 1930s—the time of the genocide of the peasants—was also, of course, a time when society was morally corrupted. Fundamental to the plan for the country's final demoralization was a course of training in hating the enemy and in elevating the business of informing on other people to the level of a supreme Soviet virtue.

Shortly after coming to the throne, Alexander III was handed a proposal for the training of spies, carefully worked out by a retired officer and former agent of the Third Department by the name of Liprandi. Liprandi argued that one should start training agents at the earliest possible age—in secondary school. The idea was to look out for boys who reported on their friends, encourage them and help them after they entered university, and then, once their education was completed, take them into the police as experienced and educated agents. Alexander III turned the plan down.[87] But in the era of collectivization, Liprandi's modest idea, which had not been acceptable in the Russia of fifty years before, was not only put into practice but applied on a monstrous, previously unimaginable scale.

A. Kosarev, a Komsomol leader eliminated by Stalin in 1938 for getting carried away by the "political training of young people," declared in 1931: "We have no morality applying to the whole of mankind."[88] Hatred became the slogan of the day, hatred inculcated from the earliest age. On February 13, 1932, the children's newspaper *Friendly Children* changed its title to *Collective Farm Children.* The editors explained the change thus: "Friendly is a bad title . . . after all, we aren't on friendly terms with the kulaks." One of the leaders of the Pioneer organization announced that the main task of the Young Pioneers was "to cultivate hatred."[89] *The Pioneers' Pravda* printed a "Poem About Hatred."

Hatred aimed at "enemies" was directed at those who were close to the children—their relations, members of their family, friends, and acquaintances. The first commandment became, Expose the enemy. Maxim Gorky, who played a decisive role in the social demoralization of the 1930s, formulated a law of the new morality: "If a 'blood' relative turns out to be an enemy of the people, then he is no longer a relative but simply an enemy and there is no longer any reason to spare him."[90]

Denunciation—above all of "blood" relations—became a duty and a virtue. An early example of this is to be seen in a letter written by the son of one of the defendants in the case of what were called "wreckers" in the coal industry. The Shakhtin case, as it is called, took place in the summer of 1928. During the trial *Pravda* published a letter under the heading: "Son of Andrei Kolodub demands severe punishment for his wrecker-father":

> As the son of one of the conspirators, Andrei Kolodub, and at the same time a Young Communist . . . I cannot react calmly to the treacherous deeds of my father. . . . Knowing my father as a confirmed enemy and hater of the working people I add my voice to the demand of all workers that the counter-revolutionaries should be severely punished. . . . Since I consider it shameful any longer to bear the name of Kolodub I am changing it to Shakhtin.[91]

The use of children to spy on adults and the training of informers became an important element in the collectivization campaign, in which the highest Party dignitaries took part. Lenin's widow, Krupskaya, offered this advice: "Just look around yourselves, children. You will see that there are still many survivals of the property-owning past. It would be a good thing if you would discuss them and make a note of them."[92] A. Bubnov, people's commissar for education, issued an order permitting a school to hand over to the courts parents who "did not take proper care of their children": it was sufficient for a child to report to his teacher that he was not satisfied with his father or mother for the school to take the matter to court.[93] At the same time the hunt was on against teachers. The editor of *The Pioneers' Pravda* explained what the "child correspondents" did: "It means keeping an eye on the teachers, being vigilant in the campaign for the quality of class teaching."[94] On March 16, 1934, *The Pioneers' Pravda* published a specimen denunciation, a letter from a "child correspondent" named Olya Balykina. The letter, which took up three columns of the paper, began: "To Spassk, to the OGPU," and among the "enemies" she exposed was her own father.

The model for family behavior and the ideal hero of Soviet children was Pavlik Morozov, a boy whose alleged denunciation of his father led to the latter's arrest and execution. This tragedy, which took place in September 1932 in a remote village in the Urals, was used by Soviet propaganda to manufacture a legend about a child who had placed a political relationship (with the Party) above a blood relationship (with his father).

One of the leaders of the Cultural Revolution in China in the 1970s, organized on the Soviet model, said: "A hero is a product of Party leadership, the fervent assistance of the masses, and the work of a writer."[95] That is exactly the way in which the "hero Pavlik Morozov" was created, only instead of the "fervent assistance of the masses" employees of the OGPU were used. A special feature of the "case" of the informer-hero was that the family was depicted as a terrorist organization which was exposed thanks to the "faithful son of the Party," the boy who wrote a denunciation of his father, who was then arrested. Pavlik and his brother were murdered; the boys' grandfather and uncle, who were accused of the double murder, confessed after being worked over in prison, and were sentenced to be shot; their grandmother was arrested and sent to a prison camp; only the mother was left to "preserve" the memory of the hero. But beyond the known fact of the murder of Pavlik and his brother, everything had been invented in a case which ended up with this mass execution of "kulaks."[96] A second peculiarity of the case was the part played by writers in creating the mythology of denunciation. Gorky himself assumed leadership of the campaign. He was actively involved in having a monument erected to Pavel Morozov (to show his respect Gorky always called the boy by his first name), he was also the author of a new moral law—that an intellectual relationship was far more important than a blood one—and he pressed for the widest distribution of the Morozov story. Not limiting himself to general instructions, Gorky, this great humanist and writer, made some concrete suggestions: "Pioneers ought also to get busy in the same specific conditions as recently gave rise to a quite severe decree."[97] He had in mind a law concerning the "reinforcement of the campaign to combat the theft of socialist property" of August 7, 1932, which laid down as the penalty the death sentence or, in case of mitigating circumstances, ten years in a camp. Gorky, with his tremendous influence over people's minds, demanded that Young Pioneers should join in the hunt for "plunderers," mainly their own parents.

The campaign produced results. At the first Writers' Congress the Pioneers who came to convey greetings to the "engineers of people's minds" announced with pride that "we have thousands like Pavlik."[98] Later they began to talk of "millions" of Pavliks.

Children and young people were used as the most effective instrument for breaking up the family. Through them the state became a member of every family. Literature became the most important means by which to train "state" children. The importance of literature (and of all connected fields of culture) in this business of shaping the child was underlined in a special decree of the government and of the Party Central Committee concerning "the strengthening of control over children's literature."[99]

One of the most widespread slogans of the early 1920s declared: "By destroying the family hearth we are at the same time striking the last blow at the bourgeois social order." Collectivization was at the same time the final blow to the last class that was not completely dependent on the state—the peasantry—and a blow against the "old" family, which continued to exist without a state "presence."

The late 1930s saw the beginning of a "reinforcement" of the family: new laws limited the freedom of divorce, and abortion was banned; a new Soviet morality was established yielding nothing in puritanical strictness to the morals of Victorian England. Soviet historians of the Soviet family explain the change of policy by asserting that "the masses developed ever greater intolerance towards dissolute behavior in the marriage relationship." The émigré historian I. A. Kurganov suggests that the Party took into account "the people's annoyance and extreme degree of dissatisfaction" caused by a policy aimed at "destroying the basis of the family."[100] But Soviet history bears convincing evidence that the Party takes something into account only when it sees some benefit to be derived for itself.

The Party launched its new family policy at a time when it had become obvious that the Soviet family had already arrived—that it was now the basic cell of the Soviet state. Wilhelm Reich, who dreamed of a theory uniting Marxism and Freudianism, did some careful research into the connection between the socioeconomic structure and the sexual structure of society, analyzing Nazi Germany and the Soviet Union in the 1930s. He concluded that "the authoritarian state is extremely interested in the authoritarian family, because it becomes a factory providing a model for the state structure and ideology."[101] The mistake Reich made consisted only in that he regarded the Soviet Union in the 1920s as a democratic state since sexual freedom existed there. He did not understand the purpose behind the post-revolutionary sexual revolution. But Reich's formula that "an authoritarian state of necessity needs an authoritarian family" found complete confirmation in official Soviet texts: "The country has achieved decisive successes in the construction of socialism. . . . In these conditions the possibility and necessity has arisen to raise fairly and squarely the question of the further reinforcement of the family as a cell carrying out useful social functions."[102]

Hypocritical chastity became the law of Soviet life. In 1926 the American entertainer Will Rogers, on a visit to Moscow, was amazed to discover that men and women bathed naked in the Moscow River. In fact, he called the book about his trip: *Not a Bathing Suit in Sight in Russia.*[103] In 1926 there were still some left, but there was also a freedom of manners which ten years later was regarded as a crime against the state.

The attitude toward love also changed. Intimate relations between men and women were moved well into the background, making room for intimate relations between man and the Leader, man and the Motherland. Outpourings of love for Stalin acquired a sensual, erotic character. Thus, Alexander Avdenko pours out his feelings: "I write books, I am a writer . . . It is all thanks to you, Stalin, the great educator . . . I love a girl with a new love, I continue myself in my children . . . and it's all thanks to you . . . And when the woman I love gives me a child the first word it will pronounce will be 'Stalin.' "[104] All that was demanded of Winston Smith, the central character of *1984,* was, after all, that he should betray the woman he loved and transfer his love to Big Brother. A quarter of a century before Orwell, Zamyatin described this situation in his novel *We,* in which the hero betrays the woman he loves and starts to love the Benefactor.

Stalin was the embodiment of the Motherland, and the Motherland was the embodiment of Stalin. It was not surprising, therefore, that "Soviet patriotism" aroused the same erotic feelings as the Leader did: "Soviet patriotism is a burning feeling of unlimited love, of unqualified devotion to the native land, and of the deepest sense of responsibility for its fate and for its defense, and it is born deep in the hearts of our people . . . in our country Soviet patriotism burns with a mighty flame. It carries life forward. It heats the engines of our fighting tanks, of our heavy bombers and cruisers, and it loads our weapons."[105]

Wilhelm Reich, who thought that such feelings had nothing in common with natural love for one's native land, compared them with an impotent man's erection brought about by special devices.[106] There was no place left for natural feelings alongside the inflamed, politically correct feelings for objects chosen by the state. Soviet literature played an active part in the "exposure" of personal relationships—that is, of love—as individualistic feelings that keep a man from his work and from the collective. The model of the Soviet positive hero is then Pavlik Korchagin, a paralyzed impotent, living only out of love for communism and the Party.

In a 1953 article by Vladimir Pomerantsev entitled "Concerning Sincerity in Literature"—the first swallow heralding the "thaw" of the 1960s—Soviet literature was reproached for its falseness, in particular for how it treated love as an emotion subordinated to work for the good of the state. Ilya Ehrenburg's story "The Thaw," which gave its name to the period, made a tremendous impression on readers because it was a love story dealing with this subject, which till then had been banned.[107] And with unerring intuition Vladimir Nabokov chose—out of an endless collection—two examples of Soviet erotica, the first from a novel entitled *Energy* (1932–38) by Fyodor Gladkov, a classic of Soviet literature: "The young worker Ivan grasped the drill. As soon as he felt the metal surface he became excited and his whole body started trembling. The deafening roar of the drill hurled Sonya away from him. Then she placed her hand on his shoulder and tickled the hair behind his ear. . . . It was as though an electric discharge had pierced the two young people at the same moment. He gave a deep sigh and clutched the apparatus more firmly." The second extract is from Sergei Antonov's *The Big Heart* (1957): "Olga remained silent. 'Oh,' exclaimed Vladimir, 'why can't you love me as I love you?' 'I love my country,' she said. 'So do I,' he exclaimed. 'But I also love,' Olga began, releasing herself from the young man's embrace,—'What?' he asked. Olga raised her limpid blue eyes to look at him and answered quickly: 'the Party.' "[108]

Soviet people continued falling in love, getting married and producing children. To many it seemed that the family remained the only refuge for the individual. But the state had already penetrated the family and become a fully fledged member of it and, what is more, had begun to dictate standards of behavior, to determine the nature of relationships, to give instructions and set tasks. In his *Book for Parents* Anton Makarenko proclaimed that the main difference between the Soviet and the bourgeois family is the "nature of parental power": "Our fathers and mothers are empowered by society to bring up the future citizens of our fatherland and they are responsible to society."[109] Parents are thus turned into officials carrying out the will of "society."

In 1937, the year in which the *Book for Parents* was published, the terror in Russia reached its highest point: society was smashed to pieces and completely atomized. The state then set about shaping the grains and atoms into a new organism, the Soviet collective that was to replace society. Millions of people had been arrested and had left behind at home in "freedom" millions of family members branded as "relatives of enemies of the people." In 1934 the Criminal Code established a new category of criminal, the "Ch. S.," "member of a family" of a traitor to his country, who could be punished simply for being related to an "enemy." Since anybody might turn out to be an "enemy," every man and woman was exposed to the danger of falling in love with an "enemy," or with a relative of an "enemy," or of marrying a "suspected" and potentially dangerous person.* The introduction of internal passports for town dwellers made serfs of people living in the country—the collective farmers who had no passports or right to live in towns. The possibility of marriage between a person living in a town and one living in a rural village was sharply reduced. Insuperable or virtually insuperable obstacles arose in the way of marriage between people from different towns, since permission to move from one city to another had to be noted in one's passport and was very difficult to obtain.

In pre-revolutionary Russia, as in all other countries in the world, the class distinctions and barriers dividing society were obvious, as was the possibility or impossibility of overcoming them. In the first post-revolutionary years it was easy to distinguish the line separating the proletariat, the "leading class," from the "former people" and the "deprived classes." In the 1930s the state acquired the power to name the enemy. Everybody became a potential enemy. Thus was born the Soviet way of life, the world in which the Soviet family still lives. The Soviet person knows that, as Alexander Tvardovsky wrote: "Any other love diminishes love for the father of the peoples."[110] He knows that the arrest of even a distant relative, not to mention a member of his immediate family, threatens him and his relatives with incalculable disasters.

*The law of June 8, 1934, introduced the concept of collective responsibility for members of a family: those who knew of the intentions of the "traitor" were liable to be sent to a prison camp for two to five years, those who did not know to five years' exile.

At the same time he knows that "life is better, life is gayer," because the Father-figure Stalin has said so.

In 1944, once there was no longer any doubt about an eventual victory over Germany, Stalin summed up the results of the war on the family front. A new code on the family and marriage gave expression to the certainty of the victory of the Soviet family and the Leader's faith in it as a means of transmitting the will of the Party and State. All the "freedoms" preserved from the time of the campaign against the bourgeois family were now suppressed: divorce was abolished; punishment for abortion was made more severe; the idea of the "illegitimate child" was introduced; and marriages with foreigners were forbidden. The new code gave legal force to a new hierarchy: it established an inequality in principle between men and women. It preserved, of course, the right of the woman to do all the hardest and least pleasant jobs, but the unmarried woman lost the right to demand maintenance and the right to show on a child's birth certificate the name of the father, and she was given the special label of "single mother."

This restriction of women's rights took place at a time when there was a sharp drop in the number of men, resulting from the terrible bloodletting of the war. According to the first postwar census, 15 million women either had lost their husbands or were unable to find one. Alexander Dovzhenko refers to this in his film *A Poem about the Sea*: "I don't need no palace," the young woman Christina says longingly. "No soft chairs, no pictures. None of that do I need."—"But why?"— "I'm a young wife."—"So what do you want?"—"Don't you know? I can say it openly—A man!"—it was the voice of an elderly peasant woman. "It's hard for her to sleep without a warm body beside her." The state needed these human losses to be replaced, but at the same time it displayed "concern about the strengthening of the Soviet family." Men were permitted to have children outside marriage, but for women this involved a sense of guilt of illegality which was condemned by the "collective."

This Stalinist code was modified gradually after the death of the Father of the People; abortion was again permitted; divorce with the agreement of both parties was made much easier to obtain; and the "illegitimate child" label was no longer used. The Soviet family had assumed its final form. The changes in relations within the family and between the family and the state are connected to the idea of the state as a fully-fledged family member. Some historians say that in the post-

Stalin period, particularly in the 1960s and 1970s, the family in the Soviet Union was turned for many into a fortress in which all could hide from the totalitarian state. If we accept this idea of the fortress-family, we must add to it that it was a fortress that shut the gates after the state forced its way in.

Evidence of the changes in recent decades can be seen in the change of attitude toward Pavlik Morozov. He remains a hero and a model as before, but today the "Pavlik Morozovs" are not required to inform on family members but only on "outsiders." The efforts of people in the ruling sector of society to hand down "as a legacy" their privileged social position finds expression in an unwillingness to train young people to inform on their parents. (But there have been plenty of cases of older people informing on younger ones.)

All the main features of the Soviet family in the Stalin period have been preserved into the present. The socialist family was proclaimed to be "a family of a superior kind," and the most "progressive." It was, officially, a "collective." The *Dictionary-Reference Book* concerning marriage and the family, intended for a wide readership, is categorical: "A member of a family is a participant in a family collective."[111] As in every other Soviet collective (for example, a "labor collective") the highest authority is the Party. Galich's ballad "The Red Triangle" recounts how, after discussing the question of "Freedom for Africa," a general meeting examines the case of a husband's unfaithfulness to his wife, and the final decision in the affair is taken by the district secretary of the Party. This corresponds exactly with reality: the Party's assurance of its right to decide all questions, including the most intimate ones, and the acceptance of this situation by a large number of Soviet citizens. A Party secretary depicted in the documentary film *The Way to People* says: "We have a record of the difficult families—they are all known to us."[112] ("Difficult families" are those with personal problems, conflicts and quarrels.) It is the daily practice for people to apply to the Party committee for help, advice or a solution. After *Pravda* published a letter from a woman who inquired, "Is that the way the Party organization is supposed to interest itself" in one's personal life—to establish whether he is a good father or a caring husband?—a stream of letters flooded into the editorial office, unanimously stating that "there could be no two opinions on the subject." A reviewer of the film *In Love at His Own Wish* considered that the authors of the film had raised an important question: "Should one or should one not try to control such a traditionally uncontrollable emotion as love?" He concluded that the film, which analyzes the subject "on the practical as well as the scientific level," proves that it is both possible and necessary.[113]

The shaping of the Soviet person is no easy matter: love "according to one's own wish" has not yet become obsolete and continues its advance across the Soviet Union. But efforts to control the whole person are not limited to desires and slogans. The framework of the Soviet way of life creates conditions permitting the state to interfere in the family and intimate life of its citizens.

Equality of the sexes, one of the few "achievements" of the Revolution that no one disputes, has led to one of the most amazing paradoxes of the Soviet system. The main burden of life in the USSR is borne by women, who have practically no voice in the solution of problems affecting them. In the early 1980s more than half the country's working class consisted of women, while in 1980 59 percent of women, but only 41 percent of men, had a professional education. Women do the heaviest physical work. During a visit that Yury Andropov made to a Moscow engineering plant, a women worker told the General Secretary that the workers in her shop were mainly women. "The men are not very keen on coming to work here," she explained. When Andropov asked "Why?" she replied: "It seems to them that it's very tough here, since the production process is dangerous, and they like to take good care of themselves." The finishing shop she was talking about used toxic lacquers and the polishing machines "weigh two kilograms and when in use vibrate so that your whole body shakes."[114] Women are employed mostly as textile workers, as cleaners, and on the collective farms, but they also work as teachers and doctors—poorly paid professions enjoying little prestige. All the administrative jobs, in both the cities and country, not to mention leading positions in the Party, government and economy, are virtually inaccessible to women.

"Our women suffer from equality," an anonymous woman in Moscow explained to Swedish journalists asking about the position of Soviet women.[115] Their sufferings are primarily the result of the fact that, in addition to her work in a trade or profession, Soviet woman has also to carry out all the domestic duties. "Domestic work" includes shopping for goods not to be found in the shops, preparing meals, washing clothes, and cleaning house. According to calculations by experts, the rational amount of time spent on domestic work need not amount to more than 12½ hours a week. According to official statistics the actual time expended in the Soviet Union is more than three times that.[116] Soviet economists have concluded that in 1984 275,000 million hours a year were spent on domestic work, "which is more than is spent on work for society (accounting for about 240,000 million hours)." The author of the article from which these figures are quoted is a man, and he found it necessary to add that "the lion's share of the work is borne by women."[117] In 1979, 180,000 million man-hours were spent on daily, family jobs.[118] There is no disputing the change. Plans for improving the service trades envisage the possibility of "reducing the time spent on domestic work" by 8,500 or 9,000 million hours a year.[119] The insignificance of this "planned" figure speaks for itself.

The state also determines the nature of family life when it plans the construction of new housing. Despite an improvement in the housing situation compared with Stalin's time, even the Soviet press does not conceal that "for many people the housing problem remains very acute."[120] This is partly because of recent curtailment in housing construction—"In two years of the current Five-Year Plan the amount of housing completed for occupation was 13 million square meters less than planned."[121]—but the main thing is that the state still continues to plan the housing program in terms not of rooms but of square meters. A new housing code of 1983 raised the maximum permitted area of housing per person from 9 to 12 square meters, but the minimum area, for example, in the Krasnodar region, is 6 square meters.[122] That means that a two- or three-generation family of three or four persons is obliged to live, at best, in two rooms. The promise made long ago—to give every member of a family a separate room and every family a separate flat— cannot be realized in the present century. Moreover, the promise was given to city dwellers: on the collective farms the very idea of a "separate room" does not exist. And the extremely hierarchic structure of the Soviet system has led to the creation of castes which impose strict controls over the possibility of "mixed" marriages. The new Soviet "upper class" does not allow itself to mix with the plebs. Marriages between workers and "educated" people and between collective farm workers and people living in cities are becoming steadily more difficult because of social barriers.

The state further determines the nature of family life when it lays down rules of sexual morality and controls sexual education. In his novel *We,* Zamyatin depicted the one State in which the sexual problem had been solved by the introduction of a "Lex Sexualis": "Every number has the right—as to a sexual product—to any other number."[123] The Soviet Union has not reached this level, but the material conditions of life that are destroying the family, the continuing imbalance between the number of men and the number of women (in 1979 there were 100 men to every 115 women), and the ease with which divorces are obtained (for every 1,000 marriages taking place in 1981 there were 333 divorces)[124] produce a situation which the handbook on scientific communism calls "the maturing and shaping of the new monogamy." (The handbook took into account the fact that in 1963 there was one divorce for every nine marriages.)[125]

A general looseness of moral behavior exists alongside the state's merciless condemnation of the "lack of moral standards" and "amorality," which means everything connected with sex. In the period of the "thaw," it was said that Stalin had apparently been responsible for having "the treasures of ancient sculpture classified as pornography because they were not covered with shirts and trousers."[126] A professor of anatomy who has emigrated to the United States recalls that examinations in the Moscow medical school never included questions concerning the structure of the sexual organs. Dr. M. Stern, a sexologist, saw a Soviet woman faint when she saw a magazine with pictures of naked men and women. At the same time current Soviet writing makes it clear that couples are easily unfaithful to each other. "I didn't resist," a woman confesses to her husband who has learned of her seduction by a stranger. "I didn't resist. . . . It was as though it wasn't me."[127]

For more than twenty years doctors and educationists have been campaigning to have sexual education in the schools and for the publication of popular booklets about sex. A decade ago, unsuccessful attempts were made to talk to schoolchildren on these "embarrassing" subjects. Some booklets were published, written by experts. S. Tylkin, an educationist, said in his *Chats About Love,* intended for young people, that "close relations between young boys and girls can interfere with studies." Moreover, he claimed, "The physiological aspect of love between man and woman plays a subordinate role." H. Khodakov, a psychiatrist and sexologist, states categorically in his book *To Young Couples:* "Efforts to obtain sexual satisfaction and above all an orgasm are not the most important thing in sexual life." V. Chertkov, a doctor of philosophy, defines in a booklet entitled *About Love* what does play "the principal role": "The sexual instinct, according to Marx, is humanized by the joint labor and struggle of man and woman."[128]

The presence of the state in the family extends to the most intimate aspects of life. In 1966 Aleksei Kosygin, then Prime Minister, refused in the name of the USSR to sign the United Nations charter on population which was intended to increase control over the birthrate, saying that having children was a private family matter that ought not to be subject to planning by a state or an international organization.[129] But the real reason was an unwillingness to leave family planning to the husband and wife and agree that it was a private matter. The regime's stubborn refusal to organize the production of contraceptive devices while permitting abortions is not to be explained by technical difficulties but by its wish to maintain control over people. According to doctors, a Soviet woman has on average six to eight abortions in the course of her life. This easily available and inexpensive operation, performed with a curette, as in the nineteenth century, requires preliminary registration at a hospital—i.e., it is controlled by the state.

In February 1980 a newspaper in Riga published a feature under the heading "Connections" in which advertisements could be placed by individuals seeking to meet a lonely woman or a lonely man. Talks dragged on for years about whether to set up a special service for this purpose. The objections were "ideological": sociologists claimed that in Soviet society there was no reason for people to be lonely, because "there are no class or economic barriers to prevent individuals from getting to know each other." In 1970, when the *Literary Gazette* carried out the first opinion poll among its readers, 20 percent said they were opposed to such a way of getting to know people, which they regarded as immoral. Seven years later only 1 percent of the people were opposed. The first questionnaires with the question "Do you feel lonely?" produced an unexpected reply: 35 percent of the men and 43 percent of the women replied "Yes."[130] There are descriptions in Soviet writing of instances of tragic loneliness of Soviet individuals even within the family. Male writers put the blame on women. Vasily Shukshin, one of the most talented Soviet writers of the 1960s, accused women of being excessively attached to worldly goods, to things, and of binding men down and depriving them even of such freedom as remained within the framework of state control. Pavel Nilin *(The Folly)* and Vladimir Voinovich *(Through an Exchange of Letters)* complete the picture of woman drawn by Shukshin with some picturesque strokes suggesting the complete incompatibility of men and women in the Soviet family. The woman is the custodian of the home and so becomes in the man's eyes the embodiment of the chains that he has to bear. Not having the courage to revolt against the state, he fights with his wife.

The uncensored underground ("samizdat") women's magazines that began to appear a decade ago provide further evidence of the tragic situation in which Soviet woman finds herself. Six decades after the revolution that was to have brought about their "emancipation" and given them "equal rights" and "free love," women bore witness to the real situation. There were stories of the nightmare conditions in which women have babies, of the humiliations involved in obtaining the papers necessary for an abortion, of the operation itself performed without anaesthetic ("two and as many as six women are aborted at the same time in one operating theatre. The chairs are so placed that the women can see everything that is going on opposite them"), of nursery schools in which the food intended for the children is stolen, of the five rubles a month paid, after much formality and humiliation, for maintaining an illegal child. The editors of the samizdat magazines and the authors of their articles place the blame on men, on a patriarchy that has "degenerated into a phallocracy." They argue in much the same way as feminists in the West who are fighting for their rights in democratic countries.[131]

An even more convincing explanation of the position of women in the USSR and of the causes of the war between the sexes is to be found in Valentina Ermolaeva's story "Male Walks." This Soviet writer paints a picture of women bearing the brunt of the system but suffering most of all because they receive nothing from men—no help, no sharing, no affection, and no love. She puts the way men treat women down to Soviet education, and the fact that Soviet man remains a child all his life. She asks:

How can he be a free person within himself if from his childhood he is taught only discipline? At home—don't do that, don't touch, don't dare! In the kindergarten—Fialkov, stand up straight, take your neighbour by the hand! Fialkov, what's the matter with you, lagging behind again, what have you seen there—a street, people walking—so what? Other children behave like children, but he has to stare around all the time. At school— Fialkov, just leave your imagination at home, and listen to what you are told in lessons, and do what your elders tell you! At college—Fialkov, you think you are smarter than all the others? Don't ask silly questions! We're having a colloquium, not a question-and-answer session![132]

Then Soviet man, brought up to submit to his elders, gets married and remains a capricious boy, working off on his wife all the insults and humiliations of his subordinate status. And it is only the state—the Party—that remains as arbiter, judge, and confessor.

Soviet sociologists have concluded that "the most dangerous enemy of the family today is alcoholism."[133] No one in the Soviet Union has any doubt on this score. An all-union conference on problems of Communist education found it necessary to record an important element of "Communist education": "On an average throughout the USSR the Soviet family spends every tenth ruble on spirits. In the villages up to 30 percent of a family's income goes on spirits. Every year 12–15 percent of the adult population fetches up in medical detoxification centres."[134] These are official figures, and independent researchers paint a much gloomier picture.

Soviet sociologists say that "the cause of alcoholism has not been finally established."[135] There are, undoubtedly, many causes, but one cannot fail to take note of a strange phenomenon: at a time when there is a chronic shortage of all products and goods in Soviet food shops, in both the city and country, spirits are available everywhere. The need to fulfill the sales plan in the absence of other products obliges the shopkeepers to sell as much as possible of the ever-available alcohol. It is, according to a samizdat author, "commodity number one." In 1972 the revenue from the sale of alcohol amounted to 19,000 million rubles, which was more than the expenditure on the health service and social security.[136]

Tatyana Mamonova—a Soviet feminist and one of the editors of the samizdat magazine *Woman in the USSR*—who was expelled from the Soviet Union along with two other editors, agrees that men in the USSR drink to make it easier to bear life under the Soviet system. But she adds that women live in even more difficult conditions but drink less.[137] Soviet conditions have made it possible to carry out what might be called a biological experiment. In spite of the fact that women bear an incomparably greater burden than men, the difference between the life expectancy of men and women in the Soviet Union is greater than in any other advanced country, and it is increasing. In 1968–71 the difference was nine years, in 1980 twelve years. This increase is taking place simultaneously with a general fall in life expectancy and rise in the death rate. According to official figures, in 1981 in the Soviet Union there were 10.2 deaths for every 1000 of the population, while in the United States the figure was 5.68.[138] A characteristic feature of Soviet demography is the decline in the birthrate. Officially the fault lies with women: "The fundamental reason for the decline in the birthrate in the USSR was the increase in the number of women employed in production, the result of granting women equal rights in the political, cultural and economic fields and raising their educational and cultural level."[139] But it would have been difficult to accuse women of responsibility for the sharp increase in the child death rate (according to official figures, between 1970 and 1975 the rate rose by a third), and not wanting to give the true explanation—the acute crisis in Soviet medicine caused by a reduction in the funds allotted to it, which are being spent on the army and weapons—the Soviet leaders simply gave orders that publication of statistical data on the birthrate was to cease from 1975.

Women are more law-abiding than men: in spite of the additional burden of their domestic work, there is less absenteeism among them than among men, and they tend to change their place of work less frequently. Women constitute the firm basis of the Soviet system. Their role as custodians of the home and of such moral values as are left is used by the state to keep the regime stable.

The Party affirms insistently, stubbornly, and incessantly its obligation and its right not to let a Soviet citizen slip out of sight, wherever he may be and whatever he may be doing. "Everybody knows that a man is busy at his place of work for a third of his time," the secretary of the Kropotkin district committee of the Party in Moscow wrote in *Pravda*. "The rest of the time he spends at home. But what does he do there?" The Party secretary did not agree with those who considered that "it's his own affair." He declared: "The employment of free time, a man's behaviour in everyday life and in public places . . . is a matter which concerns the whole country and demands the most serious attention on the part of the Party, Soviet, trade union and Komsomol organs."[140] The first secretary of the Party Central Committee in Belorussia announced proudly that "the Party and Komsomol committees and the ideological institutions" in the towns and regions of the republic "are trying to bring under their influence every micro-district, every block, every household, and every courtyard and to ensure that useful and rational use is being made of free time, and to find means of counteracting any deviation from the norms of Communist moral-ity."[141] Roughly half a century ago Hitler's minister of labor said the same thing: "There are no longer any separate citizens. The time has passed when everybody could do or not do what he wished."[142]

The central character in Zamyatin's *We,* a citizen of the One State identified by the number D-503 speaks with bewilderment about the past of mankind: "And is it not absurd for the state . . . to leave sexual activity uncontrolled? Who wanted it, when and how much . . . it is utterly unscientific, like animals."[143] The Soviet state has not yet suc-ceeded in establishing complete control over its citizens' sexual life, family relations, or free time. But that is not for want of trying. Resist-ance by the human material proved to be more stubborn than had been expected according to the scientific laws derived from Marxist-Leninist teaching. Nevertheless, much has been done: the Party—the state—has become a member of the family.

THE MYTHOLOGY

> . . . Myths represent the first form in which things and the universe were explained— an explanation by means of feelings and not reason.   LAROUSSE DICTIONARY

The role of myths in Nazi ideology was obvious to everybody. The main theoretical work of Nazism—along with *Mein Kampf*—was called *The Myth of the Twentieth Century.* But the part played by mythology in Soviet ideology and the place occupied by the myth in the arsenal of weapons used to form Soviet man remain unresearched. This is primar-ily because ideologists had already established the myth of the "scien-tific nature" of Marxism-Leninism and the rationality of a Soviet sys-tem founded on "the laws of history."

If we define ideology as a system providing the only possible answers to all questions, then Soviet ideology might be called a system that gives irrational and mythological replies to all questions. A collection of myths creates a magic ring around a Soviet person, blocking all the exits to the outside world. Indeed, it creates the impression that there is no outside world. As Ostap Bender, adventurer and wit, put it, "abroad" is a myth about life beyond the grave.

The myth about "abroad" makes it appear to be hell, the lair of an animal preparing to swallow up the "Soviet world," and, most important, it prevents people from seeing it as it really is. In his *School for Dictators* Ignazio Silone wrote of Don Ferranet, a Milanese philosopher of the eighteenth century, who knows that according to Aristotle there were only two categories: accidental things and essential things. Since cholera, which had broken out in northern Italy, did not fall into either of these fundamental categories, the philosopher concludes that there is no cholera—which does not prevent him from becoming infected and dying. Mythology makes it possible to believe in what does not exist and to reject what is real. The unreality of the myth makes it difficult to expose it with the aid of logic and reason. Having rejected the myth about abroad being hell, it was natural to conclude that it was heaven.

Klaus Mehnert, a young German journalist who arrived in the Soviet Union in 1932, reported with enthusiasm:

A new mythology has arisen in Russia, a mythology of the creation of the world by human hands. "In the beginning there was Chaos—capitalism. The parasites lived in luxury; the slaves were starving. Then came Marx and Lenin and Red October. After violent battles with internal and external foes and at the cost of immense sacrifices made by the chosen Russian proletariat, Chaos was cast out. Now Stalin with the Five Year Plan is building a world of order, harmony and justice, while the remaining five-sixths of the earth, as punishment for their opposition to Communist doctrine, are being smitten with the plague of world crisis and the scourge of unemployment. The nations can never enjoy peace and happiness until the Hammer and Sickle are gleaming over them as well."

On this Mehnert commented: "This mythology is simple and plain. In our myth-less and myth-hungry times it has a fascinating effect."[144]

The German visitor made a very shrewd observation. He noted that, like all myths, the Soviet myth about creating a new world also created its own moral code, "a moral code that is already accepted by millions and that is spreading from year to year in influence." The new moral code was no less simple and plain than the myth that gave birth to it: only by fighting against the whole world, which fears and hates us, can we achieve our aim; in this battle there can be no mercy either for the enemy or for our own people if they have committed some offense or shown signs of weakness. "That is a moral code for fighters," Mehnert concluded.[145]

Mehnert visited the Soviet Union fifteen years after Red October, and nearly sixty years have passed since that visit. But the myth that so impressed him has remained the foundation of the Soviet mythological system and of Soviet ideology. Also unchanged is the moral code of the fighters for a new world, the conquerors who promise mankind happiness and peace under the hammer and sickle. But the permanence of the principal myth does not mean that every single link in the magic chain keeping Soviet man in his heaven has been preserved. Just as worn-out parts of a machine are replaced, so, in the course of seven decades, the obsolete and worn-out myths that had begun to get in the way have also been discarded.

For the first time in the history of mankind an experiment lasting several generations has been carried out in creating myths—creating irrational explanations of the world and man to satisfy the regime's practical needs and replacing them if they cease to be useful or become obsolete. Carrying out this process was made possible by the possession of total power over all the instruments that shape human consciousness.

Power over myths and the right to engage in myth-creation give the Communist Party a powerful weapon for wielding authority over man and the country as a whole. To become master of the mythology the Party had first of all to kill the myth of revolution, as Zeus killed Cronos. Zamyatin was the first to point out that the first thing a victorious revolution does is to declare itself "the last revolution." Only having rejected the possibility of further change can the Party that has seized power set about constructing the new world and the New Man. It has abolished time and opened the door to utopia. In September 1934 Hitler confirmed the accuracy of Zamyatin's observation: "The revolution has brought us everything we expected from it in every single sphere. . . . There will not be another revolution in Germany for the next thousand years."[146]

The myth of revolution was replaced by the myth of the State. In the first years after the Revolution, when the leaders still believed that everything was proceeding in accordance with the laws of history as revealed by Marx, the withering away of the state was depicted as close at hand. Soon, however, the more perceptive Party leaders discovered what was for them an unexpected interconnection between the state and the Party. In 1923 Grigory Zinoviev recalled sadly "the first, military period of our revolution," when "mutual relations between the Party and the state were simple and clear. The uprising was organized by the Party. The Army was formed by the Party. It was the Party that assumed responsibility for dealing with the collapse of rail transport. The food crisis was resolved by the Party, and so forth."[147] Nothing could have been simpler or clearer—the Party was the State. But after the Civil War, questions arose and proposals were made suggesting in particular that the Party should stick to "its own Party affairs," should deal with "agitation and propaganda and not claim a monopoly over the political leadership of Russia."[148] The Party categorically rejected all such questions, proposals and doubts. For all its leaders, despite the internal strife, it was axiomatic: power belongs to the Party and the Party won't hand it over to anyone else. In the 1920s, in the period of factional fighting among the Party leaders, they realized that the withering away of the state would lead to the withering away of the Party.

It became obvious that the Party was a parasite on the body of the state. Consequently, the bigger the state, the stronger the Party. The Prussia of Frederick II was described as an army that possessed a state. The Soviet system was from the day it was born a party possessing a state.

The process of making a myth out of the state was completed in the mid-1930s when the state began also to employ a synonym—the Motherland, and when the State-Motherland acquired a Father—Stalin. The most popular song of the time said: "We love our Motherland like a bride. . . ." The official way of addressing Stalin was "Beloved Father!" During the Second World War soldiers would die with the words "For Stalin! For the Motherland!" on their lips.

The myth of the Soviet state comprised other myths: of the omniscient and omnipotent Party; of the immortal Leader embodying its wisdom and strength; of the people who have risen to a higher level of development and have, as *Pravda* put it, "begun the new, genuine history of mankind," convinced of the need to serve the State–Party–Leader.

Creation of the myth of the state made it possible to halt the advance of history and put a stop to the passage of time. The six-hundredth anniversary of the battle of Kulikovo, at which the Russians for the first time defeated the Tatars, was celebrated in 1980 and then made into a regular Soviet festival. According to the poet-laureate: "That battle marked the beginning of the great principality of Moscow and later of ancient Rus—Russia—itself. . . . this complex, multinational state, which in the long perspective of history was fated to become Lenin's birthplace, the first state of workers and peasants in the world."[149] The author of a novel called *Thy Name* permits Saint Sergei Radonezhsky, who in 1380 blessed the Moscow Prince Dmitri Donskoi before Kulikovo, to appear in a dream—six centuries later—to the secretary of the regional committee of the Party, thus underlining the mystic role played by the CPSU in the liberation of the Motherland from the Tatar yoke.[150]

Pravda is quite categorical. "Time has no power over Leninism."[151] The cessation of history after Lenin's Party seized power means not only that—as the most popular myth asserts—"Lenin lived, Lenin still lives, and Lenin will continue to live," but also that the immortality of the Leader of the Party expresses the immortality of the Party itself. After a visit by President François Mitterrand to Moscow in 1984, journalists described Konstantin Chernenko in these terms: "The General Secretary of the Soviet Party can still express himself fairly clearly; he is not obliged to read previously prepared monologues, although he does so very often even in face-to-face meetings, but an exchange of views is sometimes possible. We also assume that his brain functions normally."[152] The need to replace a Leader who had ceased to function normally would seem obvious; but there was no need to replace the mythical person who existed "by having resort again and again to the pure, inexhaustible spring from which the ideas of Ilich flow."[153] Brezhnev hit on a marvelous ritual formula for the myth of the Leader's immortality: when the renewal of Party membership cards was taking place he issued Party card No. 00000001 to Lenin. He took card No. 2 for himself.[154]

The mythical character of the Leader of the CPSU legitimizes his power, which he can use within limits determined by himself and which permits him to remain in his post even when moribund. The fall of Khrushchev was the result of a blasphemous interference with the myth of the Leader: the General Secretary's behavior was blasphemy, whereupon a conclave of priests overthrew the high priest who had meddled with the myth. The mythical nature of the power of the General Secretary explains its inviolability in moments of crisis. In the first days following Hitler's attack on the Soviet Union, when Soviet troops were suffering the most terrible losses, the high command was completely paralyzed because for at least ten days Stalin issued no orders whatsoever, shutting himself away from the world in his country house. During the years when Brezhnev, Andropov, and then Chernenko were successively ill and unable to function, Soviet policy was also paralyzed. The collective nature of the leadership means that members of the Politburo, even the most influential, have the right to say "No." Only a move by the General Secretary, the mythical Leader, makes it possible to say "Yes." For a train to move, a collective effort by a group of people, the staff of the train, is necessary. But if the driver does not switch on the engine the train remains in the station.

The People is the least concrete of the elements that make up the myth of the state. Only the state and the Party have concrete form and a real structure to do myth-creating. The people has no structure, if we exclude the state frontiers—the lock on the gates of heaven, in Khrushchev's words, which prevent the Soviet people from dissipating into mankind at large. The definition of the people is provided by expert ideologists who decide who belongs to the people and who does not. The myth of the people replaces the myth of the proletariat, the ruling class. Stalin's Constitution of 1936 abolished the myth of the proletariat as the dominant class enjoying inalienable privileges. Having abolished the privileges and having restored their rights to former "deprived persons," it realized Shigalev's dream of a country in which all were equal because all were slaves.

In the mid-1960s a new term came into use: the "all-people state" (this was a literal translation of the Nazi *Volksgemeinschaft*), the native land of the "new historical community of people, the Soviet people." According to the definition in the *Political Dictionary,* the all-people state "expresses the interests and will of all working people, of the whole people." Half a century earlier Hitler had defined the *Volksgemeinschaft* as "a genuine community of labour, a union of all interests, the rejection of individual citizenship and the creation of a dynamic, united and organized mass."[155]

The final hypostasis of the myth of the Soviet state as an "all-people state of the Soviet people" ideally fulfills the first function of the myth as defined by Larousse: it explains "things and the universe" without resorting to reason. The "all-people state" represents the highest form of democracy, of which the "initiator and main guarantor" is the CPSU.[156] The Soviet state is at one and the same time an "all-people state" in which all peoples are completely equal and a Russian state in which the Russian people are "first among equals." The Russian element is seen as the essence of what is Soviet, as the motive force behind the "civilization of socialism," the future of the world. Alexander Prokhanov, an author of political novels, sings the praises of the "burden borne by Russian Soviet man" in bringing Communism to the world. According to him: "The world is drawn towards socialism, into an inescapable, irreversible process." This is due primarily to the Russians. They live impoverished, poor, hungry lives. In the Smolensk region, in the heart of Russia, sixty-five years after the Revolution, it is impossible in the winter to travel from one village to another. But that is because the Russians have to feed the Afghans and build roads in Nigeria and Kampuchea.[157]

The Soviet press explains away the shortage of goods and the absence of roads, which is felt acutely in the Russian republic, by talking of corruption, idleness, and the luxurious life in the non-Russian republics. Yet only rarely does it report on court cases or on cases of corruption. On the occasions when it is instructed to publish some facts it usually turns out to be about corruption in the Kazakh or in the Central Asian republics, or about crimes committed by people with Jewish surnames.

According to the census of 1979, the Soviet Union included twenty-one non-Russian nations with a population of more than a million, from the 42.3 million Ukrainians to the 1 million Estonians. Together they amounted to almost half the population of the country. In the non-Russian Soviet republics the sense of national oppression and of being exploited by the Russians provides an excuse for the difficulties, shortcomings, and unsatisfactory situations. In a series of jokes that circulated in the early 1980s the main target was now—after Lenin, Radio Armenia and Chapaev—the Chukchis. Before the Revolution, according to one anecdote, the Chukchis had only two feelings—cold and hunger; now a third has appeared—deep gratitude. If one turns the point of the joke on the Russians themselves, one might say that the Soviet regime has presented them with the feeling of being part of a great state.

The myth that the Soviet state is the final product of thousands of years of Russian history perverts natural national and patriotic feelings and uses them as instruments with which to shape Soviet man. Every effort is made to ensure that in people's minds "Russian" should be identified with "Soviet" and "anti-Soviet" with "anti-Russian." Russian nationalism comes to be included in the Soviet ideological system—national feelings are assimilated, rendered harmless and replaced by substitutes. Or, as Soviet ideologists say, in conditions of developed socialism "the concepts of Fatherland and State merge."[158]

Yet the history of the last seven decades shows that feelings of nationalism have been, along with religion, important strong points making possible some resistance to the advance of Soviet mythology. That is why the state has waged and is still waging fierce warfare against the nationalisms of the non-Russian peoples, which cannot be used for the purpose of myth-making, and against those religions that are immune to being phagocytized and refuse to serve the state.

The use of Russian nationalism in Soviet ideology involves the danger of its being turned into national-socialism. Among Soviet ideologists quite a few favor such a transformation, but they are kept on a short leash, although it is sometimes lengthened enough for texts to be published that yield nothing to Nazi texts in their xenophobia. To describe what is "excessive" in lauding Russian nationalism, when defining the framework that restricts the spread of Nazi ideas, the term "anti-historicism" is used. Curiously, this term was borrowed from Nazi philosophers who disputed with Descartes, whom they accused of "anti-historical emptiness," rationalism and individualism.[159] "Anti-historicism" was declared in 1972 to be an excessive interest in Russian nationalism leading people to forget that "the question of relations between peoples . . . in such a multinational country as ours is one of the most complicated in social life." This Soviet historian, writing approvingly of the numerous instances of Russian nationalism in political writings and literature, reminded his readers that one effect of this was to strengthen "local nationalism": the Georgians sang the praises of their queen Tamar; the Ukrainian author Ivan Bilyk, "in his efforts to heap praise on the mythical Kievan Prince Bogdan Gatilo, went so far as to claim that Attila, leader of the Huns, also used that name"; the Kazakhs make a great hero out of Kenesar Kasymov, who led the war with the Russians in the nineteenth century.[160] In 1984, under an almost identical heading—"The Battle with Anti-historicism"—*Pravda* returned to the theme, reminding people again and again of the danger posed by local nationalisms, of "revanchists in West Germany who are revealing greater-Germany ambitions," and of "Zionists, who see in the Jews, in whatever part of the world they are living, representatives of the mythical worldwide Jewish nation."[161]

An important place in Soviet mythology is taken by the myth of the monolith, or unity. It is one of the most important elements in legitimizing the Soviet state, the Soviet camp and the world Communist movement. Based on the only true science, Marxism-Leninism, and knowing the laws governing the historical process, the state, the camp and the movement are always right. Every crack in the monolith, every doubt about the correctness of its direction, and every political deviation tends to undermine the very foundations of the system. The myth of the monolith is one of the factors restraining Russian nationalism from going further, as some Soviet ideologists would wish.

The conflict between the multinational nature of the Soviet state and the myth of monolithic unity is resolved by simultaneously asserting the ideas of the "all-people state" *(Volksgemeinschaft)* and of the "Russian people" as a model and as first among equals. This duality between contradictory concepts is another threat to the monolith. The regime's need for the myth of the monolith to give it legitimacy explains the acute tension in relations among national groups in all Communist countries—not only in multinational Yugoslavia or China, but also in Poland, where national minorities are an insignificant part of the population; in Bulgaria, where they deny the existence of Macedonians; in Vietnam, where they are fighting the Chinese; in Kampuchea, where they hate the Vietnamese; in Romania, where they persecute the Hungarians; and in Cuba, where "blacks" have been removed from power.

The myth of monolithic unity makes it impossible as a matter of principle for Communists to enter into stable alliances with other parties. The only experience that Lenin's party had of this (the inclusion of the Left SRs in the government) lasted six months. In Western Europe attempts to include Communists in the government have always ended in failure. Finding themselves too weak to swallow up their "allies," the Communists either leave the alliance or are driven out of it when their pretensions begin to exceed their legal possibilities.

One function of the myth of the monolith is to provide enemies. Anyone who undermines unity, threatens to destroy it, or is potentially capable of doing so is declared an enemy. At the same time every enemy is presented as a violator of unity, an enemy of the monolith. The transformation of unity into a myth turns the enemy into a mythical, irrational concept. The decision to let Jews leave the Soviet Union taken in the early 1970s was one of the most successful moves on the part of the Soviet mythmakers. In a country that nobody has the right to leave, a group acquiring that right becomes an enemy, encroaching on the "unity" and the "monolith," even if later the state makes it impossible for them to leave and even if not all of them want to. The irrationality of the enemy explains the success of the "conspiracy theory" that lies at the foundation of Soviet foreign and domestic policy. From the conspiracy of "imperialists" and the CIA to the worldwide Jewish conspiracy and the conspiracy of Freemasons which acquired special popularity in the early 1980s because of the search for motives for the attempt on the Pope's life and the exposure of the "Gelli lodge" in Italy, all "conspiracies" are regarded as attacks on the myth of monolithic unity and as a challenge to the truth that explains the world and creates the New Man.

The myth of the monolith, including as it does the myth of the enemy who tries to destroy unity, justifies any decision to go to war against those who threaten the monolith and obstruct the process of turning the whole planet into a single system and the only correct one. Bitter, unceasing warfare will end inevitably in victory because "Communism is invincible."

Another important feature is the infallible, omnipotent, and omniscient secret police. The most successful literary impression of this aspect of the mythological nature of the Soviet state can be found in the novel *Tarzan Triumphant* by Edgar Rice Burroughs, which tells the story of how Stalin, mythical Leader of mythical Soviet Russia, sends an agent of the OGPU into the jungle with orders to kill the most popular mythological figure of the twentieth century—Tarzan. The encounter between the two myths ends with the triumph of the king of the jungle. Burroughs could have ended the novel with the prophecy Tarzan lived, Tarzan lives, and Tarzan will live. But happy endings happen only in novels.[162]

The basic myths of Soviet mythology constitute the foundations of the totalitarian state. Hitler's triad—one state, one people, one Führer—is repeated in the Soviet triad of one party, one state, one (Soviet) people.

Myths are links in the magic ring in which Soviet man is born, lives, and dies. By alienating other feelings and thoughts, the myths of utopia, the all-people state, the monolith and the inevitability of the victory of communism lay mines under the exits from the magic circle. Nationalism becomes an instrument for arming the mighty state: religion—mainly well-organized religions—are made into channels for the prevailing ideology; the family, of which the state has become a member, ceases to be a refuge from the collective. Leszek Kołakowski has rightly pointed out that the Soviet state combats religion not because it is an atheistic state, but because it is a totalitarian one.

Klaus Mehnert, one of the very few foreigners to travel in the Soviet Union in the early 1930s, had a good knowledge of Russian. His description of the atmosphere during the period of the first Five-Year Plan is interesting because, when he talked to young Russians, the "country's elite," he never stopped thinking about what was going on in his own country, and continually compared the Soviet experiment with what might happen in Germany. "In the eyes of Soviet young people," he reported, "the two elements—'socialist' and 'national'—merge into one." He explained in very simple terms his enthusiastic conclusion: the Revolution "has eliminated the class—relatively small by comparison with the size of the nation—the parasitic class, which had moreover become very degenerate," as a result of which even by 1932 the words "I" and "my" had been rejected in favor of "we" and "our." "A new conception of the world has been born in which the question of personal happiness and satisfaction has ceased to play a part," and in particular "for Russian young people the problem of religion has disappeared." In short, "the general line [of the Party] has become the generally accepted truth."[163]

Mehnert believed what he wrote and was convinced that everyone in the USSR believed as he did. It happened at the same time as, in a letter to Andrei Bely, Boris Pasternak was writing of his horror at finding that the "phantasmagoria" conceived by Dostoevsky and Bely had been "overtaken by reality" and that it was impossible to tell "what is a copy and what is the real thing."[164] But Mehnert had grounds for believing what he did, for he was meeting people who believed in what they were doing and intended to do.

Stalin's death in 1953 separates the "era of faith" from the subsequent period of confusion, doubts, the awakening of dissidence and the eventual return to the mainstream of "developed," "mature" and "advanced" socialism and of what Pravda calls a "socially homogeneous society," in which "the integrity of standard views" was confirmed.[165] But in the process of overcoming doubts that arose as a result of the death of the Father and Teacher, the faith and enthusiasm of youth which had been so admired by foreign visitors in the 1930s and which had been revived in the war years, were lost. Irreparable mistakes were made. In the first days following Stalin's death the myth of the infallibility of the secret police was refuted—the doctors who had been arrested on charges of organizing a "Jewish plot" were set free: in 1956 the myth of the infallibility of the Leader was destroyed by Khrushchev with his speech denouncing the "cult of personality"; in 1964 a palace revolution was carried out, removing Khrushchev, First Secretary of the Central Committee and the man who had destroyed the calm. The calm was restored, but the faith had gone forever. The steel and concrete framework that had supported the system's mythological structure became a ritual: political and everyday rites.

Soviet scholars of religion argue that there are two basic components of religion: religious consciousness and religious ritual, to which correspond the believer's religious experiences, revealed to him in his thoughts about religion; and his religious behavior, which finds expression in the observance of ritual participation in the world of religious organizations, and the preaching of religious views. If we replace the word "religious" with the word "Soviet," the formula can be regarded as an excellent definition of the demands made today on Soviet man. He can believe in communism—nobody will stop him doing that, although the open preaching of communist views tends to arouse suspicion. Soviet man is expected to observe rituals or, as the scholars say, "to carry out certain religious acts."[166] Carrying out the rituals is obligatory, irrespective of one's opinion of them. As Ernst Neizvestny, one of the best authorities on the Soviet system, writes: "The personal views of an official may be thoroughly opposed to the official line, but this has no political effect—that is his night-time conscience. It is what he says on the platform that has political weight."[167] The same thing applies to every Soviet person, because everybody is an official serving the state in some job or other.

Ritual and the strict observation of the rites close the magic circle that surrounds the Soviet person. The rites can be divided into two categories—political and social—but their significance is identical and they perform the same function. Each rite—voting at a meeting, signing a letter to a newspaper to expose an "enemy," applauding at the right time, as well as seeing that the width of your trousers or the length of your skirt is the same as everybody else's—is a sign of your devotion, loyalty, and indestructible links with the State, the Motherland, the Party and the Collective. The rites create a system of signs to escape from which is a political offense. The unknown author of the most remarkable words of the Stalin era, the warning always issued by guards to prisoners—"a step to the right or a step to the left is treated as an attempt to escape and the guard shoots without warning"—defined brilliantly and precisely the function of Soviet ritual.

The history of the dissident movement in the Soviet Union can be told as the history of an attempt to break out of the magic circle and to disturb the ritual. A Soviet person became, or did not become, a dissident or a renegade according to whether he decided to vote "for" or "against" or simply abstain or to sign a letter condemning or protesting something. Alexander Solzhenitsyn recounts in his *Gulag Archipelago* the true story of a Communist who was arrested for having been the first to stop applauding a reference to Stalin, after eleven minutes of stormy applause. Don't ever be the first to stop applauding, the investigator told him. In his novel about the "historic schism" between Moscow and Tirana, the Albanian author Ismail Kadare, who took a strong dislike to Soviet "revisionists" and was a great admirer of the true Marxist Enver Hoxha, tells an entirely credible story—that in the intervals between sessions in the Kremlin, after speeches by Stalin, the delegates to a congress were offered buckets of salt water in which to bathe their hands, swollen from clapping.[168]

Solzhenitsyn's appeal to people "not to live by the lie" can also be regarded as an appeal to break out of the magic circle and to stop observing Soviet rites. Everybody behaves in the same way and consequently everybody thinks in the same way and remains in the ranks of the collective. At the end of a working day Ernst Neizvestny stood in front of the offices of the Central Committee and watched people leaving—the "leaders" and "the country's brains." And he says he discovered, to his great surprise, that he was looking at a "monotonous, well-fed herd. The people walking past me all looked exactly the same, with all marks of individuality erased. Differences in weight and height were of no significance."[169]

It is perfectly obvious that, if "the country's brains" are so indistinguishable from one another, the people who inhabit the country, ordinary Soviet citizens, have no right to stand out, to "take a step to one side" or to "break away from the collective." Unification, or what the Nazis called *Gleichschaltung,* may lead to a revolt, but it usually produces boredom, an acute form of discontent with one's situation. Ostap Bender, the adventurer and hero of satirical novels written in the early 1930s—an appealing but rather negative character—had the audacity to announce: I have recently found myself to be in disagreement with the Soviet regime: it wants to build socialism, but I find building socialism boring. This was in 1931, at a time when it could still appear amusing. Yury Alexandrov, a driver who had been made chairman of his trade union in the settlement where he lived on the shores of the Arctic Ocean, was given a ticket to go on a trip round Europe. When he reached Paris he decided to stay there—he "chose freedom." When asked his reasons for doing so, he replied that he found it very boring living in Russia.[170] The Leningrad prima ballerina Natalya Makarova, who was able to enjoy all the good things of Soviet life, also decided to stay abroad, giving the same reason as the driver—boredom.[171] Sergei Muir, a professor of biology, who succeeded in obtaining permission to emigrate, explained: "Here in the United States I have gained the degree of freedom that I lacked in the USSR—the freedom not to get involved in games I'm not interested in."[172] He refused to take part in the rituals.

Soviet psychologists admit that "in conditions of standardization of work in production and in everyday life there arises an increasing demand for the unusual and the non-standard."[173] But they regard that "demand" as a breach of the framework of Soviet life, a violation of the ritual. Strict conformity is the ideal. In the textbook of social psychology used at Lumumba University in Moscow, which trains revolutionaries for the "third world," conformism is defined as "conduct which accords fully with the norms, values and opinions and spirit of the group." As an example of "nonconformism" the textbook cites "petit-bourgeois anarchism," which "reflects a tendency on the part of the individual to set himself against the demands of the group, even if they are reasonable and accepted by the majority of the group's members."[174]

Strict observance of the ritual can lead to a loss of personality and its merging with the collective. An effect of "ritualistic training" is a lack of desire to choose or to take independent decisions. Khrushchev recounts in his memoirs how he frightened Malenkov by telling him that he was going to submit to Stalin a draft plan the Leader had not asked for. "What on earth are you doing?" Malenkov exclaimed in horror, pointing out that the Leningrad leaders had been arrested for displaying "independence"—for organizing a fair without permission.[175]

On the night of June 22, 1941, Soviet commanding officers did not issue the order to fire on the Germans even after war had broken out, because they were waiting for permission "from above." That was, one might say, in Stalin's day. But Neizvestny tells the story of two Soviet officers who were arrested in 1969 after having on their own initiative given orders to fire on Chinese who crossed the Soviet frontier. Only after the order came from Moscow to resist the Chinese were the officers freed and made Heroes of the Soviet Union. There can hardly be any doubt, therefore, that in 1983 the order to shoot down the Korean Air Lines plane flying over Soviet territory came "from above"—no Soviet person at a lower level, even with the rank of general, would have dared to take the initiative.

The fine dialectical distinction between faith and ritual (in his book *The Captive Mind* Czesław Miłosz used the Persian word *Ketman* to signify the dialectic that contributes to the self-enslavement of a writer) permits the Soviet state to overcome the difficulties that result from "standardization of perception," i.e., the obligation to observe the rituals. The difficulties are caused by the raising of the average level of education, the effect of new forms of communication technology, and a definite improvement in the standard of living in the 1960s. There is every reason to assert that alcoholism is regarded by the Soviet leaders as a lesser evil compared with the tension that would develop if there were no vodka. Alcoholism has become an important rite bearing witness to a person's attachment to the collective. In 1980 the Soviet Minister of Health declared to a journalist: "We are glad that statistics show an increase in the number of people suffering from the effects of alcohol," and explained his remark by saying that the doctors had begun to "identify the sufferers more intensively."[176] The Minister did not, of course, produce secret statistics, but according to the reckoning of an American scholar, the number of people who died of alcoholism in the Soviet Union in 1976 was a thousand times greater than in the United States and consisted mainly of adult able-bodied males.[177] In 1982 the *Literary Gazette* reported that research in schools in Perm had revealed that 31.2 percent, nearly one in three, of the pupils of the first to third classes (7–9 years) had tried drinking spirits; as a rule it was the parents who had offered their children alcohol—thus preparing them for life in the Soviet collective.[178]

Conducting a bitter battle with the "temptations of the West"—American music and jeans—the Soviet state does everything it can to establish its control over the use of "forbidden goods." Soviet figure-skaters have permission to dance to the latest Western tunes, and since figure-skating is a favorite Soviet sport, people can listen to that music on television; after long years of battle against jeans the Soviet Union purchased a factory for manufacturing these "subversive" trousers in Italy. Writers, artists, musicians, and film directors are permitted, in specific circumstances, to depart from the doctrinal norms on condition that they strictly observe the ritual. This was why Dmitri Shostakovich signed letters condemning people he admired and why Chingiz Aitmatov never fails to write approvingly in the papers about everything the Soviet state does.

Permission has been given in recent years to "liven up" the unbearably boring quality of Soviet writing by the use of Soviet erotica. But when writers began to be carried away and seemed as if they might go beyond what was considered proper, a warning article appeared in the press. Its author admitted that "only about twenty years ago" such an article could not have been written "because of the lack of material." Now there was more than enough. He quoted dozens of examples from novels and stories published in magazines in 1981. A typical example: "His eyes slid down the cleavage of her dress, seeking to catch a glimpse of her breasts with their blue veins and long brown nipples." The most frequent erotic subject was a man catching sight of a woman undressing, bathing or taking her clothes off in front of a mirror. Reminding his readers of the influence art had on people's behavior, the author of the article was upset by the numerous scenes of marital infidelity he came across. He agreed that "one has also to write about *that*" (author's italics) but insisted on the necessity of sparing the nerves of the Soviet reader and not arousing him excessively with "fresh-frozen strawberries."[179]

The article evoked a great number of letters from readers, most of whom agreed with the author. But one reader asked a reasonable question: if an author wanted to write a novel about the starting up of a rolling mill, could he manage this without "livening up" the subject if he wanted the novel to be read?[180] The question can be framed differently: if a publisher who has commissioned a novel about a rolling mill wants people to pick it up and read it, can he fail to permit some "livening up"? The answer is the same in both cases.

Great use is made of "livening up" in the relatively few Soviet novels about "life in the West," which are always entrusted to reliable authors. There is a tremendous interest among Soviet readers in how the "old world" is disintegrating while "positive" Soviet heroes look with revulsion on the degradation, recalling nostalgically the joyful, healthy life they enjoyed back in their native land. When he finds himself in the rotten West, a Soviet person—in the pages of Soviet writing, at any rate—does not forget to observe the rituals. In Paris, for example, there are three places which the real Soviet man is obliged to visit—the Père Lachaise cemetery, Lenin's flat on Rue Marie-Rose, and the Place Pigalle, so as to see with his own eyes how enslaved women are exploited.[181]

At the end of the 1950s Soviet ideologists returned to the post-revolutionary idea of creating new rituals, and a campaign was started to "introduce a new non-religious ceremony."[182] In 1964 the first nation-wide conference on socialist ceremonial was held, and fifteen years later a second conference-seminar took place. Remarkable successes have recently been achieved in developing a "theory of socialist ceremonials," in "ritual creation," declared to be "a matter of state importance."[183]

Soviet man is beset on all sides by rituals, like a wolf surrounded by hunters. All his actions have been given a ceremonial character: there are festivals to celebrate the winter, the summer, the harvest, plowing the first furrow, opening new factories, victory in a competition, getting married, receipt of the first passport, meetings with cherished foreign guests, elections to the Soviets, and the "red Saturday" when everyone has to go to work. Moscow saw the birth of the ritual visit to the Mausoleum—astronauts go there before a flight, newlyweds after their weddings, and young Pioneers to take their oath of allegiance.

In the 1960s the Soviet Union "invented" the idea of the eternal flame on the grave of the Unknown Soldier, and in the many towns where it was introduced it also became a place of pilgrimage for Pioneers and young couples. The decoration of many citizens with orders, medals and titles was yet another ceremony. In old photographs of writers it was impossible to tell by their appearance who was the better artist—Turgenev or Dostoevsky, Gogol or Belinsky. Today, photographs give the necessary information—the best is the one with the most medals on his jacket. At the second conference on socialist ceremonial there was much satisfied talk of success in the construction of monuments. They were being put up everywhere: on the Mamaev hill at Stalingrad in memory of the victory over Hitler; on the field of Kulikovo, in memory of the victory over the Tatars; in Yasnaya

Polyana, to record Lenin's happy exile there. Like the sect of hole-makers, who believed that it was sufficient to bore a hole in the ceiling of a cottage to pray to the ubiquitous god, so Soviet "ritual-makers" assume that every Soviet monument will evoke in Soviet man the correct conditioned reflex—a prayer of thanksgiving, even if sub-conscious—to the Soviet state.

Some of the new rituals are supposed to replace religious festivals and they are timed to coincide with the old ones. Instead of Christmas there is the Festival of Winter, and instead of Whitsun the Festival of the Russian Birch.[184] Similar "ritual-making" takes place in the non-Russian republics, and the general tendency is to create new festivals and ceremonies out of elements of pre-Christian, pagan rituals. Taking advantage of this tendency, the Latvians managed with great difficulty to keep their "Ligo" festival (St. John's Day), arguing that it was an "anti-Christian, anticlerical and plebeian festival."[185] In Tadzhikistan they succeeded in preserving the traditional festival of the Muslim spring new year, "Nauruz," on the grounds that it was "a festival of the Magi, fire-worshippers—a pre-Muslim festival."[186]

The campaign against religion plays a secondary role in "socialist ritual-making." The main task is to affirm the Soviet myths. The Festi-val of Soviet Youth organized in the Ukraine on the traditional Ivan Kupala day repeated all the ritual of the ancient festival, but, at the end, "high in the sky above the lake an enormous red flag was unfurled with words in gold letters: Long Live Communism!"[187] It is impossible to think of a more eloquent example of substitution.

"Ritual-making" has become organized, planned, and bureaucratic. Every republic had its Commission on New Ceremonies and Festivals, like the congregations in the Vatican. They employed ethnographers, sociologists and ideologists. It has not mattered that, in order to attract people to the "new festivals," plenty of liquor was put on sale, or that during elections some much sought-after sausage could always be found near the polling-booths: what mattered was to accustom people to the new rituals, to create the habit and draw them into the magic circle of Soviet mythology. Lévi-Strauss has noted that a freedom which people often especially value is the possibility of remaining true to customs, traditions, and small privileges inherited from a distant past.[188] To produce a substitute for those customs and traditions not only deprives a person of his freedom but can often create the false illusion that he has retained them.

I want the pen to be on a level with the
bayonet.   MAYAKOVSKY

12

Culture

It is dangerous to mention some wishes out loud—someone
might hear you. Half a century after the great poet of the Revolution
voiced his wish, his metaphor became an axiom of socialist culture.
"Good writing was ever the sharpest weapon in the struggle for the
triumph of Marxist-Leninism, in the ideological confrontation between
the two world systems," declared a 1982 decree of the Central Committee of the CPSU. Not long before he died, Yury Andropov also reminded people in the worlds of art and literature of their "responsibility
for seeing that the powerful weapon they have in their hands serves the
cause of the people, the cause of Communism." For their part, people
involved in Soviet cultural affairs are thoroughly in agreement with the
notion that they hold a weapon in their hands. Alexander Prokhanov,
a prolific author of political novels who has recently become well
known, brought Mayakovsky's metaphor up to date, saying that
"today's artist or writer should really be like . . . a gun." Another writer,
Yury Bondarev, after having received the highest Soviet decoration and
the title Hero of Socialist Labor, which means he has been made a
classic in his lifetime, declared: "I am a soldier. I was one then, when

I shouldered a rifle, and I remain one now—a soldier of our Party which promotes the great idea of Communism."[1]

The central character in a play by the Nazi dramatist Hans Jost speaks one of the most remarkable sentences of the twentieth century: "When I hear the word culture I reach for my gun."[2] These words are often interpreted as an expression of hatred for culture. Actually Jost's hero drew the revolver of Nazi culture to kill non-Nazi culture. The task the Nazis set themselves after coming to power consisted in creating the kind of culture they needed, in turning culture into a weapon of their regime. The men who created the Nazi culture of the bayonet, above all Goebbels, made extensive use of the experience of creating a new culture in the Soviet Union. Goebbels' assertion that true art is inspired by the people and intelligible to the people was essentially a repetition of Lenin's famous statement concerning the need for art "intelligible to the popular masses."[3] Goebbels declared: "Freedom of artistic creation is guaranteed by the New Reich. But the extent to which it is used must be clearly determined by our needs and our sense of responsibility for the nation, the limits of which are set by politics and not by art."[4] This was a translation into the Nazi language of Lenin's basic idea concerning the "Party's control of literature," which is expressed today in the slogan "The Party leads"—"the Communist party's supervision of creative work and the Party's Leninist policy assist the writer to make the historically correct choice."[5] The novelist Mikhail Alexeev, one of the leaders of the Union of Soviet Writers, showed surprising honesty when he translated the "theoretical" formulas into everyday language. Referring to *And Quiet Flows the Don* and the films *Chapaev* and *The Cruiser Potemkin,* he announced: "If such masterpieces can be produced in conditions of non-freedom, then long live 'non-freedom.' "[6]

The history of Soviet culture is still waiting to be researched properly. Everything written so far treats Soviet cinema, music, and graphic art by analogy with the art of non-Soviet countries and peoples, of the pre-1917 history of mankind. Mayakovsky's posthumous fate offers the most compressed example of the nature of Soviet culture. At a meeting held in 1983 to mark the ninetieth anniversary of his birth, seats on the platform were occupied by Stalin's successors, members of the Politburo headed by Geidar Aliyev, for many years head of the KGB in Azerbaidjan and an art-lover; speeches about Mayakovsky were made by poets of no talent but holding important posts in the writers' organization, and they drew attention only to those of Mayakovsky's works that could be used as a "bayonet." Bringing the celebrations to a close, a cadet from the Lenin Military-Political Academy spoke of the "tremendous role played by Mayakovsky's poetry in patriotic education and ideological training of the young defenders of our Motherland."[7]

The creation of a new world requires the creation of a new man. The creation of a new culture requires a creator of a new type. Alexei Tolstoy has offered an excellent explanation of the difference between the old and the new: in the old days, he explained, they said that writers ought to seek the truth, but in the Soviet Union private individuals do not spend their time seeking the truth, because the truth has been revealed by four geniuses and is preserved in the Politburo; the task consists rather in cultivating a new type of artist who would not only be content with the knowledge that Marx-Engels-Lenin-Stalin had found the truth once and for all but also agree to receive, like a food ration, doses of the truth released by the Politburo. In order to get this new kind of artist the Party decided to become its co-creator and penetrate into the genes of art.

The history of Soviet culture is the history of its nationalization, which opened the door to this co-authorship, and the history of its transformation into weaponry for the regime. This was a previously untrodden path, and for the first few years the Party had to feel its way and to overcome, among both Party officials and writers and artists themselves, the old ideas about culture, art and literature. Very soon after the Revolution the Party found the instrument it needed for this task: the decree of the Central Committee of the Party. From the very first in 1922, dealing with young writers, to a decree of 1984, which set the current tasks for the film industry, the basic feature remains the same—the conviction that the Party knows what, how, and when. In the first decrees this knowledge of the truth is expressed cautiously, but from 1932 on it has been proclaimed crudely, brazenly, and categorically.

The decrees and directives issued by the Party, based on a conviction that the Party knows the truth and on a system of censorship introduced only ten days after the Revolution, has grown over the decades into a gigantic apparatus that controls every single word that is printed or spoken, from novels to the labels on matchboxes. Their practical basis is a nationalization of all the tools the artist or writer uses to produce his work, but that is only one factor in the system of co-authorship. The other has been the willingness of people concerned with cultural matters to accept the Party as a colleague. Artists, writers, and filmmakers certainly did not understand what they were doing, since the Party leaders themselves did not fully understand what was happening. Some artists thought they were serving the Revolution; others felt the need to be protected from proletarian writers who were trying to produce "state art."

In 1922 "a group of artists regarded as realists decided to approach the Party and inform it that we are placing ourselves at the disposal of the Revolution and wish the Central Committee of the Party to indicate to us artists how we should work."[8] In 1925 the most important writers of the period wrote to the Central Committee and asked it to come to their defense, promising to serve the Soviet regime loyally. In 1928 the leading Soviet non-party film directors, including Eisenstein and Pudovkin, wrote to a "party conference on the cinema" requesting it "to establish a rigid ideological dictatorship" and a "planned ideological leadership" in the cinema. They asked to be given a "red kulturnik," "a governing body that should be primarily a political and cultural body linked directly with the Central Committee of the Russian Communist Party [Bolsheviks]."[9]

Less than ten years passed before the two tendencies came together. There emerged the "new spirit of the new slavery," which the Marxist critic P. Kogan urged writers to create. The playwright Vladimir Kirshon put this confession into the mouth of a character of his play *Bread:* "The Party . . . is a ring, an iron chain that unites people. . . . The chain sometimes hurts the body, but I can't live without it." It turns out to be impossible to create without the Party. The joint authors Ilf and Petrov asserted that it was not sufficient to love the Soviet regime: it was essential that it should love us. Alexander Dovzhenko agreed: for him "the genuine artist of the country" was not the one with talent or even genius dedicated to the cause of the Revolution, the working class, and the advance of socialism, but the one who said "yes."[10]

The collaboration between artists and the regime took various forms. Lenin, who understood very well the idea of culture as a weapon, limited himself to general instructions. He had no time for details and in any case was not very interested in cultural matters. As Mark Aldanov has pointed out, he concerned himself with culture as German officers spent time on the Russian language—enough to get to know the enemy. But Stalin understood co-authorship in the literal sense. He collaborated directly with leading people in all forms of artistic creation. In 1933 A. Afinogenov, following the tremendous success of his play *Fear*, sent Stalin the manuscript of a new play called *The Lie*. Having studied it, Stalin wrote to him: "Comrade Afinogenov! The idea behind the play is very promising, but the actual writing of it is not successful." At the playwright's insistent request the Leader set about improving the writing, striking out some lines and substituting others.[11] The film producer Grigori Alexandrov recounts that, having seen his latest film, Stalin announced that it was "good," but offered some criticisms of the title; some time later Stalin sent the producer "a sheet of paper with twelve titles to choose from," thus confirming his attachment to the idea of freedom of creation—the producer was given the opportunity to make his own choice out of the various titles proposed by Stalin. In the end he apparently chose the first, *The Bright Path*, and it was under that title that the film came to be a favorite with the Soviet public.[12] Dmitry Shostakovich tells the story of how, when Stalin came to the conclusion that "The Internationale" should be replaced by a new national anthem, and, after he had listened to a good number of new melodies submitted, he decided that the best thing would be for Shostakovich and Khachaturian jointly to write a new anthem. Shostakovich describes this as the "stupidest" idea, but it was only by chance that the Leader and Co-Author's order was not carried out.[13]

Stalin's successors adopted a less personal way of ruling the cultural world. Still, Khrushchev did gather writers, artists and filmmakers together in 1962 and 1963 not only to criticize them and praise them but also to tell them what and how they had to write or to sculpt. He was particularly sharp in his criticism of the Soviet theatre, which wanted to put on the plays of Shakespeare, who was, in the opinion of the First Secretary, "out of date." Brezhnev was the first of the Leaders to venture into the field of belles-lettres, putting his name to three booklets of reminiscences that were declared a major achievement in Russian prose-writing and were awarded the Lenin Prize for literature.

Irrespective of whether he is personally involved in the production of literary or other works, and of his own cultural level,* the leader of

---

*Neizvestny called Khrushchev the most uncultured person he had ever met, but he appears not to have known Khrushchev's successors personally.

the Party is the supreme authority on all cultural matters, because it is his duty as the high priest, as laid down in the ritual, and because the criterion of talent in Soviet culture has been replaced by the idea of "ideological content." Brezhnev's "trilogy," written by professional ghost writers, was no worse in quality than the average of Soviet writing awarded the Lenin Prize.

Béla Balazs, a Marxist aesthetician, took the view that "every animal likes what it finds useful, and that aesthetic taste is an attempt by an intelligent being to defend itself," and went on to proclaim: "Class taste is an organ of the class instinct for self-preservation. Taste is ideology." The conclusion is simple: "In an advanced socialist society the degree of talent displayed by an artist is measured by his ideological grasp, the clarity of his philosophical views and his public spirit." When *Pravda* wanted to urge artists and writers to fulfill the demands of the latest plenum of the Central Committee it headed a lead article on the subject "Ideology and Talent." Praising the latest officially approved work of Soviet literature, a reviewer stressed: "It is remarkable that in Kuranov's novel you keep coming across references to the tasks laid down in the country's Food Program. This says a great deal about the author's awareness of social problems."[14]

The process of transforming culture into Soviet culture began in the 1920s. Shostakovich recounts a story that was going the rounds in those days: Mayakovsky published poems regularly in *Komsomolskaya Pravda,* and when the poems failed to appear for several days one of the Soviet leaders phoned the newspaper to find out what had happened. He was told that Mayakovsky was out of town. So let Mayakovsky's deputy write them, came the leader's order.[15]

The transformation of culture means the transformation of the artist and writer, of his place in society and of his relationship to reality and culture. People active in the world of art and writing were offered the choice—surrender or perish. "The basic literary problem of the period is how to be a writer," wrote B. Eikhenbaum, and he concluded poignantly, "In our days the writer is a grotesque figure."[16] Eikhenbaum was right, but only if his formulation of the issue was completed. The problem was that the writer had to choose whether to remain a writer or to become a Soviet writer. The image of the writer became grotesque when it was squeezed out by that of the victorious Soviet writer, the Soviet artist. Osip Mandelstam put the alternatives in brilliantly compressed form: "Hat in hand or hat in sleeve." Hat in hand meant being like a servant; hat in sleeve meant being sent to prison, to a camp, to death.

Art can mirror reality or it can create a world of its own. But now a third, Soviet art emerged that was supposed to perform as an instrument, a weapon in the struggle to create a "new world" and a "new man" that would rise as a product of the Party's efforts. This transformed culture emerged slowly; the attributes of traditional art, traditional genres and styles, were at first preserved, but from the second half of the 1920s at an ever increasing speed the innovative forms of art— "degenerate art," as the Nazis called them, or "decadent bourgeois art," as Soviet critics said—were banished from the world of culture as having served their purpose. The idea of genuine talent was gradually excluded from cultural affairs, although there were still talented artists in all fields of literature, cinema, theatre, and graphic arts. But their talent did not help them; it was more likely to hinder them. In public statements they defended themselves and tried to explain away or distort what they had done. The film producer Lev Kuleshov announced: "To make good films you have to observe what is fundamental, and that is that art must serve the Party."[17] The model Soviet writer was Gorky, whose emergence in Russian literature Eikhenbaum has explained by the growing "need for bad writing." It was Gorky who introduced the lie into Soviet culture as the basis of style. In a concluding speech at a writers' congress, in the presence of many West European writers, Gorky asserted that in the capitalist world "any day of the week a book written by an honest writer can be burned in public—in Europe the writer suffers ever more keenly from pressure by the bourgeoisie and fears the rebirth of mediaeval barbarism which would probably not exclude the introduction again of the Inquisition for dealing with heretical thinkers." Gorky spoke those words in August 1934, three months before the murder of Kirov which marked the beginning of the period of the Great Terror that, among its millions of victims, took the lives of thousands of people from the world of culture.[18]

By the early 1930s the nationalization of culture was completed and culture became, as in N. Erdman's play *The Suicide,* "a red slave in the proletariat's harem." The play was written in 1928; a few years later one would have had to speak of the harem of the Party and Comrade Stalin himself.

In *The Captive Mind,* one of the very first accounts of the Sovietization of culture, Czesław Miłosz has written: "People in the West are inclined to consider the fate of these peoples only in terms of compulsion and the use of force. Apart from ordinary fear and the desire to save oneself from deprivations and physical destruction, there is also a longing for internal harmony and happiness."[19] Miłosz had in mind Polish culture which, as recent decades have shown, has turned out to be remarkably resistant to Sovietization. Russian culture, which was the first to come under attack, surrendered to repressive measures, administrative pressure and the effect of fear, but also because of the temptations offered by the myths and the promise of power.

Gorky opened the first congress of Soviet writers with the words: "We speak up as the judges of a world doomed to perish."[20] The role of "judges of the world" proved to be unusually attractive. In 1922 Sergei Tretyakov proclaimed: "The worker in art must stand side by side with the scientist as a psycho-engineer and a psycho-constructor."[21] Ten years later his futurist dream was realized: Andrei Zhdanov, secretary of the Central Committee, informed the Congress of Soviet Writers:

> Comrade Stalin called our writers "engineers of human souls." What does that mean? . . . It means . . . that they have to depict life not in a scholastic or lifeless way nor simply as "objective reality," but to depict reality in terms of its revolutionary advance. In so doing truth to life and historical accuracy in literary works must be combined with the task of the ideological transformation and training of the working people in the spirit of socialism. . . . This method . . . we call the method of socialist realism.[22]

The "judges of the world" and the "engineers of human souls" were given a law on the basis of which to make their "judgments." It rejected reality and truth and replaced them with a decision of the supreme authority as to what did and did not correspond to "reality in terms of its revolutionary advance," and what was or was not suitable for use as an instrument for "transforming and training." The law defined ethics and aesthetics. In one of Kipling's stories Adam draws two lines on the ground and the devil who witnesses this says: that's very nice, but is it art? After the imposition of the method of socialist realism all doubts disappeared: art was whatever the supreme authority declared to be art. This law acquired absolute force wherever the arms of socialist art could reach. Luis Buñuel relates how the French Communist

Party decided that his film *Los Olvidados* was bourgeois and unworthy of attention. By chance Pudovkin saw it and wrote an enthusiastic review of it for *Pravda;* whereupon the French Communist Party's attitude to the film changed the very next day.[23]

When Gorky said at the writers' congress, "We are judges of the world," and when Zhdanov said, "We call this method the method of socialist realism," their "we" referred to quite different sets of people. Gorky was talking about writers, while Zhdanov was referring to leaders. At the first congress of Soviet writers (to be followed by congresses of filmmakers, artists and musicians) the writers were included for the first time in the *nomenklatura*. They, followed by everybody working in the field of culture, gave an "iron pledge" to serve the Leader, the Party and the State, and in return they were allotted a place in the hierarchy of power. The number of writers who were not admitted to the congress because there were doubts about their willingness to serve can be counted on the fingers of one hand—A. Platonov, Mikhail Bulgakov, Osip Mandelstam, Anna Akhmatova and N. Zabolotsky.

Ernst Neizvestny has provided a vivid description of the top echelon of the Soviet leadership. In the crowd of people, "the brains of the country" leaving the offices of the Central Committee, at the end of the working day, all looking as alike as chickens in an incubator, Neizvestny, studying them closely, discovered two different species: he gave them different colors, distinguishing "reds" from "greens." The "reds" are the ones who take the final decisions, always irreproachable, because "according to the laws of society they cannot make a mistake." The "greens" are those who have the job of turning the mumbling of the "reds" into intelligible language. They have to guess what the "reds" want and formulate it in such a way that the collective brains recognize the language as their own, as though the "reds" had written it.[24]

The "green" category includes the court researchers—assistants, ideologists and philosophers—who compose the "theoretical" tracts for the leaders who want to have their multivolume "works" published, and prominent cultural figures who are also leaders in the unions of writers, artists, filmmakers, and musicians. Pre-revolutionary Russia knew nothing like this; the fact that some writers belonged to the aristocracy was a purely personal affair. Pushkin or Tolstoy were known in court circles not primarily as writers but as representatives of the hereditary nobility. Soviet writers, however, are included in the *nomenklatura* not on a personal basis but as representatives of a special service class. The peculiarity of this position is a result of the totalitarian nature of the state they serve. The state is the only client disposing of all the material resources necessary for artistic creation; it is also the only censor; and it is the supreme authority determining the limits of what is permitted and the source of the primary and secondary myths. A propaganda booklet intended for American readers stresses "the tremendous role art plays in the life of the Soviet people" and says that works of art (pictures, sculptures, etc.) "are acquired by factories, workshops, clubs, restaurants, trade unions, departments of state, soviets, the cultural and educational organizations in the Red Army, nursing homes, hospitals, public baths and railways." This colossal market for art is available to artists in three ways: the state will pay for trips to various parts of the country to produce works conceived by the artist but taking into account the needs of clients, or a professional body will offer a contract enabling the artist to work for a year on chosen subjects, also taking account of the demands of the state; or the artist can obtain commissions for specific works.[25] Joint authorship with the state is organized similarly in all fields of artistic creation.

A writer who, unlike the filmmakers, for example, needs only paper and pencil, has to buy them in a state shop. But what he needs most of all is a printer. Again Klaus Mehnert suggest some interesting factors here. Returning to the Soviet Union half a century after the publication of his first book, he collected material on the literary tastes of the Russians. His work is of interest, firstly because statistics of this kind are not published in the Soviet Union and, secondly, because Mehnert, an experienced Sovietologist who did not want to spoil his relations with the authorities, left out of his survey all "suspect" writers—those who had been expelled from the Union or had emigrated or were disapproved of by the authorities. Mehnert also presumed that all the Soviet citizens he questioned, whether by chance (taxi drivers, cashiers in shops) or by pre-arrangement (librarians, writers), would answer him honestly and speak frankly about their tastes. With some qualifications he presents the results of his survey as though they represented a free choice on the part of all Soviet readers today and a true reflection of their current (1980–83) taste.

The principal merit of Mehnert's *The Russians and Their Favorite Books* is that it demonstrates the technique of how to evoke love. Mehnert drew up a list of the twenty-four best-loved Soviet authors. By a strange coincidence, which he does not comment on, twenty-one of these were members of the management committee of the Union of Soviet Writers. The other three were the Strugatsky brothers and the Wainer brothers, excluded either because their kind of writing is not considered "serious" enough or because the quota of Jews on the committee had already been reached, and Valentin Pikul, possibly excluded because his historical novels are too chauvinist and anti-Semitic. Eight were members of the Union's secretariat, including its chairman, Georgi Markov.[26]

These quoted figures permit one to conclude (as Mehnert does) that Russia's favorite (i.e. best) writers are in charge of their Union. But one can also draw the opposite conclusion—that the leaders of the Union automatically become "favorite" writers, and that the possibility of a free choice of goods is determined by the presence of the goods on the market. Mehnert comments quite rightly on the amazing shortage of books in the USSR, and concludes from this that the cultural level of the Soviet people is unusually high and that people are consumed by a great thirst for knowledge. But one might point out that there is a shortage in the Soviet Union not only of books but also of all other consumer goods. Like other goods in short supply, books have taken over a function they do not perform in other countries—they have become a special kind of currency.

The shortage of books is organized deliberately by the state, which thus acquires an additional instrument for influencing literary output, writers and the reading public. It is all very simple. According to data in the UNESCO annual for 1981, in 1979 the Soviet Union occupied the last place among industrialized countries in the per capita use of paper "for printing and writing." The comparative figures included: United States, 65,603 kg; West Germany, 51,172 kg; Japan, 31,936 kg; Great Britain, 31,794 kg; and the USSR, 5,117 kg. Since the entire supply of paper in the Soviet Union is in the hands of the state, it publishes what it pleases. "In 1969–70 alone the print runs of Lenin's works and of books about Lenin exceeded 76 million copies."[27] In 1978 and 1979 Leonid Brezhnev's "trilogy" was published in an edition of 17 million copies. Mehnert reckoned that 12.5 million copies of books by Julian Semyonov, who sings the praises of the KGB and whom Mehnert considers to be one of the three best Soviet writers (he does not name the other two), are available. A total of 5,162,060 copies of the novels of Markov, former Chairman of the Union of Soviet Writers, were printed, while the works of one of the most important Russian writers of recent years, V. Rasputin, had a print-run of 1,427,000 copies. That unquestionably meant success, but the print-run of the political novels by another of Mehnert's favorites—Alexander Chakovsky—was three times larger.

The print-runs of books by Soviet authors are not determined by the taste of readers: their taste is determined by the number of books available. Moreover, the true success of a literary work is determined today not just by the number of copies printed but by the extent to which it is adapted for use in other media—radio, television, and film. "Popular" books are usually adapted for television and cinema and broadcast over the radio, and some are used on the operatic and dramatic stage. Works by the leaders of the Writers' Union are obviously among the first to be used in this way. One of the most successful operations for advertising the KGB was a television series based on Semyonov's novel *Seventeen Moments in Spring*, which brought fame to both the author and the KGB. In the summer of 1984, at the time of the Olympic Games, boycotted by the USSR, Soviet television transmitted a serial based on Semyonov's latest novel to pacify Soviet viewers.

In 1974 an attempt was made to solve the paper shortage and satisfy readers' tastes: it was announced that in exchange for 20 kilograms of paper brought in and deposited for pulping, a Soviet citizen could receive a coupon entitling him to a copy of Alexander Dumas's *Queen Margot* or Hans Christian Andersen's *Tales.* It quickly became clear that Soviet readers were bringing in so much paper that, to satisfy the demand for Dumas and Andersen the printings of Brezhnev and Markov would have to be halted. Moreover, as should have been expected, there were no warehouses in which the paper for pulping could be kept.

Mehnert's list of the twenty-four "favorite" Soviet writers reminds one of an X-ray picture of the body of a cancer victim: alongside the healthy organs lie those affected by the disease. Rasputin, Astafev, and Trifonov appear together with "greens" like Markov, Chakovsky, and Semyonov. Of course, in every country the publishing business shows figures for books that sell in the millions. In many cases the successful authors' work has nothing in common with real literature: this social phenomenon has attracted the attention of sociologists, psychologists, and historians. Mehnert would hardly be likely to put the West German authors Konsalik and Böll side by side, though the total sale of Konsalik's novels is much greater. Nor would he put Harold Robbins and Saul Bellow on the same level. But in Soviet writing they are not just put side by side: works produced by the "greens" are brought to the forefront, awarded prizes, orders and medals, and are used, as one critic said, as "a base and a launching pad for the cinema, the theatre and radio and television productions."[28]

Mehnert concluded that "the literary pot is boiling; the stew has many ingredients and tastes; the lid is not on so tight as it was forty or fifty years ago."[29] But it is impossible to agree with him. In the 1930s, when the transformation of literature into Soviet literature was at its height, not only was the memory still fresh of what a writer ought to be, but there were some writers still alive who had begun their literary careers before or just after the Revolution. This may explain the literary explosion of the 1960s, which produced works by Boris Pasternak, Alexander Solzhenitsyn, Yury Dombrovsky, Vladimir Maximov, Vasily Grossman and a number of others, all of whom, without exception, had been thrown out of the "literary pot" which pleased Mehnert so much. They were struck out of literature and their names removed from dictionaries, encyclopedias and textbooks, and their works were destroyed. The late Andrei Tarkovsky, explaining why he had decided not to return to Russia, said that his name had been removed from the list of film directors by an official who did not approve of any of the work or behavior of the man who had produced the films *Andrei Rublev* and *Stalker*. Another official crossed out the name of the great cellist Mstislav Rostropovich, and another did the same for the dancers Rudolf Nureyev and Mikhail Baryshnikov. Soviet culture can get along without them: only geniuses appointed by the ideological department of the Party are put into the "literary pot."

So the truth is that Soviet culture has deteriorated in comparison even with its own past. Censorship has grown steadily in importance and has become a gigantic mechanism of control. At its birth in 1922 the censorship bore an obscure name: the Chief Administration for the Affairs of Literature and Publishing (Glavlit). In the mid-1950s it came to be known officially and openly as the Chief Administration for the Protection of Military and State Secrets and the Press. This was followed by the emergence of departmental censorships, in the Ministry of Defense, and in the atomic, computer, space, radio-electronic and chemical industries. Today Glavlit is called the Chief Administration for the Protection of State Secrets and the Press. Anything in a book which at a given moment is listed in what is called the Index of Information Not to Appear in Print (running to 300 pages of small print) is struck out by the censors at the Chief Administration. Every manuscript in which there may be references to military officers or engineers, for example, must pass through an additional departmental censorship. Apart from what the censors at Glavlit do, every manuscript is censored by an editor. After the editor has passed it the manuscript is sent to the printer, who prepares galley-proofs, of which he sends two copies to the censor. After the censor has cleared the text again, the printer produces corrected proofs, of which one goes to the censor and three to the authorities in the Central Committee, the KGB and the Chief Administration who check on the work of the censor. If any "mistakes" are found in the book by any of the controllers the book is confiscated, even if it has already been printed and bound and is on sale.[30]

The official censorship represents only the first, external ring that surrounds the Soviet writer, artist, or performer. There is another, much more oppressive, internal censor: self-censorship. This consists in a magic circle of obligatory myths, of characters who may be written about, of signs that may be used. No Soviet writer who wishes to be published in his own country can escape from that circle.

It is easy and quite simple for the most popular and most published writers. They have no desire to "escape." In the last year of Alexander Tvardovsky's editorship, of *Novy Mir,* the magazine published an article in which the author asserted that the print-run of books in the Soviet Union was in inverse proportion to the author's talent and literary ability. "It is the least gifted, the most primitive and those who pander to vulgar taste who are encouraged and popularized."[31] The author could not, of course, say "those who pander to ideological taste."

To achieve "best-seller" status in the Soviet Union it is essential to choose the correct main character. A high-ranking Party official can be followed from one novel to another among the "best-sellers." Secretaries of regional Party committees who appear in the novels of Pyotr Proskurin, Anatoly Ivanov and Georgy Markov are indistinguishable, like the "reds" that Ernst Neizvestny discovered. Antonov Sobolev in Markov's *The Coming Century* ("externally calm and restrained, the secretary of the regional committee takes to heart everything going on around him. He wants passionately to see changes take place. But he has no intention of rushing thoughtlessly into experimentation."[32]) could be transferred to Proskurin's *Thy Name* or Ivanov's *The Eternal*

Summons and the reader would not notice the substitution. In "best-selling" novels the regional Party secretary naturally has some kind of encounter with the "brilliant secretary" Stalin. Alexander Chakovsky managed to bring Stalin and Brezhnev together in a single novel, *The Victory*. A reviewer underlined especially Chakovsky's skill in depicting "the image of a man, a worker and the son of a worker, a soldier in the great anti-fascist army who stood at the helm of the Country of the Soviets."[33] He meant Leonid Brezhnev.

Three basic myths are spread by the "best-selling" literature. The first is the myth of the Party (in the person of its leaders)—the father of the people, teacher and master. In a popular play of the 1930s, Kirshon's *The Rails Are Humming,* the young Communists sing: "The Party is my dream; the Party is roses; the Party is my happiness," which describes exactly the attitude of today's leading Soviet writers to the Party. The second myth is that the Soviet regime—Russian power, Revolution and the Communist Party—is the culminating achievement of Russian history. The third myth is that the chronic poverty and everlasting shortages are a sign of being the chosen people and a means of educating the soldiers of the new world. One foreigner who visited the Soviet Union in the 1930s was delighted at the country's poverty and commented that the country of Diogenes could manage without a furniture industry. The "best-selling" writers persuade their readers that they are indeed like Diogenes and consequently it is best for them to do without furniture. Of course, the writers themselves can acquire furniture abroad and live in a state of luxury that Western best-selling authors may envy. For Markov, Chakovsky, Proskurin, Semyonov and the other "millionaires," service to the state, which pays them generously with privileges, power and material goods, presents no problem. It is the writers with real talent who have problems, because they are looking for an opportunity to tell the truth and they try to avoid sermonizing.

In the last twenty years it is the countryside that has most frequently attracted talented writers as a subject, and the books written about rural and village life seemed at least until the late 1970s to provide evidence of the vitality of Soviet literature. Mehnert's list of popular writers included the well-known writers of books on village life, and they are unquestionably significant. Village life became a popular subject primarily because it was officially authorized. It attracted the genuine writers because it gave them a chance to discuss intellectual problems and eternal values.

It is only at first glance that permission to treat the subject of village life may seem paradoxical. The Nazis regarded the peasantry as the healthiest part of the nation which should preserve its roots in the soil, reject the city's depraving influence and carry on the nation's genuine traditions and values. The difference between Hitler's Germany and the Soviet Union here is that in Germany the peasantry whose praises were to be sung actually existed, while in the Soviet Union collectivization has exterminated it. Soviet literature about village life sings the praises of a peasantry that had passed away—it is in fact an elegy. That is the first reason why the censors allow the subject to be written about: having been eliminated, the peasantry ceases to inspire fear. The second reason is that books about village life conveyed a picture of meek acceptance of the destruction of the Russian countryside. *Farewell to Matyora,* the title of a story by Valentin Rasputin, one of the most important of the "village" writers, can serve as an epitaph for all their works—destruction is inevitable, so one had better accept it. The "village life" writers popularize the submissive hero who preserves his human qualities and eternal spiritual values but is powerless and helpless. The best work in this school, Rasputin's novel *Live and Remember,* is the only genuine tragedy in Soviet literature in the last few decades. Nastya, who lives in a Siberian village called Atamanovka, hides her husband, a deserter from the front in the war. Nastya relives the tragedy of Antigone—she has to make the choice between her duty to the state (to inform on her husband) and her duty to her husband. What is unusual is that Nastya hesitates, makes her choice, saves her husband, and then the Antigone from Atamanovka perishes. Soviet literature knows the "optimistic tragedy," but Rasputin wrote a real tragedy. It was allowed to be published not because the censor was impressed by the writer's talent, but because the philosophy behind *Live and Remember* was considered useful. Rasputin sings the praises of basic forces that, in his opinion, shape a man's character and determine man's fate—soil and blood. Nastya's husband runs from the front not because he is afraid to die but because he does not want to die without leaving a child behind him. The desire to continue the family drives him inexorably back home, and the author does not condemn him for committing such a crime against the state. For Rasputin, as for the majority of writers in the same genre,

226 I THE INSTRUMENTS

the history of the Soviet system is of no interest; what is important is the history of the people and the land. The Soviet state thus becomes as natural a feature as the seasons of the year.

A special place in the literature of the post-Stalin period was occupied by Yury Trifonov, the best-known exemplar of a writer about city life, much less popular than those who dealt with life in the village. A great deal in Trifonov's books, which described in detail the ethos and lifestyle of loyal servants of the regime, the intelligentsia, did not please official critics who disliked the unheroic central characters and the depressing atmosphere. Yet these qualities made Trifonov a truly popular writer. From the point of view of the censors the "shortcomings" of Trifonov's books were compensated for by their "merits." Readers identified themselves with his heroes—weak people, capable of doing mean things, of betraying their friends and teachers, suffering in their weakness and meanness, but not knowing how to cure themselves.

In Trifonov's last novel, *Time and Place,* published posthumously, he formulates "the Nikiforov Syndrome," a law of Soviet literature named after one of the characters. A Soviet writer, the law states, will never be able to write what he wants, for a complex of internal censorships—the Nikiforov syndrome—prevents him. He cannot escape from the magic ring. The novel treats of the impossibility of rejecting the state and its ideological apparatus as co-author. In varying degrees the writer's or artist's own intentions are undoubtedly important, but the "co-author" inevitably takes part in everything produced by Soviet culture.

The technique of possessing the "soul" of the creative artist, developed over the decades, has now reached a high level of perfection. The historian Rene Fülop-Miller, who visited the Soviet Union in the late 1920s, called an important aspect of this technique the "Bim-Bom Effect." He had been struck by the popularity of two circus clowns who made some fairly cutting criticisms of the regime, and he guessed that "if it had not been for the humour with which the two clowns performed, universal discontent would have burst all bounds." Bim-Bom therefore were "one of the most important supports of the Soviet regime," and he stressed one exceptionally important detail: the clowns "never attacked the regime as a whole but only parts of it, thus diverting attention from essentials."[34]

In the process of perfecting the technique of "phagocytosis," satire, a genre that excludes co-authorship, was gradually eliminated from

Soviet writing. A determined campaign was also waged against irony, because "irony is *never* neutral."[35] The "Bim-Bom Effect" was extended to certain sensitive subjects which writers were allowed to treat on condition that any criticism was aimed only at details. The illusion was encouraged that "critical" and "penetrating" independent writers were free to write as they pleased. This gave birth to the myth that it was possible—even virtuous—to write and read "between the lines" and to use lies to spread the truth. The old Russian saying that a spoonful of tar can ruin a barrel of honey was converted into the maxim that a barrel of tar could be improved by adding a spoonful of honey. There were even arguments about the proportions in which tar and honey were most beneficial to the organism. Many of the most talented figures in the world of Soviet culture have recounted their efforts to obtain permission to have a few drops of honey for a barrel of tar. Sergei Eisenstein admits in his biography that, like Tsar Ivan, he too "set about achieving self-destruction. . . . Too often even, too successfully and sometimes even too eagerly, and also . . . unsuccessfully."[36] Neizvestny relates that he felt himself to be experiencing "an internal contradiction with the established regime" when he discovered that "a great state, the whole world and history itself could be violated by such unattractive gnomes and such little kitchen dwarfs."[37] Eisenstein and Shostakovich were violated by Stalin and his minions, but over a long period each of them went along with the violation, which could be called "co-authorship," in the hope of obtaining the larger portion of honey to which he was entitled.

The argument continues about the fate of a culture that has been nationalized by the state and of the people for whom that culture is provided. The Soviet public, locked in the magic circle of the Soviet system, seek truth and information everywhere about themselves and the outside world, even in the molecules of honey dissolved in the barrel of tar, just as people with scurvy will search everywhere for vitamin C, even in places where it cannot be. The argument is between those who assert that without a molecule of honey, even in the most unpleasant solution, all hope of a revival of genuine culture will fade, and those who reckon that the poison of the lie has a stronger effect when it is mixed with a molecule of truth. On the one hand there are those who say: better something than nothing at all, while on the other side are the opponents of compromise and of any kind of collaboration with the state in matters of culture.

Meanwhile the state never ceases, consistently, stubbornly and tirelessly, to strengthen the magic circle. Those who appreciate the reality of the chains and try to break out of them are expelled from the Soviet Union; the names of "harmful" and "unwanted" people in the world of culture are struck out. Books are destroyed. Scraps of information about book-burning are reported in the press when the fires become excessive. In the summer of 1983 a reader in Tadzhikistan wrote to a newspaper to say that the destruction of "unwanted literature" by the libraries of the republic was giving rise to "serious concern." In the republican capital the libraries had "destroyed practically everything published before 1940." Replying to this letter, the "Department of Communist Education" of the *Literary Gazette* asked first of all a rhetorical question: "Why are libraries both big and small obliged to destroy books in the 'age of the book boom'?" Its reply was: "These are complicated questions requiring thorough and deep research."[38] Books published before 1940 have become forbidden, harmful literature and it is impossible to obtain many books published in the 1950s and 1960s. The reader is expected to forget the names not only of the "harmful" authors but also of the Soviet leaders who have become unpersons. George Orwell's fantasy turns out to be much closer to reality than was suspected even by admirers of the author of *1984*.

Bertolt Brecht told a story about a man whose house is entered by an armed stranger who asks: Will you make room for me in your house, give me food and drink and take care of me? The owner of the house lets the armed intruder have the best part of his house, provides him with food and drink and looks after him. Seven years later the visitor dies and the owner of the house gives his answer—No.

Seventy years have passed. The intruder is still living in the house and wants the question to be forgotten. The purpose behind the nationalization of culture and its inclusion in the magic circle of co-authorship consists in ensuring that the signs, the language with which other ways of thinking can be expressed, should disappear or be replaced.

The Russian intelligentsia could not forgive Dostoevsky for his appeal: "Restrain yourself, proud man!" The author of *The Devils* was appealing for submission to God. Mayakovsky's words—"But I restrained myself as I stood on the throat of my own song"—a haughty admission of submission to the Party, became the symbol of the faith of the Soviet intelligentsia, of those who work in Soviet culture.

In the beginning was the word.

Caption under a print depicting Hitler addressing his colleagues

The principal means of conveying information is the word.

From "Language in an advanced socialist society," Moscow 1982

13

Language

In 1920 Evgeny Zamyatin, when he came to describe the One State in his novel *We*, pointed out that the inhabitants of that future state spoke in a special language. It was Russian, the language Zamyatin wrote in, but at the same time it was not quite Russian. In it words could mean what the State wanted them to mean. Zamyatin was the first to draw attention to the emergence of a new, Soviet language. Soon other, perceptive writers like Mikhail Zoshchenko, Andrei Platonov and Mikhail Bulgakov detected the same phenomenon. They recorded the appearance of a new system which some decades later Miłosz was to call a "logocracy." Alain Besançon has formulated its law: "In a regime in which power is 'on the tip of the tongue' the extent to which the *langue de bois* extends its influence determines exactly the limits of power."

Language is the most important and the most powerful weapon in the hands of a state that has decided to transform human beings. The creation of a new language serves two aims: to obtain, as Orwell put it, "an instrument with which to express the philosophy and thoughts that are permitted," and, secondly, to make "all other sorts of thinking impossible."[1] The new language is consequently at once a means of communication and an instrument of oppression.

It is a peculiarity of the new, Soviet language that the word plays the principal role: it loses its generally accepted meaning and becomes an empty shell which the supreme authority fills with whatever meaning suits it. After one of his arrests Andrei Amalrik was found guilty of "libellously asserting that there was no freedom of speech in the USSR."[2] Here "freedom of speech" meant the need to find a dissident guilty. In a telegram to the potato-growers of the Bryansk region General Secretary Brezhnev informed them that "the potato is the most valuable feeding and industrial crop."[3] The people of Bryansk, who had been growing potatoes for two hundred years, correctly deciphered his message to mean that there were no potatoes to be had.

The word conceals reality, creates an illusion, a surrealist impression, but at the same time it preserves a link with reality and puts it into code. The Soviet language is a code in which the signs are determined by the supreme authority. The meaning of those signs is communicated to everyone using the language, but in varying degrees. One's place on society's hierarchic ladder determines the extent to which one will be admitted to the secrets of the code. There are various degrees—first, second, third and so on.

The Soviet language, still developing, has not yet reached the state described in Orwell's *1984* where, for example, the ministry of the police is called the ministry of love—in the USSR it is still frankly called the Committee of State Security. The word "security" (which appears in police nomenclature in all countries of "mature socialism") warns us that the period of "universal love" has not yet arrived. In his story *Lyubimov* Andrei Sinyavsky describes a leader possessing magic power who declares river water to be vodka. That is the ideal—the word transforming reality. But the people who drink the water complain that, though it tastes like vodka, it doesn't make them drunk. In Alexander Galich's song about Klim Petrovich, the model Soviet worker whom the Party orders to denounce Israeli militarists, Klim is handed the wrong set of notes. So he reads out: "All the world knows what the Israeli militarists are like! I speak as a mother, and as a woman I demand they be brought to book!" No one at the meeting notices the mistake and the speaker is warmly applauded.[4] That is the reality. People using Soviet language are at least half intoxicated by it. They know what is meant by the code-words "Israeli militarists," and their use is expected to evoke, and in many cases does evoke, the necessary conditioned reflex.

The word acquires a magical character and becomes a sort of oath. Marshall McLuhan's formula—the medium is the message—very precisely defines the unlimited possibilities of the Soviet system: the state is both the message and the medium; it creates the language and extends its use while controlling the content and the technique. What in the non-Soviet world are called the mass media, the means of mass information, are openly described in the Soviet Union as "means of mass information and propaganda," known as SMIP for short. It is only the conjunction "and" here that is misleading, because the information is propaganda and propaganda is presented in the guise of information.

The official description of the nature and function of the Soviet system of mass information and propaganda could not be more precise: SMIP "has at its disposal a well-organized system of model views which it transforms into reality by means of speech, which is also well thought out and organized."[5] Possessing absolute power over the word and the means of transmitting it, the Soviet state spreads the "well-organized system of model views" methodically and according to plan. The state decides what a word means and the circumstances in which it can be used, and creates a magic circle into which everyone must step who wants to understand and be understood, within the boundaries of the Soviet system.

An attempt to escape from the circle, to speak in another language, or to understand something your "rank" does not allow you to is treated as a crime. A sentence passed in 1983 on two Siberian workers, Alexander Shatravka and Vladimir Mishchenko, for "spreading fabrications known to be false which defamed the Soviet state and social system" said that they had acquainted workers with an "appeal" to set up independent groups for the organization of a dialogue between the USSR and the USA. According to the court, this appeal had called for "the creation of groups which would be independent of the campaign for the salvation of mankind which the Party, Government and the whole people are conducting."[6] The two workers' crime consisted in having destroyed the myth of unity, in encroaching on the "well-organized system of model views" and wanting to think independently.

In a science-fiction novel, *The Inhabited Island,* the brothers Strugatsky describe an imaginary model world in which total power over the word and its transmission has been established. The story is about an unknown planet whose inhabitants are continuously subjected to radiation. As a result of this the brain loses all ability to engage in a critical analysis of reality and "any doubt about the words and deeds of the authorities" vanishes from the minds of the inhabitants of the totalitarian planet. It is just a dream, but it is also the ultimate aim of a totalitarian regime.

To achieve that aim it is essential to have a language which has been made into a weapon and a means of transforming people. It is essential to have a special technique for using it. The first peculiar feature of the Soviet language is that it is being created in a planned way and that its foundations were laid even before the Revolution.

Hitler believed that all great revolutions have owed their origin and their success to the choice of slogans launched at the right moment and to the people who were able to attract followers by means of powerful speeches. He placed Christ, Lenin, and Mussolini on the same level, having himself also in mind, of course. There is no doubt that the Great October Socialist Revolution owed its origin and success to Lenin, but it is also well known that he was a mediocre orator. His strength lay in the *written* word, in his awareness of the power of the word, in the technique of using the word that he invented, and in his creation of a model for the Soviet language.

Sixty years ago, immediately after Lenin's death, the most distinguished Russian linguists analyzed the Leader's language and his way of expressing himself politically. It was a dispassionate, objective study of the model of the new language. The scholars could not have foreseen the deification of Lenin or the ultimate fate of his model for the language. For them Lenin was a great politician and a very original orator. They based their judgment on what was for them an undoubted fact: "The most important branch of modern prose-writing consists of social and political works. The most distinguished world figure in modern social and political literature was Lenin."[7] Lenin was studied as the greatest writer of his day. Five years later a new Leader was to put on the crown of the greatest writer and the crown would become an appurtenance of the general secretary. The words of the Leader were made sacred.

The linguists discovered in Lenin's words the technique used to produce the "sacred word" which, with the aid of that technique, was transformed into a "revelation," a voice from Sinai.

It was the word, the meaning injected into a particular word, that played the most important part. "A quarrel begun by Lenin with his opponents, whether they were his enemies or his comrades in the Party, usually begins with a quarrel 'about words'—claims that the words had been altered." Lenin "reduces the weight of the revolutionary phrase," fights against "revolutionary language," "big words" and "smooth words." He set about debunking the words "Freedom," "Equality," and "People." For example, he wrote: "Let's have a bit less talk about 'labor democracy,' about 'freedom, equality, brotherhood,' about 'people's power' and that sort of thing."[8] Having correctly taken note of this tendency in Lenin's style—his criticism of pseudorevolutionary words, phrases and slogans—the linguists took this to be a positive development, an effort to free the language of empty phrases and the smooth, "big" words. They can hardly be blamed for this, since they did not know what was going to happen later. Lenin's efforts were seen as tantamount to a clearing of the air and the elimination of words with definite, historically formed meanings. All those "smooth words" that had entered the revolutionary vocabulary since the time of the French Revolution were ridiculed; Lenin exposed them and drove them out of use, insisting on his right to give words their true meaning and denying his opponents the right to use revolutionary language without the permission of the Leader.

The process of debunking revolutionary language was in reality a process of replacing it with another, approved language, taking away a word's immanent meaning, and this was the first element in the Leader's style, which the linguists called "Lenin's dissuasive speech." The second element was "persuasive speech," the principal feature of which was the transformation "of general statements . . . into slogans, verbal directives for political action." Lenin strove to construct out of words "formulae and slogans having a compact, concrete, topical meaning."[9] As Goebbels was to say later: we speak not in order to say something but in order to obtain a particular effect.

Leninist speech is composed of words the meaning of which is determined by the speaker himself; the word becomes a brick in the construction representing the "formula-slogan." Lenin developed a special way of writing that made it possible to establish the "formula-slogan" in the mind of the reader or listener: his speech was divided into paragraphs intended to create an impression of consistency and so be more persuasive. Then, as the most important compositional element, there is the use of *repetition*, by means of which a rectangle is formed which concentrates the attention, narrows the field of possibilities, and squeezes thought into a tight ring from which there is only one exit. For example, Lenin would repeat a verb in three tenses: "there was, there is and there will be," "relations are improving, must improve and will continue to improve." As a rule he used this three-part formula; in linguistics the triad is a synonym for "many," and thus he created the illusion of verbal richness. The repetitions sound like a logical argument. The listener or the reader is left without choice: they have been given the decision, the answer—the only one because it is the right one, and the right one because it is the only one. The relative lack of verbs, the turning of them into nouns, makes Lenin's speech seem like an order.[10] Thus the finished model of the language of the Soviet Leader was created: the word, deprived of its immanent meaning; the slogan composed of similar words; a composition which imposes this formula-slogan as the only answer-decision-order.

It is no accident that this research into Lenin's political language appeared in the magazine of the *Left Front in Art (LEF)*. The futurists who favored formalism regarded themselves as the only representatives of the revolution in art and assumed the task of formulating the laws of the new language. For them it was quite clear: "The Revolution has set us some practical tasks—to influence the minds of the masses and to give direction to the will of the working class." The Revolution had an aim: to forge the new man. The futurists provided the means: "Art . . . is one of the sharpest class weapons for influencing people's minds." They set themselves a maximum program: to carry out "the conscious reorganization of the language and adapt it to the new reality" and to campaign for the "emotional training of the mind of the producer-consumer."[11] Developing these thoughts expressed by Sergei Tretyakov, the theorist of futurism, the linguist Grigory Vinokur set forth the main features of a previously unknown concept, linguistic policy. According to his definition, "linguistic policy is nothing other than interference (based on precise, scientific understanding of the matter) by the will of society in the structure and development of the language with which the policy is concerned." The interference begins with phraseology, that is, with vocabulary. "It is in the dictionary that it is easiest to bring social influences to bear on the language," Vinokur wrote. "It is far easier, for example, to replace one word by another than it is to change the declension of a noun." Thus "the rationalization of phraseology is the first problem of linguistic policy."[12] For Vinokur the "rationalization of phraseology" meant "making it younger," which in turn meant a return to the slogans, set formulae and terms.

This reveals Vinokur's amazing naïveté, which derived from the equally astonishing political naïveté of the futurists and representatives of "left-wing art." They talked of the need to influence people's minds with language and proposed a technique for doing it, but they did not understand the system that was being created or the nature of the ruling party. Vinokur said: "The phraseology of revolution has justified itself. Beyond the limits of that phraseology it has been impossible to think in a revolutionary way or about revolution." This is a correct and important observation—without revolutionary slogans and a revolutionary vocabulary, neither a change in people's way of thinking nor the Revolution itself would have been possible. The successful phraseology to a large extent determined the success of the Revolution: the Bolsheviks found "the right words . . . and the transition from hearing them to acting on them was not complicated by any secondary associations— read and act!" This is an excellent definition of a slogan—a word that is uncomplicated by secondary associations and demands to be translated into action. For example, the most famous slogan of the Revolution, "Steal the stolen property!" combined a content "as simple as the lowing of cattle" and a form characterized by "an exclamatory intonation with a monotonous but catching tune."[13]

When the Revolution was over and the Civil War came to an end, the Communist Party continued to use this tested technique. In 1923 *Pravda* wrote: "Our press is always setting forth, in an especially striking way, the main slogans, key issues, and main campaigns, and it keeps hammering away at them stubbornly and systematically—'boringly,' our enemies say. Yes, our brochures, newspapers, and leaflets do indeed drum into the heads of the masses a certain number of the main 'key' formulae and slogans." The writer insisted on those words—"hammer away" and "drum into." He continued: "A real Communist article is not just a newspaper article but a magazine article too, not only a piece of political persuasion but also a scholarly treatise, and is distinguished by its exceptional clarity and precision of style. It is harsh and coarse, elementary and vulgar, our enemies say. It is truthful, sincere, bold, frank and merciless."[14] For Vinokur such a style was acceptable during the Revolution, but now, he argued, it was necessary to "rejuvenate our phraseology." He suggested introducing new words, more lively and more human, and to get away from stock phrases. He cited examples of the cliché-slogans—Down with Imperialism! Long Live the Victory of the Indian Workers and Peasants! Long Live the International Solidarity of the Working Class! Long Live the Working Class of Russia and its Vanguard—the Russian Communist Party! "It's just a lot of mumbo-jumbo," he concluded, "a collection of sounds which have become so familiar to our ears that it would seem completely impossible to react to them in any way. . . . There is no real thought and no real feeling behind those stilted phrases."

Vinokur was certain that slogans were just verbal clichés that had long ago lost any real content. You could think in images and you could think in words, but you couldn't think in clichés, and if you did, it would only be "senseless."

He was making a serious mistake. He presumed that the new world needed a new kind of man, capable of thinking logically and rationally, and he was warning people of the danger of the effect of empty phrases on people's minds. He did not understand that that was in fact the aim—to destroy the capacity for logical thought and to create a language "shutting our eyes to the true nature of things." The introduction of censorship just ten days after the October Revolution began was for the new regime an essential act of the greatest importance. The next step, in July 1918, was equally important: the closing down of all non-Communist newspapers and periodicals. The creation of a new language was possible only in the absence of anything to compare it with. Only in such conditions could the senseless "thinking in clichés" be born.

Vinokur was the first to describe, without suspecting what he was doing, the foundations of the logocracy: "We cease to think logically . . . hackneyed phraseology shuts our eyes to the true nature of things and their interrelationship, and it makes us use their terminology, a very inaccurate one, instead of dealing with real things."[15] We are thus faced with a paradox: a scholar discovers a remarkable weapon, defines its lethal power, and advises the person who was going to use the weapon to refuse it and be disarmed. Sixty years after Vinokur called "revolutionary phraseology" "mumbo-jumbo" containing no real thought, newspapers were writing:

Writers and artists, cultural workers! Create works worthy of our great Motherland! Workers in the food industry! Increase the production of foodstuffs of high quality! Peoples of the Arab countries! Close your ranks in the struggle against Israeli aggression and the dictates of imperialism! A fraternal greeting to the peoples of Angola, Mozambique and the other countries of Africa that have chosen the path of socialist development![16]

Historians still argue about the legitimacy of the Stalinist period in Soviet history. Was he Lenin's disciple, and did he continue Leninism or distort and betray it? Stalin was in fact Lenin's best and only successor, because he understood better than anyone the importance of the word and of power over the word. He completed the work begun by Lenin, turning the model of a Soviet language into a working language and a mighty instrument for working on people's minds. And in his struggle for power Stalin showed the remarkable possibilities he could exploit for using words in new ways and his own talents as a master of semantic tricks. His conflict with Trotsky, for example, was conducted over the meaning of two slogans—"building socialism in one country" and "permanent revolution." Stalin would label each of his opponents with a slogan and then criticize the slogan and its supporters. Thus did the struggle for power assume a tone of scholarly dispute.

As Stalin's power grew, so did the part played by slogans—which marked the magical decisions that set the path to be followed by the Party, state and mankind. And it was the General Secretary himself who first pronounced the slogans. Lenin's famous formula—Communism is Soviet power plus electrification—changed in the early 1930s to: Communism is Soviet power plus sloganification. Stalin said, The tempo decides *everything!* Cadres decide *everything!* Man is the *most* valuable capital! Mayakovsky was and *remains* the best and most talented poet of our age! Such slogans related to *all* spheres of Soviet life and always provided a definitive solution for *everything,* determining what was *the most* valuable and *the most* important. The Leader's word bore a universal and total application. Like a shaman's oath, upon it depended people's lives, the fate of the country and whether the weather was to be good or bad.

In their novel *The Golden Calf* the satirical authors Ilf and Petrov described a pre-revolutionary official of the Tsarist regime who now takes exception to such Soviet terms as "Proletkult" and "sektor." He hates the Soviet regime, but when he falls asleep he dreams Soviet dreams. The Soviet regime took over the dreams even of a monarchist.

As time went on, there emerged a linguistic hierarchy. The Leader's words acquired a value irrespective of their content, purely because

they had been uttered by the Leader. The central character in Platonov's story *The Foundation Pit,* a worker who is out to make a career
for himself, tries learning new words by heart. Every day Kozlov "on
waking would stay in bed reading books, and once he had learned the
phrases, slogans, verses, words of wisdom, theses, resolutions, words of
songs and so forth he would set off to visit various organizations and
offices, where he would scare the already scared employees with his
learning and his opinions."[17] Kozlov does make a career—he becomes
a trade union official—simply because he knows the right words, the
language of the State. As in the Roman Empire, when someone in a
remote province could make a career only if he knew Latin, in the
Soviet Union only a knowledge of the Soviet language opens the way
to advancement.

Rene Fülop-Miller was among the first of the few foreigners to
understand the true nature of this hierarchy. The aim, of the Soviet
regime, he said, was

> to produce an eternally subordinate, *ecclesia militans,* propagandist and
> Soviet bureaucrat. . . . It might be said that the Bolsheviks have organized
> their education system in such a way that nobody can go beyond the
> officially permitted level of knowledge and education, so that there should
> be no danger that the citizens of the proletarian state might acquire too
> much knowledge and become a "subversive element."[18]

The Soviet language became the most important means of preventing
people from acquiring more knowledge than the state wished.

A sacred pyramid of the Soviet language emerged, in which political
language was more important than literary, the Leader's word more
important than that of a lesser official, which was more important than
that of a worker, and so forth. As Leader Stalin named the vice-leaders.
In Russian literature it was Pushkin; in Soviet writing it was Gorky;
in the theatre Stanislavsky, and in biology Lysenko. With Stalin's bless-
ing they became sacred and their words became obligatory truths.

Soviet speech lost its freedom. The language was put together out
of slogans and quotations from the Leader, Pushkin, the current vice-
leader, and excerpts from *Pravda.* It was turned into a *cento,* but
without the humorous quality of that patchwork form of Latin verse.
The sense of the Word was determined by the authority of the person
who spoke it. It could be spoken without being understood, like an oath.

A correct quotation was confirmation of a person's reliability; an incorrect one might have very serious consequences. In Marek Hlasko's novel *The Graveyard,* about the Stalinist years in Poland, a skilled worker who called his dog "Rumba" is arraigned at a factory meeting. His accusers declare that if today he calls his dog "Rumba," tomorrow he'll be setting fire to Korean children with napalm.[19] Only a few years later the rumba became famous in Russia as the national dance of Cuba (known as Freedom Island), and the use of the word ceased to be objectionable. In his novel *Incognito,* the Romanian writer Petru Dumitriu, describing a party meeting, noted that "Only speech consisting entirely of ritual formulae was safe from criticism."[20]

The "quotability" of Soviet language is encouraged because a quotation includes in itself the answer to any question that might be asked. The authoritative, assertive word is expected simply to evoke the unconscious reflex the regime needs. Soviet language is an assertive, answering language, not intended for asking questions. A Polish joke illustrates this quality beautifully: A Polish computer is asked, Why is there no meat? It cannot answer because the word "meat" has not been programmed into it. An American computer is similarly unable to answer because the word "no" is not in its program. But the Soviet computer which had not been provided with the word "why?" is also unable to reply.

The crushing, unquestioned authority of the Leader's word is the result to a large extent of his right and power to name the Enemy. Lenin set the pattern for this. The word that signifies the enemy must be striking, easy to remember, implying condemnation by its very sound, and always imprecise, so that everyone who at a given moment does not please the Leader can be included under its rubric. Lenin's first brilliant idea was to use the word "Mensheviks" in this way, when his opponents in the Social-Democratic Party agreed to apply it to themselves. Lenin went on to think up labels to attach to all his opponents—*otsovisty,* "liquidators," and so forth. When he came to power and to be declared an "enemy" meant prison or death, he continued this pattern. The history of the Soviet Union can be told in terms of the words signifying enemies that appear and disappear only to make place for others: wreckers, kulaks, *podkulachniki* (kulak supporters), Rights, Lefts, Trotskyists, Bukharinists, cosmopolitans, Mendelians, and Morganists. The word may have a pejorative meaning (wrecker), a favorable one (Leftists), or a neutral one (genetics). But when the Leader chooses a particular word to signify an enemy he invests it with a new meaning. In 1930 the *Soviet Encyclopedia* defined the word "cosmopolitanism" as "recognition that the whole world is a person's fatherland." It was a good word, an international word. But by 1954 "cosmopolitanism" was defined as "a reactionary attempt to persuade people to renounce their patriotic traditions, national independence and national culture. Today aggressive American imperialism is trying to exploit the false theory of cosmopolitanism."

In the post-Stalin period two new enemies appeared: "Zionism" and "dissidence." The 1930 encyclopedia gives an objective definition of "Zionism": "a bourgeois trend among Jewish communities caused to a considerable extent by the persecutions of the Jews and by anti-Semitism." By 1954 the disapproval of the supreme authority is apparent: "a bourgeois-nationalist movement . . . Zionism aims to divert Jewish workers from the class struggle." In the *Political Dictionary* of 1969 the negative aspects of Zionism are stressed even more: "a reactionary bourgeois-nationalist movement. The centres of Zionist organization are in the USA and Israel." Finally, in the *Political Dictionary* of 1975, Zionism has become an enemy: "The ideology of Zionism reflects the interests of the wealthy Jewish bourgeoisie, closely linked with the monopolist circles of the imperialist states. . . . Zionist propaganda is closely connected with anti-Communist propaganda. . . . At the thirtieth session of the General Assembly of the United Nations, Zionism was recognized as a form of racism and racial discrimination." This was the first occasion when a country or movement declared to be an enemy by the supreme Soviet authority became at the same time the enemy of all mankind.

Until the late 1970s the word "dissident" had no application to Soviet life. In 1930 it was defined as "the name given to a non-Catholic in old Poland," in 1954 as "a Christian professing a faith different from the prevailing one." The *Political Dictionary* of 1978 said: "(1) persons who abandon the teaching of the prevailing faith (the heterodox): (2) The term 'dissidents' is used by imperialist propaganda to signify the small number of renegades, people who have put themselves outside Soviet society and who oppose socialist construction." In the period when Solidarity was challenging the Polish government, the Soviet press was for a short time in a state of confusion because it found it difficult to put a name to the enemy. When it was at last decided to declare "KOR" to be the main enemy, everything fell into place and the campaign against Solidarity took the familiar form of exposure of a current enemy.

The power to name the enemy makes the Leader, the Supreme Authority, complete master of the vocabulary. The dictionary, and along with it the language, is nationalized. As a result the censorship acquires a special function. The first, normal task of the censorship is to ban works and indicate what must not be written. But in addition, Soviet censorship indicates *how* people are to write and *what* they are to write about.

The existence of a linguistic authority makes the Soviet language into a system strictly defined by a norm. All languages are more or less normative by nature, but the Soviet language has a pattern to go by— the speech of the Leader—so that it is possible to know precisely not only what is right and wrong but also what is permitted and what is not. The vocabulary is checked regularly both by the censor's office and by linguists working for the censorship. "Incorrect" words are thrown out, disappearing altogether or being described as "obsolete." Even songs have words removed from them. There is a Russian saying that you can't throw words out of a song. That's true, but it turns out that a word can be changed. A popular song with lyrics by M. Isakovsky entitled "Birds of Passage Fly By" contained the line: "We don't need the coast of Turkey and we don't need Africa." In the 1960s, after Isakovsky's death, the line was changed to: "We don't need a foreign sun, we don't need a foreign land." Specific geography was replaced by an abstraction. Fourteen years after Stalin died his name was removed from a song. In the original version of the Soviet national anthem one had to sing: "The Party of Lenin, the Party of Stalin leads us from victory to victory." The corrected version went: "The Party of Lenin, the strength of the people, leads us to the triumph of Communism." In this case the abstraction "from victory to victory" was replaced by a specific destination—to Communism.

Words that are still needed but are given a changed meaning are transformed by the addition of an adjective ("real humanism," for example) and with the aid of commentary. This process is well described in the story by Ilf and Petrov entitled "Bound in Gold." Radio Moscow had decided to broadcast Offenbach's operetta *La Belle Hélène*. Before the program started a list of the characters was read out: "1. Helen, a woman whose beautiful exterior conceals total spiritual emptiness: 2. Menelaus, whose royal mantle skillfully conceals the pitiable instincts of a small man of property and a great tyrant; 3. Paris, whose external charm conceals a selfish character; 4. Agamemnon, on the surface a hero but actually a coward; 5. Three goddesses, a stupid myth," and so on. The commentary concluded with the words: "The music for the operetta was written by Offenbach who tries, beneath a quite unnecessary external tunefulness, to conceal the complete spiritual emptiness and the grasping instincts of a wealthy man of property and a small-time feudal lord."[21]

An example of the treatment meted out to Russian and its transformation into Soviet language can be seen in the use of suffixes, primarily the -ism suffix. In Vladimir Dal's *Explanatory Dictionary* (published in 1880) there are a total of seventy-nine words ending in -ism. In Ushakov's four-volume dictionary (1935–40), the dictionary of mature Stalinism, there were 415. According to Ushakov, the -ism suffix is used in words referring to "false systems, harmful political tendencies and negative features in Soviet life."[22] It is not surprising that the word "liberalism" is defined in this way: ". . . 4. Criminal tolerance, laxity. Rotten liberalism." Ushakov's distaste for such political trends as "Menshevism" and "Maximalism" is obvious, but his attitude is no less hostile towards other trends and "harmful sciences": "Freudianism—an idealistic bourgeois theory in psychology and psychopathology"; "Feminism—a bourgeois political movement in capitalist countries"; "Utilitarianism—a bourgeois ethical teaching concealing distinctions in a class society"; "Urbanism—a decadent culture of the ruling sections of a capitalist city."

The question naturally arises: What about Bolshevism, communism, socialism, Leninism? But that is a logical question only in a non-Soviet system of thought. Since the Word, like every other written system of communication, is in the hands of the Leader, the Supreme Authority, it has only the meaning given to it officially. Consequently the suffix "-ism" in most cases itself evokes by its very presence a negative reaction on the part of the recipient, while in some cases the same suffix produces a positive reaction.

Total power over the Word gives the Master of the Word a magical power over all communication. Soviet speech is always a monologue because there is no other party to talk to. On the other side is the enemy. In the Soviet language there are no neutral words—every word carries an ideological burden.

Receptivity to the spoken or written word is an important condition for its penetration into the human consciousness. That is why in Soviet language the same words are repeated over and over again, until they become a signal that acts without any effort of thought. The effect of set phrases and slogans is also assured by their always being repeated in absolutely the same form.

I do not know of research into the effect on a human being of the unceasing action of repeated, identical hypnotic magical phrases and slogans. But surely it was not when he described the telescreen that saw everything that Orwell showed such amazing perception, but when he stressed that the apparatus could not be turned off. Andrei Platonov described in *The Foundation Pit* the nightmarish reality of the never-ending voice on the radio from which one could not escape and which could not be switched off. Verses written by the Soviet poet Nikolai Dorizo, which in literary terms can be classified only as hack-writing, offer a model of Soviet linguistic hypnosis. "The chimes ring out in the silence—the heart of the Party. The atom fuses in the fire—the power of the Party. The grain pushes through in the fields—the wisdom of the Party. The wisdom of the Party is eternal." This is exactly what Goebbels had in mind when he said that we speak in order to have an effect. Dorizo composed a self-hypnotizing text of a prayer to the idol. When a Party philosopher says: " 'In the world of the mind we must never retreat,' these words of Pushkin's sound unusually topical when applied to the concept of advanced socialism," the purpose of the operation is obvious: the name of Pushkin must be linked in the reader's mind with the "concept of advanced socialism." Pushkin and "advanced socialism" are intended to become synonymous signals, so that one of the phrases will automatically evoke the other.[23]

The way language can be used to bring pressure to bear has been described by Wlodzimierz Lechowicz, former Polish minister of supply, who was arrested in Warsaw in 1948 and spent eight years in prison. Among the tortures to which he was subjected was torture "by the word." Lechowicz called it "torture by whisper." It consisted in "the monotonous repetition day and night in a quite intelligible whisper (as though the walls were speaking) of sentences that were supposed to produce in me a state of mental depression or agonizing physiological reactions." For example, at the end of 1949 for several days and nights he could hear nothing but a sort of dialogue between two other prisoners that consisted simply of such sentences as: "See how frequently he swallows his saliva," "Saliva appeared in the corner of his mouth," and so forth. At the end of a day Lechowicz found he could no longer swallow the enormous quantity of saliva he was producing. Some time later a similar program was arranged on the subject of sweating. Though the cell was very cold, it being winter, the many hours of whispering, repeating the words "he is sweating," caused Lechowicz to perspire profusely.[24] It is worth noting that Lechowicz's experience (the torture was an experiment and the experiment a form of torture) occurred at the time when Stalin was preparing his work of genius *Marxism and Linguistics*. Stalin's book could serve as the theoretical basis for research into the practical possibilities of developing a technique for establishing a direct link between the spoken or written word and human behavior.

The Soviet language is a semiological system in which the principal sign is the word. As Soviet theorists say: "The main material vehicle of information is the word."[25] It is therefore natural that it should be kept under close supervision. Precisely for this reason it becomes a political crime to try to introduce a new sign or to use a new literary form for a work not dealing at all with political or social problems—a lyric poem, for example—or to use a new or unapproved form of graphic art. This is why such a campaign is organized against nonconformist painting, sculpture and graphics. The danger of abstract art is that it leaves the viewer free to give his own meaning to the work. (Music, most abstract of the arts, does not escape the attention of the guardians of the Sign, and the Central Committee of the party has issued many special decrees about the language of music.) The hierarchy of signs is clearly to be seen in Soviet cinematography: the foundation of the film is considered to be the scenario, the written word, and the visual image is subordinate. It is easier to control and to censor the word than the image. Some Soviet film directors try to use the Image to outdo the Word. That was what Eisenstein did: in his films the political speeches are always insufferably conformist, but the picture is often quite independent. In Tarkovsky's film *Stalker* the words put into the mouths of the main characters are highly orthodox, but the use of sepia to signify the world they live in and of green to suggest the place where they seek to liberate their souls permits Tarkovsky to carry on a dialogue with the audience beyond the limits set by the words. Osip Mandelstam defined very precisely the importance of the word in the Soviet system when he said that it was only in the USSR that poetry was taken seriously—nowhere else were poets killed because of a word.

Some artists and writers who perform special services for the state may be permitted to use a symbol not permitted to others. Only the poet Andrei Voznesensky, for example, is allowed to write God with a capital letter. This serves to underline his special place in the hierarchy of Soviet art and the Soviet system of signs and symbols: it is meant to symbolize the liberalism of the regime and a freedom typical of the Soviet system. Tarkovsky's films are practically never shown in Soviet cinemas—only three or four copies are made—but they are shown abroad to demonstrate the high quality of Soviet art and the Soviet regime's tolerance.

Khrushchev was overthrown for a number of obvious political reasons but also because he violated the Soviet system of signs and symbols. In particular, he was never forgiven for using his shoe to bang on the desk at the United Nations to express indignation. To bang with your shoe at a gathering of foreigners was a sign of bad manners. A Soviet leader was by definition a model of good manners.

The importance and role of the official Soviet system of symbols have not changed since the early 1920s despite changes in terminology. Above all, the role of the Party is unchanged. In a textbook for philology students, *Socio-linguistic Problems of the Languages of the Peoples of the USSR: Problems of Linguistic Policy and Linguistic Construction,* it is indicated that the work has been approved by the Institute of Marxism-Leninism at the Party's Central Committee. There is no change in the treatment of language as a weapon in the struggle against enemies and an instrument for molding Soviet man. Or, as it is said in another scholarly work, *Language in an Advanced Socialist Society,* "the main task of mass communications in a socialist society is the purposeful development and perfecting of the minds of all its members."[26] The principal word in this statement is "purposeful." Soviet language is teleological. It serves "the worldwide historical process of establishing and developing a new Communist social and economic mentality." Its task is to help a person "to understand his optimal place as a cell in the social organism."[27]

Any violation of the state's monopoly over the Word was declared to be a crime in the very first Soviet Criminal Code. The punishment for it was laid down in chapter I, article 58, dealing with "counterrevolutionary crimes." Article 58-10 stated: "Propaganda, written or spoken, containing an appeal for the overthrow, undermining or weakening of the Soviet regime . . . and also the distribution, preparation or possession of texts with such a content entails the deprivation of freedom for a period of not less than six months." That meant—and from 1928 it was mandatory—ten years' detention. This first Criminal Code, drawn up with Lenin's direct participation and perfected by Stalin, was replaced in 1960 by a new Code. As before, any encroachment on the state's monopoly over the word was dealt with in the first part of the first chapter which referred to "especially dangerous crimes against the state." Article 70 repeats Article 58-10 almost word for word but extends its application: to "written and spoken propaganda conducted with the object of undermining or weakening the Soviet regime" is now added: "the spreading for the same purpose of slanderous fabrications likely to discredit the Soviet state and social system." The possibility of being prosecuted for an "incorrect" word was considerably increased. It was not now even necessary to "appeal for the overthrow of the Soviet regime," but sufficient to voice a "slanderous fabrication," which covered everything that had not been published in the Soviet press, to be exposed to a period of detention of from six months to seven years.

The articles of the Criminal Code are applied in specific circumstances, but the censorship is constantly at work on the language. The way the censorship works, placing its mark on every printed word, every picture and every note of music, can be judged by studying a number of works that were first published in censored form and later in the original, complete form. It is sufficient to compare, for example, the first edition of Bulgakov's novel *The Master and Margarita* with the next one, or the version of Fazil Iskander's novel *Sandro of Chegem,* published in Moscow and the one published in the United States; or the various editions of Soviet encyclopedias or of the works of Marx, Lenin, and Stalin.

In 1977–78 a previously top-secret document reached the West containing the official text of the instructions issued to the censors in Poland. It is entitled "Book of works banned and advice given by the Chief Administration for the control of the press, publishing and performances." It was brought to the West by a Polish censor, Tomasz Strzyżewski, and was published as *The Black Book of Polish Censorship.* Strzyżewski said that the Polish censors made roughly 10,000 interventions every year (in the 1970s)—either stopping some written work from being published, a play from being produced or a film from being shown, or demanding that changes be made in texts or pictures, or "recommending" how something should be written, put on the stage or filmed. *The Black Book,* a remarkable document, reveals more about the nature of the Soviet language than anything else that has been written about it. There can be no doubt that the Polish censorship was based on the Soviet model.

Marshall McLuhan considered the world as a semantic system in which information could give a true or false idea of reality. But censorship regards the world as a semantic system in which the information that is let through is the only reality. So there is no sense, from this point of view, in studying Soviet information or the Soviet language in terms of truth or falsehood. The lie penetrates the word and the word becomes a lie. Printed information, by virtue of having passed the censor and been printed, is transformed into a *fact,* the only reality. The best example of this is provided by the censor's instructions concerning river pollution: "It is forbidden to publish material about actual pollution by Polish industry of the Polish parts of rivers of which the sources are in Czechoslovakia. At the same time, information about pollution of these rivers by industrial activity on Czechoslovak territory is permitted."[28] Socialist industry never pollutes the rivers in its own socialist country! Mistakes may be made in a neighboring socialist country (Czechoslovakia, for example) and then there is pollution, but only up to the Polish frontier.

Censorship becomes a magic wand in the hands of the regime. It does not protect the socialist state from open criticism (there are other institutions for doing that) but it creates a semantic system that protects and defends socialism's ideal model. People appear and disappear at a wave of the censor's magic wand: writers, musicians and public figures whose names are banned from the press simply disappear. Later they may, in the event of a change of political tactics, be resurrected, that is to say, reappear in the press. Historical events disappear from books and newspapers and later return in a distorted form. (In 1975, for example, the Polish censors permitted, "in scholarly works, memoirs and biographies," the use of the phrase "died at Katyn" or "perished at Katyn" on condition, however, that the date of death was not earlier than 1941. This was intended to support the view that the Polish officers killed at Katyn had been executed by the Nazis.) Censorship puts a categorical ban on the reporting of any natural disasters or catastrophes. After it has gone to work on the flow of information, one is left with an impression of the ideal state and a country advancing confidently from socialism to communism. This impression is—it has to be—the only reality.

The censorship in Poland operates according to the same principles as govern the censorship in the USSR and other countries of "mature socialism." A similar kind of censorship operated in Hitler's Germany, because language as an instrument to control the human mind and to transform reality was also understood by the Nazis from the very beginning. And once they were in power the Nazis set about constructing a new language, Lingua Tertii Imperii, the Language of the Third Reich.

Throughout the twelve years of the Nazi regime the German philologist Victor Klemperer kept a diary in which he devoted special attention to the changes taking place in the German language and to the process of turning German into a new language of the Third Reich. Above all, he noted, "Everything that was printed and spoken in Germany was wholly under the control of the party bodies." The main feature of the new language was its extreme poverty, i.e., the exclusion of all "complicated" and "ambiguous" words; the absence of any distinction between the written and spoken word, the written word of the party documents becoming part of everyday language; changes in the value of words and the frequency of their use; and an emergent hierarchy in the vocabulary, with the words that the people in charge of linguistic policy found less important and unnecessary gradually disappearing (like those described as "obsolete" in Soviet dictionaries). Klemperer wrote: "Nazism enters into people's very flesh and blood through individual words, turns of speech and linguistic forms that are forced on people through being repeated millions of times and are absorbed mechanically and unconsciously." He underlined the significance of the "individual word" and the endless repetition of ready-made clichés.

The amazing similarity between the Nazi and Soviet propaganda techniques, treatment of the language, and symbols used is immediately apparent even with a fleeting study of Soviet and Nazi texts and iconography. Klemperer is of the opinion that the main symbols in Hitler's language, the model for the Nazi language, can be found already in *Mein Kampf,* published in 1925–26. New words—people, party, struggle—and new formulae were used with increasing frequency from the day the Nazis came to power. They made extensive use of military terminology in peacetime, just as, on Trotsky's initiative, the Bolsheviks did after the October Revolution. The "labor front," the "battle for the harvest"—that is the language of both Nazi Germany and the Soviet Union. Hitler took over from Soviet propagandists the famous triple portrait with the profiles of Marx, Engels and Lenin, replacing them with the profiles of Friedrich II, Bismarck and Hitler. Stalin borrowed Hitler's formula—governments come and governments go, but the German people remain—changing it to read, Hitlers come and go, but the German people remain. Stalin said: Marxism is not a dogma but a guide to action. Rosenberg said: Nazism is not a dogma but an attitude to the world. At the entrance to Hitler's concentration camps was written *Arbeit macht frei* and at the entrance to Stalin's: Labor is a matter of honor, of valor and heroism. On today's Soviet camps it says: Hard work is the road to early release. Germany was decorated with posters saying: Adolf Hitler means victory! In the Soviet Union the slogan said, Where Stalin is, there is victory![29]

The censorship exercised by Goebbels as minister for propaganda is almost as well known today as the work of the Polish censors. The technique for handling information and the word is identical. There is the same attitude to the word as the vehicle for a magical force. Goebbels banned the pejorative use of the word "propaganda," for example—"enemy propaganda." In the summer of 1942 he forbade the use in propaganda of the words "murder" and "sabotage," so as not to give rise to wrong ideas. In February 1944, when German losses on the Eastern front reached an incredible level, he forbade use of the expression "cannon fodder" even in reference to the enemy, so as not to evoke associations. By changing the words Goebbels was trying to change reality—reality was to be what Goebbels said it was. The history of Hitler's Germany is the most convincing evidence of the power of the word and the technique for manipulating it. The population of Germany, surrounded on all sides by mighty enemies, with daily proof of the reality of bombing from the air and by artillery, and the victorious advance of the enemy's armies, continued to the last minute to believe in Goebbels's propaganda. Klemperer reports that in April 1945 in Berlin under siege the Germans expected that on April 20, the Führer's birthday, there would be a miracle and the enemies would vanish like a mist in sunshine. The miracle—the faith in Hitler and in the reality created by his Word—is called by the American historian Herstein "the war Hitler won."

In the Soviet Union, the influence of the Word, of Soviet language, has continued now for seven decades. Poland has been within the "magic circle" of the Soviet language for four decades. Throughout that period Poles have had at their disposal another language, the language of the Church, which can serve as a point of comparative reference. Its example shows that, even in the most favorable conditions, total power over the language allows the regime to exert a powerful influence both on the language and, above all, on people's minds. In 1979 an unofficial Warsaw publisher produced material about a colloquium organized by the unofficial Society for Scientific Courses on the subject of the language of propaganda.[30] Linguists, historians, and writers analyzed the phenomenon I have called the Soviet language and which the Poles call *nowomowa,* a translation of Orwell's Newspeak. *Nowomowa* is a Soviet language with all its peculiarities, only sounding like Polish. The sociologist Stefan Amsterdamski distinguished four main features of *nowomowa:* the first and most important forces upon every word an obvious indication of its value of which there must not be the slightest doubt—the meaning is subordinate to the value; the second feature is a special synthesis of the pragmatic and ritual elements—the pragmatism connected with a word's function as propaganda and the need to take into account the circumstances and the audience; the ritual aspect connected with the specific situations in which only a particular language may be used (the ritual aspect puts strict limits on the pragmatism); the third is the magical quality of *nowomowa,* i.e., its presentation of what is desired as if it were real; using a word to create a reality, and failing to use it in order to condemn the thing, person or fact to non-being; and the fourth feature is that the word appears or disappears at the will of the supreme authority.

This Warsaw colloquium showed that the linguistic construction of which Vinokur wrote in 1923 has succeeded wildly, even in Poland. The Polish *nowomowa* constructed on the Soviet model has acquired all the qualities of a new language that Vinokur had described half a century before. Historians of "Solidarity" have pointed out the important role played in the emergence of their independent trade union movement by a free, uncensored press. Numerous underground books, newspapers and magazines appearing in the period 1976–80 tore open the magic circle of *nowomowa* and of Soviet language.

The nature of Soviet language has enabled it to become a universal language, the Esperanto of the late twentieth century. Today the world wants to dress in the American way, to eat in the American way, and to watch American films. But the world speaks in the Soviet way and gives expression to its fears and hopes in the Soviet language. This is true not only of the "progressive press," of which Moscow says that it "possesses certain features of the socialist press,"[31] and not only of the people whom Moscow calls "progressive public opinion in the world," but also of all the people who use the Soviet language without being aware of doing so. Monsieur Jourdain is a typical hero of our time.

The Polish writer Tadeusz Konwicki has written that, since time in socialist Poland is relative, the only calendar is kept in a safe at the Central Committee of the Polish Communist Party. The Western press and the speeches of statesmen and politicians in the non-Soviet world give the impression that the words defining the time around the entire planet are kept in a safe at the Central Committee of the CPSU. Moscow decides who are enemies and who are friends.

The use of Soviet language and Soviet vocabulary is essential for entering into the magic circle of progress and the bright future. In the Soviet sphere *nowomowa* is essential for upward advancement and becomes, in different countries at different speeds, the main means of communication. In the non-Soviet zone *nowomowa* achieves most success in political speech, in diplomacy and in the language of the "bearers of culture," determining a person's place in the elite.

The techniques used for sovietizing the minds of people in the non-Soviet world have not been sufficiently understood, but many of the channels through which Soviet language penetrates are well known. First of all, there are the slogans published in the Soviet press, the worldwide campaigns organized by Moscow and the "Communist and Workers' Parties" of the non-Soviet world. Soviet ideologists do not conceal the names of those who help them. While "monopoly capital" uses mass media for propaganda and for spreading its so-called "mass culture" and the language of the "ruling classes," "the Communist and Workers' parties . . . try to make extensive use of the national languages for the purpose of educating the peoples and spreading advanced culture and ideology."[32] But the failure to appreciate the part played by language is especially important, the failure to realize that, in conditions of the total warfare declared on the non-Soviet world, there are no innocent words. The use of words the meaning of which is defined by the Soviet dictionary turns a person's speech into *nowomowa* whether the speaker wishes it or not.

The American senator Daniel Patrick Moynihan speaks of "semantic infiltration" and of "the process by which we take over the language of our opponents in describing political reality."[33] This is an apt definition of the phenomenon that began in October 1917. The main characteristic of Soviet language—the value judgments contained in every word—changes the sense of even the most well-intentioned speech if it includes Soviet slogans, terms and definitions. It was sufficient to name one of the sides fighting in Lebanon in 1983 "Palestino-progressives" for any doubt about the justice of their aims to disappear. "Progress" is a good word, requiring no commentary. It was sufficient to dub the latest general secretary of the CPSU a "dove" and a "liberal" who was obstructed in his progressive intentions by "hawks" and "conservatives" for hope of a "Communism with a human face" to be reborn. When Cardinal Trinh, archbishop of Hanoi, invited the Pope to visit Vietnam and said, "We shall be very glad to welcome the pastor of our Church in our dear country, which is socialist, like your dear homeland, Poland,"[34] socialism received the highest accolade from the Church.

Alain Besançon has suggested that Soviet words ought to be properly translated: the word *kolkhoz,* meaning "collective farm," for example, should be translated "a serf plantation, run by an outside bureaucracy and under the surveillance of the apparatus of enforcement."[35] The only objection to this proposal would be that so many words would have to be retranslated. Western journalists would no longer be able to write "Soviet trade union delegation," since there is no such thing as a trade union in the Western sense in the Soviet Union. They would also have to stop writing about Soviet "elections" as well as about "détente," "the struggle for peace," "reforms," "socialist democracy," and so forth.

Soviet censors know very well the value of words and will permit no ambiguity. Because "in many languages of the world the word 'red' is closely associated in people's minds either with the Communist movement or with the Left in general," it was forbidden in Russia to write about the "Red Brigades"—they were left untranslated as *Brigata*

Rossa. And the Chinese word *dazybao* was not translated so as not to besmirch the Soviet "wall newspaper." There was to be no talk of "events in Afghanistan," only of "events around Afghanistan." In using "concepts connected with bourgeois ideology or in setting out bourgeois ideas concerning various aspects of our social and political life and our ideology" Soviet linguists insist on the use of inverted commas to indicate that the word or words are not to be taken at their face value. In the following sentence for example—"Problems of 'free exchange' and 'human rights' in socialist countries was one of the main points dealt with by the ideological services of NATO"—the inverted commas around "free exchange" and "human rights" are intended to ridicule the very possibility of doubting their absence in the country of "mature socialism."[36]

A decade ago a new concept was introduced into Soviet language, that of the country's "information space," comparable with its "air space." Determined steps were taken to protect Soviet citizens from receiving prohibited information. Among the censor's instructions to the Polish mass media there were, for example, compulsory "recommendations": "The official name, Korean People's Democratic Republic, must be used and the country must not be called North Korea. At the same time it was forbidden to call South Korea by its official name of the Korean Republic. It was to be called instead the puppet government of South Korea or the Seoul regime."[37] Long before the Helsinki agreement was signed, Polish censors, on instructions from Moscow, issued precise and detailed instructions as to what, how, when and where Poles could speak, write and display.

Defense of "the country's information space," of the Soviet zone, is the first function of the logocracy. The second function is an offensive operation, an attack on the "disinformation space" of the non-Soviet world. A powerful weapon in this offensive is the "semantic infiltration" of non-Soviet languages. In the course of negotiations with representatives of countries of the non-Soviet world the main aim of Soviet diplomats is to "sovietize" the language in which the talks are being conducted and to infiltrate it with words, terms, expressions and ideas with a Soviet content. In diplomatic documents and communiqués about meetings with statesmen and so forth, the Soviet vocabulary is used, so that they become coded texts with a double meaning, one for internal and the other for external use. People who take part in negotiations with logocrats and agree to use the

Soviet vocabulary are drawn into the magic circle of utopia and become its "honorary citizens."

Marx's statement that "being determines consciousness" is entirely applicable to the Soviet system if it is agreed that the being, the reality, in which people live is created by language. It is an illusory reality. And at the same time there is a real reality—bread and love, birth and death. Soviet language creates and reinforces the illusory reality. The living language enables the reality to exist. The formation of Soviet man is to a considerable extent a battle between two languages. The "new language" not only "tries to take the place of the classical language, it uses all kinds of means to destroy it. . . . Above all, those aspects of the language are destroyed that are essential for the discussion of social problems, history, ideology and politics."[38]

Logocracy, the power of language, possesses a tremendous force that is extremely difficult to resist. There are substitute words, substitute meanings, and a substitute reality. In the 1930s people who criticized the Nazi regime in Germany were asked: And what about the improved highways and the Volkswagen? Critics of the Fascist regime in Italy were told that it was only under Mussolini that the trains began to run on time. Free secondary education and an increase in the number of doctors compared with 1913 are supposed to convince people of the advantages of "mature socialism." In 1984 Pierre Vassal, a French anthropologist, went into raptures over the "superhuman efforts" of the Albanian people who had turned marshlands into fertile fields and had constructed an iron and steel plant, and so forth.[39] The logocracy makes it possible to simulate normality, ordinary life, in totalitarian conditions. Osip Mandelstam told his wife that Soviet citizens thought everything was normal because the trams were running. The Soviet language turned them into evidence that the illusory reality was normal. The people really do build factories in Albania, but it is also true that in that tightly sealed off country, with one word from the Leader the people unanimously forget their "eternal friends" of yesterday and turn them into "eternal enemies."

Studying the nature of language in a totalitarian system, George Steiner has concluded that the German language was used as the instrument of the "planning and practical bringing about of the catastrophe." Steiner well describes what Klemperer called the "language of the Third Reich": "Refined and coarse linguistics fuels Nazi ambitions, inspires its propaganda and devises lying, reassuring parodic terms to signify tortures and gas chambers." It is difficult to disagree with that. But at the same time he writes: "Stalin's vocabulary reflects the bankruptcy of the Word (no danger here for Russian literature) while the vocabulary of the Nazis reflects the hyperbolic, inflationary wreck of the Word that Goethe speaks about in *Faust II*."[40]

That is something one has to object to: the Stalinist vocabulary is not bankrupt; it has triumphed and remained triumphant. The scholar's differing attitudes to the two totalitarian languages—the understanding of the harm inflicted by Hitlerism on the German language and the failure to understand the damage done by the Soviet language to Russian—is, in fact, the most convincing evidence of the victory of the Soviet language. It would be very strange if no harm had been done to the language in which orders were given for people to be tortured in Soviet prisons, for executions in Soviet camps, for the extermination of millions of kulaks, and so forth.

In a logocracy the language is destroyed gradually, year by year. Optimists believe that the old women will preserve the Russian language, but today's old women grew up under the logocracy—in the 1930s they were young Communists and were taught the alphabet of Soviet language. The length of time the Soviet language has been doing its work and the emergence of new generations for whom the living Russian language is merely a dead language to be found only in old books spells victory for the Soviet language, and consequently for the transformation of people's minds, and victory of the dweller in utopia over humanity. Yet the living Russian language is putting up resistance to the new Soviet language and an important focus of this resistance is Russian classical literature, which is still studied and read in Soviet schools. The "studying," however, takes place in the Soviet language, and it is officially acknowledged that "the present generation is growing up with virtually no knowledge of the classical authors. . . . This is due primarily to the fact that the teaching of literature in the schools is not always on a satisfactory level."[41] And when the Russian classics of literature are published, they are commented on, whittled down, and interpreted to make them fit into the framework of the Soviet mentality.

Another form of resistance is the use of obscenities in everyday life. The Russian language has always been rich in swear-words which have served as an embellishment or to give vent to intemperate emotions. Foul language—in Russian, *mat'* ("mother")—has now become a universally accepted form of communication, used by Central Committee members and non-party people, drunks and non-drinkers, women and children, young and old, intellectuals and peasants. While it represents a challenge to the Soviet language, *mat'* is at the same time destroying Russian, restricting its vocabulary greatly and of course reducing the feelings it expresses to a primitive level.

After Stalin's death, at the time of the "thaw," many writers took it upon themselves to try to save the Russian language, notably Alexander Solzhenitsyn. He has tried to restore to Russian the richness of its vocabulary, digging into Vladimir Dal's pre-Revolutionary dictionary and using words and turns of phrase that have gone or been thrown out of circulation. The "village" writers seek an antidote in the use of dialects and the language used by writers in regions far from Moscow. Another important weapon for resisting the spread of the Soviet language is satire. The satirists—Erofeev, Voinovich, Sinyavsky, Aleshkovsky—try to ridicule the Soviet slogan-cliché and to dismantle the cage in which Russian has been imprisoned. Solzhenitsyn, Maximov, Dombrovsky and Vladimov have written some very effective satires, and it is no accident that they and their works have been excluded from officially approved literature. Satire is a great enemy of totalitarian language.

The strength of Soviet language lies in the fact that, being an instrument for transforming people, it is a medium of communication between "top" and "bottom," rulers and ruled, and is a linguistic system equally intelligible "above" and "below." The logocrats and the recipients of the Word are equally bound in the magic circle over which it exerts its influence. There are no augurs in the Soviet logocracy who, using the Word as a weapon, can protect themselves from its influence. Everybody lives and works within the bounds of the Soviet vocabulary and Soviet thought patterns. Rulers and ruled are equally convinced of the danger represented by the enemies which the former have created to frighten the latter.

The creation of a logocracy was possible only thanks to "cultural workers" actively participating in the construction of the Soviet language. Ernst Neizvestny observed, at the summit of the Soviet regime, the "reds" who "never make a mistake" and the "greens" who turn the animal noises of the "reds" into intelligible speech. That is how the Central Committee, the brain of the country, works. The label of "greens," which Neizvestny applied only to the Central Committee's back-room officials, should be extended to many others. For example,

Gorky acted as a "green" when he put many of Stalin's ideas into intelligible language; Sergei Eisenstein and other brilliant and talented, (as well as many less talented) writers, artists, musicians, and stage and film directors performed the same service. Neizvestny, who has an excellent understanding of the nature of the system, relates, with a candor that one can only admire, how he helped a Central Committee official compose a speech for one of the "greens" who was going abroad. He gives a rather vague explanation of why he did this, saying that "it is very difficult to know where the interests of the regime end and the interests of Russia begin."[42] He might presumably have added that he was flattered to be involved with the people in power.

Another great strength of the Soviet language is that it creates the illusion of a symbiosis between the rulers and the ruled and generates a sense of unity vis-à-vis the outside world. The Soviet language becomes the distinguishing feature of "our people" who, unlike "foreigners," can take things in at the slightest hint and read between the lines. The regime becomes part of the family, its opponents becoming enemies. Even "dissidents" begin to speak the Soviet language.

In 1968, Leonid Brezhnev detected the "treachery" of Alexander Dubček above all in the fact that Dubček began to talk "differently": "Way back in January I made several comments on your speech and I drew your attention to the fact that some of your statements were wrongly formulated. But you left them in! Is that the way to go about things?"[43] Dubček, who had graduated from a Party training school in the Soviet Union, had committed the most serious offense—he had changed the Word.

In 1914 Franz Kafka wrote a story called "In the Penal Colony," a story that may be considered as a brilliant parable of Soviet language. With extraordinary foresight he described what was to happen in the future. Only one form of punishment is used in the colony: a special machine is used to tattoo the sentence on the prisoner's body. The prisoner is not told what his sentence is, but, as the officer-executioner says, "He will get to know through his own flesh." The sentence is written down on paper and then transferred to the man's body in a special script. "Of course the script can't be a simple one—it's not supposed to kill a man straight off but, only after an interval of, on an average, twelve hours; the turning point is reckoned to come at the sixth hour. So there have to be lots and lots of flourishes." After six hours of continuous inscriptions comes what the officer called the "critical moment"; "... the man begins to understand the inscription, he purses his mouth as if he were listening . . . our man deciphers it with his wounds. To be sure, that is a hard task; he needs six hours to accomplish it. By that time the Harrow has pierced him quite through and casts him into the pit."

That is the way, one inscription after another following the pattern, in which the Soviet language writes on people's bodies and minds the inscription prepared by the logocrats. Their aim is not outright execution, as in the penal colony, but the transformation of man.

In one of the most terrible and most important books of the twentieth century, Varlaam Shalamov's *Kolyma Tales,* the last story is called "The Sentence." A prisoner dying from hunger and exhaustion is by some miracle transferred to light work, and he begins to regain his strength. With the courage of a great writer Shalamov describes how the man returns to life. He regains his feelings—anger, courage, fear, pity. The dying man is restricted to a vocabulary consisting of a few essential words. And suddenly a word occurs to him—"sentence." He doesn't understand what it means, he can't remember. It is only a week later that he remembers the meaning of the word "sentence." The word that had become for the dying man a sign of his "rebirth" turns out to be his "sentence." As in Kafka's story, the prisoner makes out the sentence on his own body. The joy which Shalamov's hero experiences when he understands the meaning of the word "sentence" recalls the feelings of the prisoner in the penal colony: "But how quiet he grows at the sixth hour. Enlightenment comes to the most dull-witted. It begins around the eyes. From there it radiates . . . the man begins to understand the inscription."

A man begins to understand Soviet language. He becomes an inhabitant of Utopia. He becomes a cog in the machine.

> *Winston Smith:* "I *know* that you will fail. There is something in the universe . . . some spirit, some principle—that you will never overcome."
> *O'Brien:* "What is it, this principle that will defeat us?"
> *Winston Smith:* "I don't know. The spirit of Man."
> *O'Brien:* "And do you consider yourself a man?"
> *Winston Smith:* "Yes."
> *O'Brien:* "If you are a man, Winston, you are the last man. Your kind is extinct: we are the inheritors."
> GEORGE ORWELL, *1984*

Conclusion

This conversation between O'Brien, the ideologue of the Inner Party, and Winston Smith, an inhabitant of Oceania, takes place in 1984. In the story of the totalitarian state described by Orwell it is a year of no particular significance, merely a stage on the road to 2050, when, with the final adoption of Newspeak, mankind's collective ability to remember its past is to be obliterated forever. In *1984* the machine emerges victorious: the state has destroyed the individual by turning him into a cog. According to Orwell, who wrote his novel in the late 1940s, a century should be enough to bring about this transformation.

In the seven decades since the Bolshevik victory in October 1917 human society as a whole and man as an individual have been subjected by the totalitarian Soviet state to a planned, concentrated and all-encompassing attack of unparalleled intensity. We can already assess some of the results: there have been important successes, but the Goal has yet to be achieved. But one cannot, however, give a definite answer to the question Orwell asked on the eve of the Second World War, a decade before the publication of his novel: "Is it just as possible to produce a breed of men who do not need liberty as to produce a breed of hornless cows?" Orwell admitted the failure of the Inquisition, but explained that this was because it had lacked the resources of the modern state: "The radio, press-censorship, standardized education and the secret police have altered everything. Mass suggestion is a science of the last twenty years, and we do not yet know how successful it will be."[1] Orwell wrote this in 1939. Today, almost half a century later, we know what success has been achieved by the technique of mass persuasion, especially when practiced by a totalitarian state.

The years devoted to remolding the human material have produced secrets. One of the most important consequences of the attempt to form the new Soviet man has been the disappearance of the idea that there is any difference between the rulers and the ruled, between "them" and "us." This is in part because by 1983 the Party had more than 18 million members, and because an extremely hierarchical society can reward an entire army of big, middle and small "bosses" with tiny crumbs of power—enabling them to refuse, withhold, forbid, obstruct, steal, and give or take bribes. This is because the country's intellectual elite, both academic and cultural, has merged with the power apparatus, to which it is exclusively devoted.

The uniqueness of the Soviet system and the efforts made to conceal its true nature have led to a situation where, every ten years, the "secret" of power in the Soviet Union is rediscovered. These discoveries are made both in the Soviet Union and outside it. In 1919 Lenin discovered that the "workers' state" which he was creating was prone to "bureaucratic deviations." Trotsky, after his removal from power, discovered that power in the Soviet Union was in the hands of the "bureaucratic apparatus." In 1953 Georgy Malenkov was defeated in the struggle for power because he had assumed that its "center" was in the Government, and not the Central Committee. It is not surprising, therefore that, undeterred by their many disappointments, Western statesmen and political scientists have never ceased "waiting for Godot"—for a general secretary who would qualify as a genuine liberal and democrat: if not Stalin, then Andropov, or Chernenko, or Gorbachev, or whoever is next on the list. The transparency of the screen that separates the authorities, who operate the levers of the machine, from the cogs, who can move only within very narrow limits, is one of the most important results of the process of "human remolding." The regime has succeeded in making people come to it with their complaints about their living conditions, which the regime itself has created. In pre-revolutionary Russia, as in every normal state, the dividing line between the upper and lower strata of society was self-evident and incontestable.

In the 1930s, for example, émigrés from Nazi Germany did not hesitate to call themselves "anti-fascists." It was obvious: those who fled Hitler's Germany were enemies of the regime. But Soviet émigrés do not as a rule describe themselves as anti-communist or anti-Soviet. For them those terms are pejorative; having left the Soviet zone, they begin to yearn for their unfreedom and for the Machine, in which, as cogs, they had felt so secure.

The process that turns human beings into cogs is about to enter its eighth decade. The Soviet system which, when it first appeared, offered the whole world a new model for Revolution has by no means lost its appeal. Now that it has reached maturity it offers the world a blueprint for the exercise of power. Those who long for the revolutionary fire and youthful ideological zeal of the early years are mistaken in believing that simply because the fire has gone out, and the enthusiasm subsided, the system has become weaker. On the contrary. Searching for new political forms, and losing faith in democracy, the world witnesses a true miracle: while remaining impoverished, a country becomes a superpower whose nuclear arsenal gives it the right to decide the fate of mankind. What is more, this miraculous country is ready to share the secret of its success with all who desire it. It is a prescription as simple and reliable as a Kalashnikov gun: a single party, privileges for the ruling class and a special technique for educating its citizens, who learn to be content with the gifts bestowed upon them by the Party and the Leader, who love and protect them. If Sékou Touré's Guinea had possessed nuclear weapons, it could have become an ideal specimen of the Soviet system. Nazism limited its system's sphere of influence to the areas it occupied; Marxism-Leninism proposes a model that is universally applicable.

The successes of the Soviet system, and the extent to which it has succeeded in spreading its model and its language, have generated a myth of its invincibility. In his novel *We,* Evgeny Zamyatin was the first writer to formulate the law of the One State: a totalitarian system can exist only if it turns the inhabitants of Utopia into cogs or, as he put it, numbers. In his novel, the state wins its final victory by performing on each citizen a small operation that excises from the brain the "center of imagination." In *1984*, the authorities remove Winston Smith's love for Julia by subjecting him to appalling tortures. He becomes a cog: he loves Big Brother.

In the early 1980s, sixty years after Zamyatin and thirty after Orwell, a voice rose from "the belly of the whale." It was that of Alexander Zinoviev, who related in detail the thoughts, feelings and wishes of *Homo sovieticus.* Logician and writer, Zinoviev does not distance himself from the product of the Soviet system, declaring "I am myself a Homosos." Speaking for himself—that is to say, for all Soviet citizens—Zinoviev repeats word for word what O'Brien told Winston Smith. The ideologue of the Inner Party asserts that "the Party cannot be overthrown. The rule of the Party is forever." Zinoviev insists that "Soviet society cannot be destroyed in a thousand years. . . . The Soviet system will continue to exist for the rest of human history." O'Brien ridicules the idea that proletarians or slaves might rise in revolt. "Put it out of your mind. They are helpless, like the animals. Humanity is the Party. Those who are outside it are irrelevant." Zinoviev makes it clear that "An internal protest cannot be imagined. You don't seem to be able to comprehend to what extent Soviet society is passive and regimented. . . . Our people are resigned. They are indifferent."[2] Zinoviev's explanation is a scientific one: the Soviet system will last forever because it conforms to the laws of history and nature. It goes without saying that *Homo sovieticus,* who obediently complies with the laws of the state, is even less likely to transgress against the laws of history and nature. And he insists that no one will ever be able to do so.

The Solidarity movement in Poland was a true revolutionary event precisely because it showed that it was still possible to rebel against the "laws." The events of 1980–81 in Poland were revolutionary first and foremost because the screen separating the rulers from the ruled lost its transparency. The gulf between "them," the "reds" as the Poles call them, and "us," society, once again became self-evident.

History abounds in examples of mighty empires that collapsed, when only yesterday they had seemed utterly stable. Various internal and external factors turned out to be the beginning of the end of these "everlasting" states. At the end of the twentieth century the world stands on the threshold of a new technological revolution. In advanced industrial countries, a transition is taking place from an industrial society to one based on information technology. But the Soviet system is incapable of making this transition. Free access to information would lead to its destruction. What would happen if the unparalleled opportunities created by the new technology were to break the magic circle which imprisons the Soviet people and they were to see and hear how badly they live? Yet the Soviet system will have to find ways of adapting to the technological revolution. Otherwise, the Soviet superpower will fall further and further behind militarily and will weaken. The legitimacy of the regime as the "defender" of the country will be seriously shaken and the pride of the once mighty state will be wounded—a pride which for decades has been the people's compensation for the poverty and privations they endured.

The dilemma created by this technological revolution is one of the forms taken by the main contradiction contained in the Plan itself, in the idea of creating Utopia and turning man into a cog. The successful formation of *Homo sovieticus,* in the end, depends exclusively upon the complete and final victory of the Soviet system throughout the world. The existence of an outside world, of an "abroad," is not only a constant source of temptation but also evidence of the weakness of the "only correct teaching," whose value and influence rest entirely on force. "Capitalist encirclement," so readily invoked by Soviet ideologues, is a threat to the complete transformation of man. The destruction of the outside world thus becomes a prerequisite for the final triumph of the state over the individual. If the worldwide advance of the Soviet system could be halted, that would make it possible to stop the process which is forming the cogs without which the Machine cannot exist and which can themselves exist only as parts of the Machine.

On the threshold of the third millennium, the fate of mankind depends on an answer to the question: Is it possible to transform human nature?

NOTES

INTRODUCTION

1. M. S. Gorbachev, "O perestroike i kadrovoi politike partii" (speech to Plenum of the Central Committee of the CPSU, January 27, 1987), *Pravda,* January 28, 1987.
2. I. V. Stalin, *Collected Works,* Vol. 13, p. 357.
3. Quoted by Aleksei Adzhubei in "Vremya v litsakh i detalyakh," *Komsomolskaya Pravda,* May 17, 1986.
4. Gorbachev, op. cit.
5. Fyodor Burlatsky, "Razgovor nachistotu. Polemichesky dialog o perestroike," *Literaturnaya Gazeta,* October 1, 1986.
6. Gorbachev, op. cit.
7. *Literaturnaya Gazeta,* January 1, 1986.
8. G. Smirnov, "Revolutsionnaya suts obnovleniya," *Pravda,* March 13, 1987.
9. Ibid.
10. Quoted in *Pravda,* March 2, 1987.
11. N. P. Makarov, *Polny russko-frantsusky slovar,* Petrograd, 14th ed., 1918.
12. Quoted in *Pravda,* January 29, 1987.
13. Vladimir Shubkin, *Byurokratika, Znanie,* New York 1987, pp. 164, 169, 166.
14. *Pravda,* February 14, 1987.
15. V. I. Lenin, *Collected Works,* Vol. 36, p. 143.
16. *Kommunist,* No. 18, 1975, p. 36.
17. Quoted in *Pravda,* January 29, 1987.
18. Stalin, op. cit., Vol. 12, p. 173.
19. I. V. Stalin, "Rech na vypuske akademikov Krasnoi Armii," *Pravda,* May 6, 1935.

20. Gorbachev, op. cit.
21. Stalin, op. cit., Vol. 13, p. 354.
22. T. I. Oizerman, *Voprosy filosofii*, No. 11, 1985.
23. Gorbachev, op. cit.
24. *History of the All-Union Communist Party (Bolsheviks): Short Course*, Moscow 1950.
25. *Il Mondo Economico*, October 28, 1986.
26. Vasily Grossman, *Life and Fate*, Boston 1985, pp. 764–5.
27. *International Herald Tribune*, March 5, 1987.
28. *Pravda*, September 20, 1986.
29. Gorbachev, op. cit.
30. *Pravda*, March 21, 1926.
31. Smirnov, op. cit.
32. Lion Feuchtwanger, *Moscow 1937*, p. 174.

I THE GOAL

I. THE BEGINNING OF THE EXPERIMENT

1. N. Bukharin, *Programma RKP*, 1917.
2. Alexander Herzen, *Collected Works*, Vol. XVI, p. 28.
3. Maxim Gorky, *Untimely Thoughts*, New York 1968; November (20), 1917, p. 86; November 10 (23), 1917, p. 89; December 10 (23), 1917, pp. 106, 107; May 26, 1918, p. 211; June 6, 1918, p. 232.
4. Ibid., December 10 (23), 1917, p. 106.
5. Galina Nikolaeva, "Cherty budushchego," *Pravda*, January 7, 1949.
6. Yury Trifonov, *Studenty*, Moscow 1953, p. 369.
7. *Sovetskie lyudi*, Moscow 1974, p. 3.
8. *Pravda*, February 25, 1986.
9. Ibid., October 15, 1981.
10. Ibid., June 15, 1983.
11. Edward Kuznetsov, *Prison Diaries*, New York 1975.
12. Alexander Zinoviev, *Homo Sovieticus*, Boston 1985.
13. *Pravda*, October 18, 1961.
14. Evgeny Zamyatin, *We*, New York 1972.
15. Cited in *Le Monde*, September 1, 1982, and February 4, 1983.
16. Ibid., August 20, 1975.
17. Bertrand Russell, *The Practice and Theory of Bolshevism*, London 1920, p. 131.
18. *Che-Ka. Materialy po deyatelnosti chrevzychainykh kommissii*, Predislovie Viktora Chernova, Berlin 1922.

2. SKETCH FOR A PORTRAIT

1. Igor Shafarevich, *Sotsializm kak yavlenie mirovoi istorii*, Paris 1977, p. 374.
2. *Malaya Sovetskaya Entsiklopediya* (Short Soviet Encyclopedia), Moscow 1930, Vol. I, p. 287.
3. For the complete text of the proclamation, see M. Lemke, *Politicheskiye protsessy v Rossii 1860-kh gg.*, 2nd ed., Moscow 1923, pp. 510–18.
4. M. N. Pokrovsky, "Korni bolshevizma v russkoi istorii," *25 let RKP (Bolshevikov)*, Tver 1923, p. 24.
5. Maxim Gorky, *Sobranie sochinenii v 30 tomakh*, Vol. XXV, Moscow 1953, p. 226.

6. See A. Anenskaya, "Iz proshlykh let," *Russkoe bogatstvo*, 1913, Book I, p. 63.
7. P. N. Tkachev, *Izbrannie sochineniya na sotsialno-politicheskie temy*, Moscow 1932, Vol. III, pp. 220–9.
8. Ibid., Vol. I, p. 174.
9. A. Arosev, *Ot Zhëltoi reki*, Moscow 1927, pp. 138–9.
10. Tkachev, op. cit., Vol. I, p. 195.
11. *Cahiers du monde russe et soviétique*, No. 4, 1966.
12. N. Pirumova, "M. Bakunin ili S. Nachaev?," *Prometei*, No. 5, 1968, p. 178.
13. George Orwell, *Collected Essays*, New York 1968, Vol. IV, p. 21.
14. N. G. Chernyshevsky, *What Is to Be Done?*, New York 1961, pp. 221–41.
15. Ibid., p. 224.
16. I. S. Turgenev, *Sobranie sochinenii v 28 tomakh*, Vol. 8, p. 478.
17. F. M. Dostoevsky, *Sobranie sochinenii v 10 tomakh*, Moscow 1956, Vol. IV, p. 159.
18. N. Berdyaev, "Filosofskaya istina i intelligentskaya pravda," in *Landmarks: A Collection of Articles on the Russian Intelligentsia*, 1977.
19. L. Panteleev, *Iz vospominanii proshlogo*, Moscow and Leningrad 1934, Vol. I, pp. 53–8.
20. Cited in N. Valentinov, *Vstrechi s Leninym*, New York 1953, p. 103.
21. Pokrovsky, op. cit.
22. V. Bonch-Bruevich, "Lenin o khudozhestvennoi literature," *Tridtsat dnei*, Moscow 1934, No. 1, p. 19.
23. P. N. Tkachev, "Narod i revolyutsiya," op. cit., Vol. III.
24. Alexander Gambarov, *V sporakh o Nechaeve*, Moscow 1926, p. 123.
25. Cited in Bonch-Bruevich, op. cit., p. 18.

3. HOMO SOVIETICUS SUM

1. *Pravda*, December 25, 1918.
2. Maximilian Voloshin, *Severovostok*, "Puti Rossi," *Ekho*, 1969, p. 43.
3. Bertrand Russell, *The Practice and Theory of Bolshevism*, London 1920.
4. N. Berdyaev, *Novoe srednevekove. Razmyshleniya o sudbakh Rossii i Evropi*, Berlin 1924, p. 94.
5. V. Afanasev, "Ob upravlenii ideologicheskoi sferoi v sotsialisticheskom obshchevestve," *Kommunist*, 1975, No. 12.
6. Andrei Platonov, "Gradov City," *Russian Literature Triquarterly* 5 (Winter 1973), pp. 371–98.
7. Albert Rhys Williams, *Through the Russian Revolution*, London 1923.
8. *Sovetskie lyudi*, pp. 4–5.
9. Alexander Zinoviev, *Homo Sovieticus*.
10. L. Averbakh, *O zadachakh proletarskoi literatury*, Moscow and Leningrad 1928, pp. 18, 19.
11. *Letopis Marksizma*, 1928, No. 1, p. 35.
12. See Nicholas Bethell, *The Last Secret*, New York 1974, and Mark R. Elliott, *Pawns of Yalta*, Carbondale, Illinois, 1982.

II THE VECTORS

1. Nadezhda Mandelstam, *Hope Against Hope*, New York 1970, p. 163.
2. Cited in Averbakh, op. cit., p. 18.

4. INFANTILIZATION

1. Robert J. Lifton, *Thought Reform and the Psychology of Totalism*, New York 1963.
2. Ibid.
3. The official name for the means of communication in the USSR. The accepted abbreviation is SMIP.
4. See *Literaturnaya gazeta*, No. 22, June 1, 1983.
5. *Izvestia*, August 27, 1978.
6. Semyon Gluzman, "Strakh svobody," in *Russkaya Mysl*, August 28, 1980.
7. S. Kogan, *Literatura etikh let, 1917–1923*, Ivanovo-Boznesensk 1924, pp. 79, 35.
8. Evgeny Zamyatin, *We*, p. 189.
9. Lenin, *Collected Works*, Vol. 36, p. 172.
10. Bruno Bettelheim, *The Informed Heart*, New York 1973.
11. Ibid.
12. Iosif Mendelevich, "Vospominaniya" (manuscript).
13. *Vestnik russkogo studencheskogo khristianskogo dvizheniya*, Paris and New York 1970, No. 98.
14. The first references to concentration camps appear in official documents in June 1918. See my *Kontsentratsionny mir i sovetskaya literatura*, London 1975.
15. Speech of February 17, 1919. *Istorichesky arckhiv*, 1958, No. 1, pp. 6–11.
16. Roger Pethybridge, *The Social Prelude to Stalinism*, London 1974, p. 140.
17. Lenin, *Collected Works*, 4th ed., Vol. 33, p. 55.
18. Nadezhda Mandelstam, *Hope Against Hope*, p. 167.
19. *Narodnoe obrazovanie v SSSR. Sbornik dokumentov 1917–1923*, Moscow 1974, p. 377.
20. See B. A. Myasoedov, *Strana chitaet, slushaet, smotrit*, Moscow 1982, p. 3.
21. See *Knizhka partinogo aktivista*, Moscow 1980, pp. 159, 161.
22. Andrei Platonov, *The Foundation Pit*, Ann Arbor, Michigan, 1973, p. 212.
23. Interview with Robert Conquest, Novosti, New York, November 5, 1983.
24. *Pravda*, December 25, 1974.

5. THE NATIONALIZATION OF TIME

1. Lenin, *Collected Works*, Vol. 39, p. 89.
2. Raymond Robins, *My Own Story*, quoted in Robert Payne, *The Life and Death of Lenin*, London 1964, p. 408.
3. Speech delivered October 17, 1921.
4. Lenin, *Collected Works*, 4th ed., Vol. 29, p. 215.
5. Hayek was one of the first to reveal the essence of the planned economy in his book *The Road to Serfdom* (Russian edition: London 1944). The award of the Nobel Prize for economics to Hayek in 1982 indicates that, although belatedly, the importance of his ideas has been recognized.
6. Igor Birman, *Ekonomika Nedostach*, New York 1983.
7. *Pravda*, August 16, 1982 (leading article).
8. *Pravda*, August 29, 1929.
9. Yury Andropov, "Uchenie Karla Marxa i nekotorie voprosy sotsialisticheskogo stroitelstva v SSSR," *Kommunist*, 1983, No. 3, p. 20.
10. *Vospominaniya A. V. Lunacharskogo—Literaturnoe nasledstvo*, Moscow 1971, Vol. 80, p. 46.

11. V. Kaverin, *Khudozhnik neizvesten—Sobranie sochinenii v 6 tomakh*, Moscow 1964, Vol. 2, p. 68.
12. V. Dudintsev, *Not by Bread Alone*, New York 1957, pp. 32–3.
13. Ya. Ilin, *Bolshoi konvieier*, Moscow 1954, p. 21.
14. *Voprosy ekonomicheskogo rayonirovaniya (1917–1929)*, Moscow 1957, p. 72.
15. Archives of the Czechoslovak Communist Party. Secret documents of Rudolf Slansky. Quoted in Karel Kaplan, "Stalin: The Creation of Comecon and Czechoslovakia," in *Problems of Eastern Europe*, New York 1983, 7–8, p. 119.
16. Stalin, *Collected Works*, Vol. 12, p. 169.
17. *Istoriya SSSR s drevneishikh vremyon do nashikh dnei v 12 tomakh*, Moscow 1967, Vol. 8, pp. 250, 255.
18. Simon Leys, "L'Indignation," in *Commentaire*, Autumn 1983, No. 23, p. 641.
19. V. Lysenko, *Posledni reis*, Frankfurt-on-Main 1982, pp. 51, 220.
20. *Nedlya*, April 1983.
21. *Pravda*, August 22, 1975.
22. A. Chernousov, "Praktikant," *Sibirskie ogni*, 1975.
23. Birman, op. cit., p. 47.
24. Marshall I. Goldman, *USSR in Crisis: The Failure of an Economic System*, New York and London, 1983, pp. 31–2.
25. *Izvestia*, May 22, 1983.

6. IDEOLOGIZATION

1. *Kratky politichesky slovar*, Moscow 1983, p. 109.
2. F. A. Hayek, *Law, Legislation and Liberty*, London 1979.
3. V. I. Lenin, *Collected Works*, Vol. 45, p. 106.
4. George Orwell, *Collected Essays*, Vol. 4, p. 75.
5. Ibid., Vol. 2, p. 286.
6. Nadezhda Mandelstam, *Hope Against Hope*, p. 126.
7. Alexander Galich, *Kogda ya vernus*, Frankfurt-on-Main 1981, p. 378.
8. Stalin, *Collected Works*, Vol. 13, p. 39.
9. V. Kaverin, "Neskolko let," in *Novy Mir*, 1966, No. 11.
10. See Raïsa Berg, *Sukhovei*, New York 1983, p. 120.
11. Ibid., p. 121.
12. See Michel Tatu, *Power in the Kremlin*, New York 1969, pp. 132–6.
13. See Berg, op. cit., p. 117.
14. Stalin, *Collected Works*, Vol. 13, p. 178.
15. Ilya Ehrenburg, *Sobranie sochinenii v 9 tomakh*, Moscow 1967, Vol. 9, p. 192.
16. Nadezhda Mandelstam, op. cit., p. 21.
17. Nikita Khrushchev, *Khrushchev Remembers*, New York 1982, p. 207.
18. *Baikal*, 1967, Nos. 5 and 6; 1968, No. 1.
19. *Sovetsky Soyuz*, 1968, No. 11.
20. Stanislav Rodionov, *Dolgoe delo*, Leningrad 1981, p. 211.
21. Maxim Luzhanin, "Bessonny telefon," *Belarus*, No. 4, 1977.
22. As he watched hundreds of thousands of people who had come to take their leave of Lenin in 1924, Osip Mandelstam commented: "They've come to complain to Lenin about the Bolsheviks." Nadezhda Mandelstam, *Hope Abandoned*, New York 1974, p. 205.
23. Vasily Shukshin, *Besedy pri yasnoi lune*, Moscow 1974.
24. V. Kolupaev, "Volyevoe usilie," *Fantastika 1969–70*, Moscow 1974.

25. Vasily Shukshin, "I Believe," in *Snowball Berry Red*, Ann Arbor, Michigan, 1979, p. 94.
26. Varlaam Shalamov, *Kolyma Tales*, London 1980.
27. Tadeusz Borowski, *This Way to the Gas, Ladies and Gentlemen*, New York 1967, p. 121.
28. Alexander Solzhenitsyn, *The First Circle*, p. 83.
29. Lenin, *Collected Works*, 4th ed., Vol. 5, p. 435.
30. Ibid., Vol. 39, p. 224.
31. *Krasnaya kniga VChK*, ed. P. Makintsian, 1920, Vol. I, p. 3.
32. See George Legett, *The Cheka, Lenin's Political Police*, London 1983.
33. George Orwell, *1984*, p. 210.
34. Quoted in *Pravda*, March 29, 1937.
35. S. Tsvigun, "O proiskakh imperialisticheskikh razvedok," in *Kommunist*, 1981, No. 14.
36. See *Cahiers du monde russe et soviétique*, 1982, Vol. XXIII (I).
37. Alexander Orlov, *Handbook of Intelligence and Guerrilla Warfare*, Ann Arbor, Michigan, 1963.
38. Yury Korolkov, *Chelovek dlya kotorogo ne bylo tain (Richard Sorge)*, Moscow 1966.
39. Chingiz Aitmatov, *Buranny polustanok*, Moscow 1981, p. 168.
40. Gorky, *Untimely Thoughts*, p. 86, November 7 (20), 1917.
41. Ibid., p. 89, November 10 (23), 1917.
42. See M. Heller and A. Nekrich, *Utopia in Power*, New York 1986, p. 60.
43. *Pravda*, May 4, 1918.
44. Just one of the stories invented about Lenin. See H. Valentinov, *Maloznakomy Lenin*, Paris 1972.
45. L. V. Bulgakova (ed.), *Materialy k biografii Lenina*, Leningrad 1924.
46. Leon Trotsky, "Lenin kak natsionalny tip," *Pravda*, April 23, 1920; Zinoviev cited in *Pravda*, April 23, 1920; there was an added comment to Mayakovsky's remark: That's the way it has been for seven decades; we say one thing and mean another.
47. A. Lunacharsky, *Shtrikhi. Lenin—tovarishch, chelovek*, Moscow 1966, p. 179.
48. *Izvestia*, January 24, 1924.
49. See my *Andrei Platonov v poiskakh shchastya*, Paris 1982.
50. M. Olminsky, "Kriticheskiya stati i zametki," *Proletarskaya revolyutsia*, 1931, No. I, pp. 149–50.
51. Nina Tumarkin, *Lenin Lives! The Lenin Cult in Soviet Russia*, Cambridge, Mass., 1983.
52. Kazimir Malevich, *Iz knigi o bespredmetnosti*, Malevich archives, quoted in Tumarkin, op. cit., p. 190.
53. *Kommunisticheskoe prosveshcheniye*, 1924, No. I, p. 67.
54. Heller and Nekrich, op. cit.
55. Stalin's report to the Central Committee of the Party, March 3, 1937, reported in *Pravda*, March 29, 1937.
56. *Literaturnaya gazeta*, November 24, 1962.
57. A. Tvardovsky, *Za dalyu dal*, Moscow 1970, p. 132.
58. A. Ivanov, "Vechny zov," *Roman gazeta*, 1978, No. 2, p. 47.
59. Pyotr Proskurin, "Imya tvoe," *Roman gazeta*, 1978, No. 13, pp. 8, 26.
60. Alexander Zinoviev, *Nashei yunosti polyot*, Lausanne 1983, p. 29.
61. Andrzej Drawicz, *"Master i Margarita" kak orudie samozashchity*, in *Odna ili dve russkie literatury*, Lausanne 1981.

62. *Knizhka partinogo aktiva,* Moscow 1980, p. 115.
63. *Spravochnik propagandista,* Moscow 1975, p. 100.
64. *Pravda,* March 7, 1982.
65. B. A. Yasoedov, *Strana chitaet, slushaet, smotrit (Statisticheski obzor),* Moscow 1982, p. 23.
66. Ibid., p. 20.
67. Vasily Grossman, *Forever Flowing,* New York 1972, pp. 141, 142.
68. Yury Dombrovsky, *Khranitel drevnostei,* Paris 1978, pp. 131, 184.
69. Boris Pasternak, *Doctor Zhivago,* New York 1958.

7. TOTALITARIANIZATION

1. Leszek Kolakowski, "Totalitarianism and the Virtue of the Lie," in *1984 Revisited: Totalitarianism in Our Country,* New York 1983, p. 122.
2. Evgeny Zamyatin, *We,* pp. 12–13.
3. George Orwell, *Collected Essays,* Vol. 2, p. 135.
4. George Orwell, *1984,* p. 205.
5. Jerry F. Hough and Merle Fainsod, *How the Soviet Union Is Governed,* Cambridge, Mass., 1979, pp. 622, 526.
6. Ibid., p. 523.
7. Leonard Schapiro, *The Communist Party of the Soviet Union,* New York 1970.
8. *Konstitutsiya (osnovnoi zakon) SSSR,* Moscow 1974, p. 28.
9. *Konstitutsiya SSSR,* Moscow 1978, p. 3.
10. Basile Kerblay, *Modern Soviet Society,* New York 1983.
11. Sergei Polikanov, *Razryv. Zapiski atomnogo fizika,* Frankfurt 1983, p. 157.
12. A. Bek, *Novoe naznachenie,* Frankfurt, 1971, p. 21.
13. Stefan Heym, *Collin,* London 1980.
14. Evgeny Zamyatin, *We,* p. 157.
15. Schapiro, op. cit., p. 851.
16. Hannah Arendt, *The Origins of Totalitarianism,* New York 1951, p. 374.
17. *Pervy vsesoyuzny syezd sovetskikh pisatelei, Stenograficheski otchot,* Moscow 1934, p. 1.

III THE INSTRUMENTS

8. FEAR

1. A. Afinogenov, *Strakh,* pp. 48, 15.
2. Alexander Solzhenitsyn, *Gulag Archipelago,* New York 1974.
3. See Jean Delumeau, *Le Peur en Occident,* Paris 1978, pp. 27, 49; Gustave Le Bon, *The Crowd,* New York 1960; and Norman Cohn, *Europe's Inner Demons,* New York 1975.
4. M. Ya. Latsis (Sudrabs), *Dva goda borby na vnutrennem fronte,* Moscow 1920, p. 2.
5. See V. D. Bonch-Bruevich, *Na boyevykh postakh fevralskoi i oktyabrskoi revolyutsii,* Moscow 1930, p. 199.
6. M. Ya. Latsis (Sudrabs), *Cheka v borbe s kontrrevolyutsiei,* Moscow 1920, p. 8.
7. Interviewed June 26, 1919, in Poltava. See *Pamyat,* No. 2, p. 429.
8. Vasily Grossman, *Forever Flowing,* p. 181.
9. L. Trotsky, *Terrorism and Communism,* Ann Arbor, Michigan, 1961.

10. Pierre Pascal, *En Russie Rouge: Lettres d'un Communiste français*, Petrograd 1920.
11. See *Cheka—Materialy po deyatelnosti chrezvychainykh kommissii*, Central Bureau of the Party of Socialist-Revolutionaries, Berlin 1922.
12. Ya. Kh. Peters, *Vospominaniya o rabote v Cheka v pervy god revolyutsii*, quoted in *Byloe*, 1933, No. 11, pp. 122–3.
13. Lenin, *Collected Works*, Vol. 36, p. 280; *Dekrety sovetskoi vlasti*, Vol. 2, p. 411.
14. Ibid., Vol. 54, p. 296; Vol. 45, pp. 118–21.
15. Trotsky, op. cit., p. 58.
16. R. Abramovich, *The Soviet Revolution 1917–1939*, London, p. 312.
17. *Pravda*, December 25, 1918.
18. Quoted by I. Knizhnik, "Frantsuzsky intelligent o Sovetskoi Russii," in *Kniga i Revolutsiya*, 1921, Nos. 10–11, p. 13.
19. Quoted by Latsis, op. cit., p. 10.
20. Quoted by Lunacharsky in *V Narkomprose*, Moscow 1931, p. 182.
21. Latsis, ibid.
22. Ilya Ehrenburg, *Rvach*, in *Sobranie sochinenii v 9 tomakh*, Moscow 1964, Vol. 2, p. 798.
23. Quoted in Lev Nikulin, *Myotvaya zyb*, Moscow 1966, p. 22.
24. I. Z. Steinberg, *Nravstvenny lik revolyutsii*, Berlin 1923, p. 127.
25. Lenin, op. cit., Vol. 44, pp. 53, 54; 327–9.
26. Ibid., Vol. 45, pp. 190, 191.
27. *Pravda*, April 10, 1921.
28. Nikolai Erdman, *The Suicide*, in *Russian Literature Triquarterly* (Fall 1973), p. 44.
29. See M. Heller and A. Nekrich, *Utopia in Power*, and my *Kontsentratsionny mir i sovetskaya literatura*, London 1974.
30. Lenin, op. cit., Vol. 35, pp. 54, 55.
31. Latsis, op. cit., p. 24.
32. I. V. Stalin, *Collected Works*, Vol. 13, p. 114.
33. M. Gorky, *Collected Works*, Vol. 27, p. 509.
34. Evgeny Evtushenko, *Kater svyazi*, Moscow 1966, p. 192.
35. Lysenko, *Posledni reis*, p. 204.
36. Ibid., pp. 204–5.
37. N. V. Ogarkov, *Vsegda v gotovnosti k zashchite otechestva*, Moscow 1982, p. 68; B. Demin, "Nenavist k vragu," *Kommunist vooruzhennykh sil*, No. 13, 1969.
38. G. E. Glezerman, *Rozhdenie novogo cheloveka. Problemy formirovaniya lichnosti pri sotsializme*, Moscow 1982, p. 244.
39. Pyotr Proskurin, "Imya tvoe," *Roman gazeta*, Nos. 13–16, 1978 (circulation 1,609,-000); No. 14, pp. 57–8.
40. Evgeny Zamyatin, *We*, pp. 41–4.
41. Quoted in V. Amenqual, *¡Que viva Eisenstein!*, Lausanne 1980, p. 310.
42. *Literaturnaya gazeta*, March 19, 1969.
43. Semyon Kirsanov, "Sem dnei nedeli," *Novy Mir*, 1956, No. 9.
44. The *Small Soviet Encyclopedia* of 1930 gave this definition: "Cosmopolitan (from the Greek meaning citizen of the world)—a person who considers the whole world to be his fatherland and does not recognize himself as belonging to a particular nationality." In 1953 "cosmopolitan" was defined as "a supporter of cosmopolitanism," a "reactionary, anti-patriotic, bourgeois outlook, hypocritically taking the

whole world as a fatherland, rejecting the value of a national culture, and denying the right of nations to an independent existence as well as the idea of defending the fatherland and the independence of the state." The article concludes with a threat: "Cosmopolitanism is the ideology of American imperialism striving for world domination" (*Dictionary of the Russian Language,* by S. I. Ozhegov, Moscow). Thirty years later the four-volume dictionary said: "Cosmopolitanism—a reactionary bourgeois ideology which preaches the rejection of national traditions and culture, opposes state and national sovereignty and puts forward the idea of a 'world state' and 'citizenship of the world' " (Vol. 2, Moscow 1983). The *Short Political Dictionary* (1983) fills out this definition with a warning: "Bourgeois cosmopolitanism is the reverse of proletarian internationalism and hostile to it."

45. According to the 1979 census—1,811,000. See *Naselenie SSSR,* Moscow 1983, p. 128.
46. Vladimir Begun, *Polzuchaya kontrrevolyutsia,* Minsk 1974, p. 3.
47. L. A. Korneev, *Klassovaya sushchnost sionizma,* Kiev 1982, pp. 12, 96, 44, 45. Korneev refers to a book by one of the most active pre-revolutionary anti-Semites—A. Selyaninov, *Tainaya sila masonstva,* St. Petersburg 1911.
48. Ivan Shevtsov, *Vo imya otsa i syna,* Moscow 1970, pp. 328, 379.
49. Korneev, op. cit., p. 64.
50. *Komsomolskaya Pravda,* April 19, 1971.
51. See Marian Pilka, "Deformacje w wykladzie historii w podrecznikach dla szkol srednich," *Zeszyty Historyczne,* 1982, No. 61, p. 7.
52. Eduard Bagritsky, *Stikhotvoreniya i poemy,* Moscow and Leningrad 1964, p. 126.
53. Nikita Khrushchev, *Izbrannie otryvki,* New York 1979, p. 191.
54. Alexander Zinoviev, *Homo Sovieticus,* p. 192.
55. *Polskaya revolutsia.* Samizdat material from the Samizdat Archive. Radio Liberty Issue No. 16, 1983, p. 50.

9. LABOR

1. *Istoriya SSSR,* Vol. 7, p. 114.
2. S. N. Prokopovich, *Narodnoe khozyaistvo SSSR,* New York 1952, Vol. 1, p. 330.
3. Ibid., p. 322.
4. *Mysl* (Kharkov), 1919, No. 7. Quoted in P. A. Garvi, *Professionalnie soyuzy v Rossii v pervie gody revolyutsii (1917–21),* New York 1958, pp. 47, 48.
5. M. Gorky, *Untimely Thoughts,* p. 89.
6. V. I. Lenin, *Collected Works,* Vol. 35, p. 196.
7. Ibid., Vol. 40, p. 315.
8. Ibid., Vol. 36, p. 188.
9. L. Trotsky, *Terrorism and Communism,* p. 176.
10. Lenin, *Collected Works,* Vol. 36, p. 203.
11. Ibid., Vol. 39, p. 264.
12. A. Volsky (V. Makhaisky), *Umstvenny rabochi,* New York 1968, p. 361.
13. Lenin, *Collected Works,* 4th ed., Vol. 30, p. 260.
14. Trotsky, op. cit., p. 176.
15. N. Bukharin, *Ekonomika perekhodnogo perioda* (Moscow 1920), in *Put k sotsializmu,* New York 1967, p. 118.
16. *Sovetskoe narodnoe zakonodatelstvo,* Moscow 1968, p. 155.
17. *Izvestia,* March 26, 1919.
18. See *Kratki slovar po selskoi ekonomike,* Moscow 1983; *Upravlenie narodnym khozyaistvom,* Slovar, Moscow, 1983; *Kratki politicheski slovar,* Moscow 1983.

19. *Istoricheski arkhiv,* 1958, No. 1, pp. 6–11.

20. Speech at the Third All-Union Congress of Trade Unions, April 9, 1920.

21. *Istoriya sovetskogo gosudarstva i prava v trekh knigakh. Kniga 2,* Moscow 1968, p. 499.

22. *Ugolovny kodeks SSSR,* Moscow 1932, p. 128; *Istoriya sovetskogo gosudarstva i prava,* pp. 510, 509.

23. *Malaya Sovetskaya Entsiklopediya,* Vol. 8, Moscow 1930.

24. Quoted from *Sotsialisticheski Vestnik,* No. 11, June 13, 1931.

25. I. Stalin, "O nedostatkakh partinoi raboty . . . ," *Pravda,* March 29, 1937.

26. *Pravda,* August 21, 1975.

27. S. Shtut, *Kakov ty, chelovek?,* Moscow 1964, p. 277.

28. Stalin, op. cit.

29. O. Litovsky, "Film o bditelnosti," *Kino,* No. 17, March 30, 1936.

30. Lenin, *Collected Works,* Vol. 37, pp. 407–11.

31. M. F. Getmanets, *Makarenko i kontseptsiya novogo cheloveka v sovetskoi literature 20–30 godov,* Kharkov 1978, p. 207; A. S. Makarenko, *Collected Works,* Moscow 1951, Vol. 7, p. 13.

32. *Pravda,* December 20, 1938.

33. Ibid., January 4, 1939.

34. *Trud,* October 26, 1973; *Pravda,* April 12, 1984.

35. *Pravda,* ibid.

36. The story was printed in *Novy Mir,* No. 2, 1963.

37. Vladimir Voinovich, *In Plain Russian,* New York 1979, p. 66.

38. Alexander Zinoviev, *Nashei yunosti polyot,* Lausanne 1983, p. 124.

39. *Arkhiv Samizdata,* 5042, August 26, 1983. Also in *Survey,* Spring 1984.

40. See *SSSR: Vnutrennie protivorechiya,* New York 1982, No. 6.

41. *Pravda,* May 7, 1982.

42. *Kratki filosofski slovar,* Moscow 1954, pp. 236, 237.

43. *Filosofski slovar,* Moscow 1963, p. 197.

44. *Literaturnaya gazeta,* May 2, 1984.

45. *International Herald Tribune,* April 5, 1984.

46. *Izvestia,* August 21, 1975; April 17, 1983.

47. *Pravda,* October 20, 1983.

48. Marshall I. Goldman, *The USSR in Crisis: The Failure of an Economic System,* New York and London 1983, pp. 128, 129.

49. *Izvestia,* May 20, 1983.

50. *Pravda,* April 5, 1984.

51. *Russkaya Mysl,* July 15, 1982.

52. *International Herald Tribune,* June 9, 1983.

53. Producer V. Abdrashitov, screenplay by A. Mindadze.

54. Evgeny Bogat, "Ballada o chasakh," *Literaturnaya gazeta,* September 15, 1982.

55. See *Intermedia* (London), May 1984, Vol. 12, No. 3, p. 19.

56. *International Herald Tribune,* May 28, 1984.

57. *Intermedia,* op. cit., p. 17.

58. John Barron, *The KGB Today,* New York 1983, p. 196.

59. Henry Regnard, "L'URSS et le renseignement scientifique, technique et technologique," *Défense Nationale* (Paris), December 1983.

60. *Literaturnaya gazeta,* May 2, 1984.

61. *Pravda,* August 3, 1984.

62. *Pravda,* June 18, 1983.
63. A note taken of Khrushchev's talks with Soviet writers and artists on March 7 and 8, 1963. *SSSR: Vnutrennie protivorechiya,* 1982, No. 6, p. 192.

10. CORRUPTION

1. Konstantin Simes, *USSR: Secrets of a Corrupt Society,* London 1982; reviewed by Michael Simmons, "The Party's Never Over," *Guardian,* September 27, 1982.
2. Aron Katsenelinbogen, *Tsvetniya rynki i sovetskaya ekonomika. SSSR. Vnutrennie protivorechiya,* 1981, No. 2, p. 97.
3. Ibid., p. 90.
4. Ibid., p. 91.
5. Simes, op. cit., p. 91.
6. Alexander Nekrich's conversation with Yury Alexandrov, *Obozrenie,* No. 7, November 1983.
7. Lev Timofeev, *Tekhnologiya chornogo rynka ili krestyanskaya iskusstvo golodat,* 1982, p. 81.
8. *Literaturnaya gazeta,* September 22, 1982.
9. Igor Efimov, *Bez burzhuyev,* Frankfurt-on-Main 1979, p. 121.
10. *Literaturnaya gazeta,* June 18, 1976.
11. Arkady Adamov, *Na svobodnoe mesto,* Moscow 1981, p. 386.
12. Evgenia Evelson, "Sudebnie protsessy po ekonomicheskim delam v SSSR" (manuscript), p. 47.
13. Ibid., p. 374.
14. *Materialy Dvadtsat shestogo syezda KPSS,* Moscow 1981, p. 59.
15. *Pravda,* June 18 and August 10, 1983.
16. Boris Bazhanov, *Vospominaniya byvshego sekretarya Stalina,* Paris 1980, p. 97.
17. Lydia Shatunovskaya, *Zhizn v Kremle,* New York 1982, pp. 149, 150.
18. Evelson, op. cit., p. 154.
19. Simes, op. cit., p. 31.
20. *Russkaya Mysl,* April 5, 1984.
21. *Bakinski rabochi,* February 4, 1984.
22. *Posev,* 1983, No. 10, p. 41.
23. Ibid., p. 42.

11. EDUCATION

1. Viktor Shulgin, *Pedagogika perekhodnogo perioda,* Moscow 1927.
2. Speech by Z. Lilina (Zinovieva), quoted in V. Zenzinov, *Besprizornie,* Paris 1929, p. 36.
3. S. A. Fedyukin, *Veliki Oktyabr i intelligentsiya,* Moscow 1972, p. 173.
4. E. N. Medynsky, *Narodnoe obrazovanie v SSSR,* Moscow 1952, p. 20.
5. *Sovetskaya shkola na sovremennom etape,* Moscow 1977, p. 20.
6. V. I. Lenin, *Collected Works,* Vol. 41, p. 313.
7. *Izvestia,* January 4, 1984.
8. *Pravda,* April 29, 1984.
9. A. Yefremin, *Opyt metodiki politgramoty,* 5th ed., Moscow 1924, p. 87.
10. E. A. Tudorovskaya, *Volshebnaya skazka. Russkoe narodnoe poeticheskoe tvorchestvo,* Soviet Academy of Science, Moscow 1955, Vol. 11, Book 1, pp. 314, 316–17.
11. I. Kikoin, *Rol uchebnoi literatury v formirovanii mirovozzreniya shkolnikov,* Moscow 1978, p. 77.

12. A. A. Maximov, "Borba za materializm v sovremennoi fizike," *Voprosy filosofii,* 1953, No. 1, p. 194.
13. A. B. Zalkind, *Pedologiya v SSSR,* Moscow 1929, pp. 6, 11, 13.
14. See I. I. Kazakov, *Teoriya i praktika lizatoterapii,* Moscow and Leningrad 1934.
15. *Pravda,* March 14, 1937.
16. A. S. Vygotsky, *Myshlenie i yazyk,* Moscow 1934.
17. Zalkind, op. cit., pp. 15, 16.
18. A. Lunacharsky, *Chto takoe obrazovanie?,* in *O vospitanii i obrazovanii,* Moscow 1976, p. 359.
19. Medynsky, op. cit., pp. 44, 45.
20. *Sovetskaya shkola . . .,* Moscow 1927, pp. 52–3.
21. Ibid., pp. 55, 57.
22. Zalkind, op. cit., p. 35.
23. *Rekomendatelny spisok knig dlya chteniya v 1–8 klassakh,* Moscow 1982.
24. *Pravda,* May 22, 1982.
25. Ibid., April 30, 1984.
26. *Literaturnaya gazeta,* November 10, 1982.
27. I. Lupamova, *Polveka,* Moscow 1969, pp. 189–90.
28. *Komsomolskaya Pravda,* September 3, 1982.
29. Ekaterina Markova, "Podsolnukh," *Yunost,* 1983, No. 8, p. 12.
30. Cited in *Rekomendatelny spisok knig . . .*
31. *Pravda,* May 22, 1982.
32. *Sovetskaya Shkola . . .,* pp. 66, 67.
33. Medynsky, op. cit., pp. 77, 89, 78; *Sovetskaya Shkola . . .,* pp. 16–17.
34. *Pravda,* August 24, 1984, pp. 64–5.
35. Bogdan Cywinski, *Zatruta humanistyka,* Warsaw 1980.
36. Hugh Seton-Watson, "Reflections: 30 Years After," *Survey,* Winter–Spring 1975, p. 41.
37. G. Nikanorov, "Otmetka . . . uchitelyu," *Sovetskaya kultura,* August 20, 1976.
38. *Oktyabr,* 1984, No. 1.
39. *Sovetskaya kultura,* August 20, 1976.
40. *Le Monde,* September 10, 1976.
41. *Sovetskaya kultura,* op. cit.
42. Quoted in B. T. Likhachev, *Teoriya kommunist-icheskogo vospitaniya,* Moscow 1974, p. 377.
43. *Sovetskaya Shkola . . .,* p. 148.
44. *Raduga,* Kiev 1983, Nos. 10, 12.
45. Vladimir Tendryakov, *Chrezvychainoe,* Moscow 1972.
46. *Pravda,* April 13, 1984.
47. Ibid., April 14, 1984.
48. Ibid., May 4, 1984.
49. Ibid., April 13, 1984.
50. Basile Kerblay, *Modern Soviet Society,* New York 1983.
51. *Pravda,* April 14, 1984.
52. Ibid., May 4, 1984.
53. *Narodnoe prosveshchenie,* July 1982.
54. *Pravda,* January 7, 1984.
55. Ibid., April 14, 1984.
56. Ibid.

57. N. V. Ogarkov, *Vsegda v gotovnosti . . .,* Moscow 1982, p. 64.
58. *Pravda,* April 14, 1984.
59. See *International Herald Tribune,* May 28, 1984.
60. Getmanets, op. cit., p. 207.
61. A. S. Makarenko, *Izbrannie pedagogicheskie proizvedeniya,* Moscow 1946, p. 33.
62. Quoted in William Shirer, *Twentieth-Century Journey,* Vol. III: *The Nightmare Years: 1930–1940,* Boston 1984, p. 123.
63. "Semeionoe pravo," *Malaya Sovetskaya Entsiklopedia* (Small Soviet Encyclopedia), Moscow 1930, Vol. 7.
64. A. B. Zalkind, *Revolyutsiya i molodezh,* Moscow 1924, p. 67.
65. Klara Zetkin, *O Lenine: Vospominaniya i vstrechi,* Moscow 1925, p. 67.
66. Alexandra Kollontai, "Dorogu krylatomu erosu," *Molodaya Gvardiya,* 1923, No. 3, p. 113.
67. Alexandra Kollontai, *Lore of Worker Bees,* Chicago 1978, p. 181.
68. Nina Serpinskaya, *Vverkh i vniz,* Petrograd 1923. Quoted in P. S. Kogan, *Literatura etikh let, 1917–1923,* Ivanovo-Voznesensk 1924, p. 50.
69. Zalkind, *Revolyutsiya . . .,* pp. 73, 86.
70. Fyodor Panferov, *Tsement,* Moscow 1978, p. 228.
71. A. V. Lunacharsky, *O bytiye,* Moscow 1927, p. 68.
72. Lev Gumilev, *Sobachi pereulok,* Moscow 1928, p. 36.
73. Sergei Malashkin, *Luna s pravoi storony,* Moscow 1926. See also N. Bogdanov, *Pervaya devushka;* I. Brazhnin, *Pryzhok;* B. Gorbatov, *Yacheika.*
74. *Molodaya Gvardiya,* 1923, No. 3.
75. Leon Trotsky, *Les Questions du mode de vie,* Paris 1976, p. 75.
76. Ibid., pp. 85, 88.
77. Mikhail Koltsov, *V ZAGS* (written in 1936).
78. Trotsky, op. cit., p. 87.
79. Gleb Alexeev, "Teni stoyashchego vperedi," *Krasnaya nov,* 1929, Nos. 2–4; No. 2, p. 15.
80. Zalkind, *Revolyutsiya . . .,* pp. 53, 54, 83.
81. A. Voronsky, *Literaturniye portrety v dvukh tomakh,* Moscow 1928, Vol. 1, pp. 98, 109.
82. *Ispolzovaniye istochnikov i literatury v kurse nauchnogo kommunizma,* Leningrad 1982, pp. 171–2.
83. Trotsky, op. cit., p. 73.
84. V. T. Chentulov, *Ekonomicheskaya istoriya SSSR,* Moscow 1969, p. 267.
85. *Plenum TsK VLKSM* (November 1962), stenographic record, Moscow 1963, p. 369.
86. Robert Conquest, *The Great Terror,* New York 1973, pp. 389–90.
87. See Jan Klucharzewski, *Od bialego caratu do czerwonego,* Warsaw 1928, III, 473.
88. *Pravda,* July 7, 1932.
89. *Pionerskaya pravda,* December 17, 1932.
90. M. Gorky, *O detskoi literature,* Moscow 1958, p. 201.
91. *Pravda,* May 27, 1928.
92. *Pionerskaya pravda,* October 18, 1932.
93. *Prikaz narodnogo kommissara prosveshcheniya RSFSR o distsipline i vospitanii rebvenka v shkole,* Moscow 1934.
94. M. Gusev, *Detkory v shkole,* Moscow 1934, p. 68.

95. Cited in A. Zhelokhovtsev, *Kulturnaya revolyutsiya s blizkogo rasstoyania,* Moscow 1973, p. 138.
96. See Yury Druzhnikov, "Voznesenie Pavlika Morozova" (manuscript), Moscow 1983.
97. M. Gorky, *Sobranie sochinenii v 30 tomakh,* Moscow 1953, Vol. 27, p. 440.
98. *Komsomolskaya pravda,* August 20, 1934.
99. *Pravda,* June 1, 1935.
100. *Narody Evropeiskoi chasti SSSR,* Moscow 1964, p. 479. See I. A. Kurganov, *Semya v SSSR, 1917–1967,* New York 1967, p. 96.
101. Wilhelm Reich, *The Mass Psychology of Fascism,* London 1975, p. 64.
102. G. M. Sverdlov, *Sovetskoe semeinoe pravo,* Moscow 1958, p. 77.
103. See Joseph Finder, *Red Carpet,* New York 1983, p. 42.
104. *Pravda,* February 1, 1935.
105. Ibid., March 19, 1935.
106. Reich, op. cit., p. 295.
107. *Novy mir,* 1953, No. 12; *Znamya,* 1954, No. 4.
108. See Vladimir Nabokov, *Lectures on Russian Literature,* New York 1981, p. 10.
109. A. Makarenko, *Sochineniya,* Moscow 1951, Vol. 4, p. 351.
110. A. Tvardovsky, "Po pravu pamyati," an autobiographical poem that was never published but circulated in samizdat.
111. *Kratki populyarny slovar-spravochnik o brake i semye,* pp. 16, 31; *Semya i obshchestvo,* p. 36.
112. See *Literaturnaya gazeta,* April 25, 1984.
113. *Pravda,* July 15 and October 10, 1982; March 30, 1984.
114. Ibid., February 1, 1983.
115. Carolina Hausson and Karin Linden, *Thirteen Interviews,* New York 1983, p. xiv.
116. *Semya i obshchestvo,* p. 60.
117. *Pravda,* May 15, 1984.
118. A. G. Kharchev, *Brak i semya v SSSR,* Moscow 1979, p. 283.
119. *Semya i obshchestvo,* p. 65.
120. *Izvestia,* January 9, 1984.
121. *Trud,* August 4, 1983.
122. *Stroitelnaya gazeta,* December 18, 1983.
123. Evgeny Zamyatin, *We,* p. 22.
124. *Naseleniya SSR,* Moscow 1983, pp. 17, 87.
125. *Ispolzovanie istochnikov . . . ,* p. 176. See also S. Laptenok, *Moral i semya,* Minsk 1967, p. 179.
126. *100 voprosov i 100 otvetov,* Moscow 1967, p. 31.
127. Ilya Glezer, "Amerikanski student," *Vremya i My,* 1984, No. 76, p. 163; Mikhail Stern, *Sex in the USSR,* New York 1980; Anatoli Kurchatkin, "Zvezda begushchaya," *Oktyabr,* 1984, No. 1, p. 115.
128. See Mark Popovsky, "Treti lishni. On, ona i sovetski rezhim" (manuscript), pp. 250–2.
129. See M. Bernshtam, "Kontrol rozhdaemosti v SSSR," *Novy zhurnal,* 1983, No. 153, p. 243.
130. *Literaturnaya gazeta,* March 24, 1982.
131. *Zhenshchina i Rossiya,* issue No. 1, Leningrad, December 10, 1979. Republished in Paris, 1980, pp. 58, 55, 53, 13.
132. Valentina Ermolaeva, "Muzhskie progulki," *Nash sovremennik,* 1978, No. 7, p. 40.

133. *Semya i obshchestvo,* p. 123.
134. Quoted in Pyotr Dudochkin, "Trezvost-zakon zhizni," *Nash sovremennik,* 1981, No. 7.
135. *Semya i obshchestvo,* p. 93.
136. A. Krasikov, "Tovar nomer odin," *Dvadtsat vek,* 1977, No. 2, p. 114.
137. "Feminism in Soviet Russia," *International Herald Tribune,* June 27, 1984.
138. Vladimir Shlapentokh, "By Soviet Evidence Women Seem Superior," *International Herald Tribune,* February 9, 1984; *Naselenie SSSR,* pp. 68, 55; *International Herald Tribune,* July 10, 1984.
139. *Naselenie SSSR,* p. 55.
140. *Pravda,* June 3, 1983.
141. Ibid., April 12, 1984.
142. R. Ley, *Soldaten der Arbeit,* quoted in David Schoenbaum, *La Révolution Brune,* Paris 1979, p. 124.
143. Zamyatin, *We,* p. 21.
144. Klaus Mehnert, *Youth in Soviet Russia,* London 1933, p. 81.
145. Ibid., p. 82.
146. See Max Domarus, *Hitler: Reden und Proklamationen, 1932–1938,* Würzburg 1962, p. 447.
147. *Pravda,* March 27, 1923.
148. Ibid.
149. *Literaturnaya gazeta,* September 3, 1980.
150. Pyotr Proskurin, *Imya tvoe,* Moscow 1973.
151. *Pravda,* January 21, 1984.
152. *Le Monde,* July 5, 1984.
153. *Pravda,* January 2, 1984.
154. Ibid., March 2, 1973.
155. Ibid., March 4, 1983; see *Kratki politicheski slovar,* Moscow 1983, p. 224; Domarus, op. cit., p. 349.
156. *Pravda,* October 7, 1983.
157. See Alexander Prokhanov, *Derevo v tsentre Kabula,* Moscow 1983, and "V ostrovakh okhotnik . . .," *Novy mir,* 1983, No. 5.
158. *Pravda,* August 3, 1984.
159. See Franz Böhm, *Anti-Cartesianismus: Deutsche Philosophie in Widerstand,* Leipzig 1938.
160. A. Yakovlev, "Protiv anti-istorizma," *Literaturnaya gazeta,* November 18, 1972.
161. V. Oskotsky, "V borbe s anti-istorizm," *Pravda,* May 21, 1984.
162. See Aleshkovsky's novel *Ruka* about a member of the "organs" of the secret police—a killer called The Hand.
163. In Mehnert, op. cit., pp. 254, 270, 206, 251, 261, 259.
164. October 12, 1930. See *Russian Literature Quarterly,* 1975, XIII, pp. 545–51.
165. *Pravda,* March 4, 1983, and A. N. Vasileva, *Gazetno-publitsicheski stil rechi,* Moscow 1982, p. 11.
166. I. A. Galitskaya, *Molodezh, religiya, ateizm,* Moscow 1978, p. 72.
167. *Govorit Ernst Neizvestny,* Frankfurt 1984, p. 114.
168. Ismail Kadare, *Le Grand Hiver,* Paris 1978, p. 157.
169. *Neizvestny,* p. 50.
170. Conversation between Alexander Nekrich and Yury Alexandrov, *Obozrenie,* November 1983, No. 7.

171. *Kontinent*, 1984, No. 39.
172. Sergei Muir, *Ulybka fortuny*, 1981, p. 168.
173. Quoted in Galitskaya, op. cit., p. 48.
174. The textbook was published in French by the school of psychology of the Institute of Social Science: *Principes fondamentaux de la psychologie sociale. Manuel*, Institut de Science Sociale, URSS, Moscow, 1980, p. 124.
175. Nikita Khrushchev, *Khrushchev Remembers: The Last Testament*, Boston 1974, p. 56.
176. Academician B. Petrovsky, "Preodolenie opasnogo neduga: problemy i zadachi borby s pyanstvom," *Literaturnaya gazeta*, September 3, 1980.
177. Vladimir Treml, "Death from Alcohol Poisoning in USSR," *The Wall Street Journal*, December 10, 1982.
178. *Literaturnaya gazeta*, September 8, 1982.
179. Sergei Chuprinin, "Ozhivlyazh," *Literaturnaya gazeta*, February 10, 1982.
180. *Literaturnaya gazeta*, March 31, 1982.
181. See Alexander Kron's novel *Bessonnitsa*, Moscow 1979.
182. L. M. Saburova, "Literatura o novykh obryadakh i prazdnikakh v SSSR za 1963–1966," *Sovetskaya etnografiya*, 1967, No. 5.
183. *Nauka i religiya*, 1979, No. 2.
184. See Natalia Sadomskaya, *Novaya obryadnost i integratsiya v SSSR* in *SSSR: vnutrennie protivorechiya*, ed. V. Chalidze, New York 1981.
185. Quoted in ibid., p. 80.
186. L. M. Rakhimov, *Ob ispolzovanii narodnykh traditsii*, Dushanbe 1966.
187. V. I. Brudny, *Obryady vchera i egodnya*, Moscow 1968.
188. "Pierre Billard fait 'Le Point' avec Claude Lévi-Strauss," *Le Point*, November 14, 1983.

12. CULTURE

1. The unpublished decree of the Central Committee of the CPSU "Concerning the creative links between literary and art magazines and the practice of Communist construction" was summarized in *Literaturnaya gazeta*, August 4, 1982. See also *Pravda*, July 16, 1983; *Literaturnaya gazeta*, January 18 and March 21, 1984.
2. Quoted in Adelin Guyot and Patrick Restallini, *L'Art Nazi*, Paris 1983, p. 87.
3. Quoted in Ilya Glazunov, "Vsegda zhivoe nasledie," *Pravda*, September 20, 1980.
4. Cited in Lionel Richard, *Le nazisme et la culture*, Paris 1978, p. 195.
5. "Partiya vedyot," *Literaturnaya gazeta*, April 25, 1979.
6. *Chetvyorty syezd pisatelei RSFSR*, stenographic report, Moscow 1977, p. 114.
7. *Pravda*, July 20, 1983.
8. *AKhRR. Sbornik vospominanii, statei, dokumentov*, Moscow 1973, p. 81.
9. *Iskusstvo kino*, 1964, No. 4, pp. 14–15.
10. See *Za bolshoe kinoiskusstvo*, Moscow 1935, p. 65.
11. See Mikhail Heller, "Poet i vozhd," *Kontinent*, 1978, No. 18.
12. Grigori Aleksandrov, *Epokha i kino*, Moscow 1976, p. 220.
13. Dmitri Shostakovich, *Testimony*, New York 1979.
14. Béla Balazs, *Wybor pism*, Warsaw 1957, p. 277; editorial article "Byt ideinym," *Sovetskaya kultura*, September 20, 1975; *Pravda*, July 4, 1983; Mikhail Sinelnikov, "Opirayas na fakty," *Pravda*, September 1, 1982.
15. Shostakovich, op. cit., p. 255.
16. B. Eikhenbaum, *Moi vremennik*, Moscow 1929, pp. 89, 133.

17. *Sovetsky istoricheski film,* Moscow 1939, p. 120.
18. Eikhenbaum, op. cit., p. 117; *Pervy syezd soyuza sovetskykh pisatelei,* stenographic record, p. 678.
19. Czeslaw Milosz, *The Captive Mind,* New York 1955.
20. *Pervy syezd . . .,* p. 1.
21. *LEF,* 1924, No. 1, pp. 199, 202.
22. *Pervy syezd . . .,* p. 24.
23. Luis Buñuel, *My Last Sigh,* New York 1984, p. 248.
24. *Govorit Ernst Neizvestny,* pp. 50–4.
25. Osip Beskin, *The Place of Art in the Soviet Union,* The American Russian Institute, New York 1936, pp. 11, 13.
26. Klaus Mehnert, *The Russians and Their Favorite Books,* Stanford, Calif., 1983, pp. 32–4.
27. *KPSS o formirovanii novogo cheloveka. Sbornik materialov (1965–1981),* Moscow 1982, p. 33.
28. Yury Andreev, *Nasha zhizn, nasha literatura,* Leningrad 1974, p. 6.
29. Mehnert, *The Russians . . .,* p. xiii.
30. See Mikhail Yakobson, "Tsenzura khudozhestvennoi literatury v SSR," *Strelets,* 1984, No. 5.
31. Natalia Ilyinas, "Literatura i massovy tirazh," *Novy mir,* 1969, No. 2.
32. Vitaly Ozerov, "Slovo i delo," *Pravda,* June 9, 1983.
33. Savva Dangulov, " 'Pobeda'—O romane Aleksandra Chakovskogo," *Izvestia,* October 7, 1981.
34. Rene Fülop-Miller, *The Mind and Face of Bolshevism,* New York 1929.
35. *Literaturnaya gazeta,* October 5, 1983.
36. S. Eisenstein, *Sobranie sochinenii v 6 tomakh,* 500.
37. *Govorit Ernst Neizvestny,* pp. 28, 29.
38. *Literaturnaya gazeta,* June 22, 1983.

13. LANGUAGE

1. George Orwell, *1984,* p. 241.
2. Andrei Amalrik, *Notes of a Revolutionary,* New York 1982.
3. *Pravda,* September 16, 1976.
4. Alexander Galich, *Kogda ya vernus,* p. 380.
5. Vasileva, op. cit., p. 11.
6. *Arkhiv Samizdata,* No. 5132.
7. *LEF,* 1924, No. 1, p. 141.
8. Ibid., pp. 55, 59, 62, 105.
9. Ibid., p. 142.
10. Ibid., pp. 118, 142, 145.
11. Ibid., pp. 197, 199.
12. Ibid., p. 106.
13. Ibid., p. 110.
14. *Pravda,* March 1, 1923.
15. *LEF,* op. cit., pp. 112–13, 115.
16. *Izvestia,* October 17, 1982.
17. A. Platonov, *The Foundation Pit,* Ann Arbor, Michigan, 1973, p. 276.
18. Fülop-Miller, op. cit., p. 243.
19. Marek Hlasko, *The Graveyard,* New York 1959.

20. Petru Dumitriu, *Incognito,* New York 1964.
21. I. Ilf and E. Petrov, *Sobranie sochinenii v 4 tomakh,* Moscow 1961, Vol. 3, p. 89.
22. See V. D. Lifshits, *Suffiksalnoe slovoobrazovanie v yazyke sovetskoi epokhi,* Moscow 1965.
23. *Sovetskaya Rossiya,* February 13, 1984; *Pravda,* March 4, 1983.
24. Lechowicz's account of his treatment was published in *Zeszyty Historyczne,* Paris 1984, No. 67, p. 100.
25. *Yazyk v razvitom sots. obshchestve,* p. 77.
26. Ibid.
27. Vasileva, op. cit., p. 18.
28. *Czarna ksiega cenzury PRL,* London 1977–78 (*The Black Book of Polish Censorship,* New York 1984), Vol. I, p. 146.
29. Victor Klemperer, LTI, *Notizbuch eines Philologen,* Leipzig 1970.
30. *Jezyk propagandy,* NOWA, Warsaw 1979.
31. *Yazyk v razvitom . . .,* pp. 87, 88.
32. Ibid., p. 8.
33. *International Herald Tribune,* June 16–17, 1984.
34. *Le Figaro,* August 7, 1980.
35. Alain Besançon, *Russkoe proshloe i sovetskoe nastroyashchee,* London 1984, p. 89.
36. *Yazyk v razvitom . . .,* pp. 103, 99.
37. *Black Book,* pp. 26, 27.
38. *Jezyk propagandy,* p. 27.
39. *Le Monde,* July 17, 1984.
40. Ibid., March 6, 1981.
41. *Literaturnaya gazeta,* February 23, 1983.
42. *Govorit Ernst Neizvestny,* pp. 54, 117–18.
43. Zdeněk Mlynar, *Nightfrost in Prague,* New York 1980.

CONCLUSION

1. George Orwell, *Collected Essays,* Vol. I, p. 381.
2. Alexander Zinoviev, *Homo Sovieticus,* p. 7; Orwell, *1984,* pp. 261, 269; George Urban, "Portrait of a Dissenter as a Soviet Man: A Conversation with Alexander Zinoviev," *Encounter,* April–May 1984.

INDEX

A NOTE ON THE TYPE

The text of this book was set in a type face called
Times Roman, designed by Stanley Morison
(1889–1967) for *The Times* (London) and first
introduced by that newspaper in 1932.

Among typographers and designers of the
twentieth century, Stanley Morison was a strong
forming influence—as a typographical advisor to
The Monotype Corporation, as a director of two
distinguished English publishing houses, and as
a writer of sensibility, erudition, and keen practical sense.

Composed, printed and bound by The Haddon
Craftsmen, Inc., Scranton, Pennsylvania

Designed by Marysarah Quinn